CAMEROON

D0863195

Politics and Society in Critical Perspectives

Edited by
Jean-Germain Gros

University Press of America,® Inc.
Lanham · Boulder · New York · Toronto · Oxford

Copyright © 2003 by
University Press of America,® Inc.
4501 Forbes Boulevard
Suite 200
Lanham, Maryland 20706
UPA Acquisitions Department (301) 459-3366

PO Box 317
Oxford
OX2 9RU, UK

Library of Congress Cataloging-in-Publication Data

Cameroon : politics and society in critical perspective /
edited by Jean-Germain Gros.
p.   cm.
Includes bibliographical references and index.
l. Cameroon—Politics and government—1960-
2. Cameroon—Social conditions—1960-

JQ3529.A15C36 2003
320.96711—dc21   2003053321

ISBN 0-7618-2590-8 (clothbound : alk. ppr.)
ISBN 0-7618-2591-6 (paperback : alk. ppr.)

In loving memory of Laura Desrosiers (1924–2002)

Contents

List of Abbreviations

AAC	All Anglophone Conference
AMEO	Association for Meritocracy and Equal Opportunity
ARCAM	Assemblée Représentative Camerounaise
ASSABENOUE	Association Amicale de Benoue
ATCAM	Assemblée Territoriale Camerounaise
CAMAIR	Cameroon Airlines
CAMSHIPLINES	Cameroon Shipping Lines
CDA	Christian Democratic Alliance
CDC	Cameroon Development Corporation
CDU	Cameroon Democratic Union
CENER	Centre National de l'Enseignement et de la Recherche
CGT	Confédération Générale du Travail
CPDM	Cameroon People's Democratic Movement
CRTV	Cameroon Radio and Television
DIRDOC	Direction de la Documentation
FECAFOOT	Fédération Camerounaise de Football
FRSC	Federal Republic of Southern Cameroons
GSO	Groupe Spécial d'Operation
HROC	Human Rights Organization of Cameroon
JEUCAFRA	Jeunesse Camerounaise Française

KNDP	Kamerun National Democratic Party
MDJC	Mouvement Démocratique de la Jeunesse Camerounaise
MDR	Mouvement pour la Défense de la République
MINAT	Ministère de l'Administration Territoriale
MINCOM	Ministère de la Communication
MINDEF	Ministère de la Defense
MINFI	Ministère des Finances
MINJES	Ministère de la Jeunesse et Sports
NCCOP	National Coordination Committee of Opposition Parties
NPMB	National Produce Marketing Board
NVCC	National Vote Counting Commission
PDC	Parti des Démocrates Camerounais
RDPF	Rassemblement Démocratique du Peuple sans Frontière
REGIFERCAM	Regie de Chemins de fer du Cameroun
SCAC	Southern Cameroons Advisory Council
SCCA	Southern Cameroons Constituent Assembly
SCARM	Southern Cameroons Restoration Movement
SCNC	Southern Cameroons National Council
SCYL	Southern Cameroons Youth League
SDF	Social Democratic Front
SEDOC	Service de Documentation
SEMIL	Service de l'Enseignement Militaire
SNEC	Société Nationale des Eaux du Cameroun
SNH	Société Nationale d'Hydrocarbure
SNI	Société Nationale d'Investissement
SODECOTON	Societé de Developpement du Coton
SONARA	Société Nationale de Rafinerie
SONEL	Société Nationale d'Electricité
SOTUC	Société de Transport Urbain du Cameroun
UNC	Union Nationale Camerounaise
UNDP/NUDP	Union Nationale pour la Democratie et le Progrès
UPC	Union des Populations du Cameroun

Foreword

Minion K. C. Morrison

The regeneration of modes of democratization has been occurring all over Africa since the mid-1980s. These changes have occurred with great regularity in previously authoritarian, military and/or patrimonial governments. They have been replaced by a variety of regimes, producing varying degrees of increased citizen participation and accountability. It is fair to say that in spite of the limited range of the "new democracy" in some of these countries, the mostly grassroots campaigns for more public expression have been everywhere present. Hardly any leader or government from the previous period has gone unimpaired in the maintenance of the *ancien regime*.

As such it is incumbent upon contemporary scholars to account for these changes and to make a careful assessment of how much change has occurred. It is once again a period that offers virtual laboratory circumstances for the generation of knowledge about politics and for conceptualizing the problem of citizen expression in an African context. Not since the independence era has there been such an opportunity to make comparisons from African experience for the understanding of democracy. The present study offers a selection of studies on politics and society that opens that window on contemporary Cameroon. And, it is a country that offers distinct circumstances for the exploration of democratization processes in contemporary Africa.

Cameroon is one of Africa's most diverse countries. Like many of its neighbors, a wide diversity of ethnic identities are present. They animate intra- and inter-group relations in the country. It has regional differences whose topography and natural resource endowments vary, affording grasslands, forests and petroleum products. Regional variations also include distinct religious, ethnic, and political orientations—e.g. North versus South, East versus West, *inter alia.*

Moreover Cameroon has one of the most complex colonial histories, having been colonized and/or administered by three European powers—France, Britain and Germany. At independence, Cameroonians, like few other Africans, had to somehow integrate territories subject to at least two of these traditions. Therefore, this nation at the bend of the Guinea Coast has had a good deal more to negotiate in making its way among the sovereign nations in post colonial Africa. It is at once a representative case of the diversity characteristic of the African states, and at the other a worse case example of the challenge of democratization. These studies so ably organized by Professor Jean-Germain Gros tell that story.

In the post-independence political history of Cameroon, the country has been both blessed and cursed. Its blessing has been long-term stability of leadership. Its long-serving President Ahidjo served from the grant of independence to the Francophone and Anglophone territories between 1960 and 1961 until his resignation in 1982. Since that time only one other leader has served as President, Ahidjo's successor Paul Biya. The nation remains one of a very small number of African states whose leaders have neither been deposed by military nor by civilian elements. At the same time, the economy has enjoyed the substantial proceeds from its oil production and reserves. By most standards in post independence Africa these circumstances would seem to indicate a promising array of resources with which to sustain robust citizen demands.

On the other hand, some of the unique characteristics of Cameroon have contributed to a spectacular failure in the integration of the nation-state and in the distribution of public resources. The discrete British and French colonial legacies since World War I have left a gap between the peoples on either side of the linguistic and administrative divide. The larger Francophone sector of the territory has always had differential power vis-à-vis the Anglophone sector. This has spawned an enduring cleavage whereby the Anglophones charge discrimination from the ruling elite on the Francophone side of the territory. Sometimes this has caused political actors in Anglophone Cameroon to adopt an exit strategy for going it alone as an independent territory, but it has mostly meant struggle between the two sides. Similarly the maldistribution and management of the considerable national proceeds from the petroleum industry have led to charges of corruption. And in any case, the considerable financial proceeds have not resulted in any basic, let alone fundamental, reallocation of resources in the society.

And ironically, what seems to be perhaps the country's greatest asset—stable leadership—has not led to sustained participation and open political expression. A widespread opinion among citizens and scholars alike is that the irrepressible regime of first Ahidjo and now Biya has been a detriment to citizen's public expression and participation. The Ahidjo regime, while relatively benign, is regarded as having established the trajectory of patrimonial authoritarianism. He tightly held the reins of government and manipulated the social forces in the society with such a profound certitude that few could brook him. Biya, the protégé and successor, is deemed to be equally skilled at the management of the political arena. Hence, despite the swirl of democratization that envelops African states, Cameroon remains fairly aloof of the process.

Professor Jean-German Gros and his collaborators investigate this enigma of despoiled promise in Cameroon. They start from the rather improbable prospects that diverse Cameroon faced at its independence, but which it seemed to allay with strong leadership and physical endowments. Nevertheless, the analysts show that the situation rapidly deteriorated from early on as Ahidjo solidified his position as virtual arbiter of all actions in the public arena. The inevitable political dominance of the Francophone sector has been unrelenting in its dislocation of Anglophones, except for the careful manipulation of a selected number of symbolic representatives or "pawns" (a kind of ethnic calculus). Professor Le Vine in the second chapter offers an analysis of the enigmatic Ahidjo and the clever way in which he maintained the relatively benign regime, while maintaining absolute authority. Le Vine argues that despite all of Ahidjo's excesses, a dictator in the classical sense, he was not. It was rather in the cultivation of his personality at the head of a power-holding elite. This group perceived itself to be the natural heirs to the French administrative legacy. In the cult of personality that developed Ahidjo then could ride above the "parochial sentiments" of opposition elements in the society.

In the introduction Professor Gros agrees, placing the President within the oft-cited administrative hegemonic leader framework. He argues that Ahidjo maintained relative order and enforcement through a competent bureaucracy, with carefully controlled ethnic balancing. The latter was often only symbolic, but provided sufficient imprimatur to avoid abject coercion for system maintenance. With this kind of bureaucratic control, it was thereby not necessary to deploy military or other police powers against the populace. Both Gros and Le Vine help to explain the mystery of Ahidjo's survival in a political environment fraught with political fissures, any of which might have caused systemic crisis.

In chapter one, Professor Gros provides a broad overview of the history of this "crossroads" of a country, and the many "moods" it presents to the analyst of politics. He sketches an outline of the indigenous political foundations of the peoples of what came to be known as Cameroon. He then describes and analyzes with alacrity the imposition and superimposition of many colonial apparatuses over what became artificial federations of traditions and interests. Therein lay the foundations for many of the succeeding problems that emerged in the superimposition of an Africanized government that ostensibly restored the self-determination of this artificial entity.

Professor Gros paints a picture of an emergent African post-colonial state that did anything but restore self-determination. It is a familiar picture insofar as it mirrors that in many other parts of Africa. The difference, of course, is the almost unique scope of the integrative challenge in Cameroon with a dominant Francophone sector and a sizeable oppositional minority Anglophone sector. Ahidjo is shown to be the flawed leader whose efforts to resolve this division ultimately failed. Moreover, because his successor and protégé Biya has proved far less skillful in maintaining a veneer of bureaucratic competence in governance, the country has come close to collapse. The response of the regime has been to introduce a level of repression and ethnic politicization rarely utilized before to maintain elite power.

The balance of the eight-chapter volume accounts for the post-colonial society in the broadest sense. There are chapters on leadership, political economy, elections and democratization, ethnicity, music, theatre, and a kind of post-modern analysis of group identities based on the French and English presences in the territory. Professor Le Vine, as has been mentioned, takes up leadership. He presents a fine exposition of Ahidjo as a personality and as a political leader. He suggests that in his moderation, except for the personalist elements, he may indeed have risen to the integrative challenge. It is less certain whether he may have ever risen to the development challenge in light of the continuing colonial linkages.

Professors Ngenge and Jua discuss aspects of the "Anglophone problem." Each agrees, in their separate ways, that the Anglophone sector has never been taken as a foundational entity to the post-colonial state. Professor Ngenge reflects upon the creation of the unitary state on the embers of the two distinct colonial traditions. There was never any sense in which the heirs to the predominating French colonial tradition ceded real power to the other side. The imposition of the unitary state, Ngenge shows to have been the art of not so clever manipulation by Ahidjo and his confreres. The evolving state never succeeded in righting this inequality. Then Jua uses a kind of post-modern approach to articulate the imaginations by which these separate sectors function. In this instance theatre is the medium and the author uses a selection of theatre pieces to illustrate these divides and their political consequences.

Along these same lines Professors Nyamjoh and Fokwang (chapter eight) discuss how music is used as a source for making political statements in a society where ruling elites both manipulate and repress such sources. They discuss the remarkable worldwide popularity of various of these creative traditions, especially *Makossa*. The latter was largely associated with the time of the Ahidjo regime and reflected an undercurrent of criticism and possibility in the inherited post-colonial state. The successor Biya regime, however, worked assiduously to sponsor indigenous music from his southern ethnic base as a "state" cultural project. *Bikutsi* then became inscribed as an exponent of the hopes and dreams of the new Biya state. It won financial and other support from the government that resulted in its primacy on the airwaves and in entertainment venues. The authors then go on to show the irony of *Bikutsi* itself becoming a major source of criticism of the excesses of the regime; and, how this spawned government infiltration and further manipulation of artistic critics. The tangled web of betrayals and ensuing recriminations did little to advance independent creativity of artists or an expansion of voices in the society.

The political economy chapter by Professor Tatah Menten brings us back to the social sector with his discussion of the sources of poverty in a country of potentially great wealth. He reminds us that Cameroon experienced a considerable economic boom with the discovery of oil, but also experienced an exaggerated bust with the worldwide oil crisis. In the machinations of the great oil cartel, Cameroon was a bit player once again at the whims of bigger fish. This was coupled with the not unrelated devaluation of the CFA, and the subsequent withdrawal of Franc backing for the currency. Like many other of the poor and dependent economies, Cameroon was forced to accept the hard choices inherent in structural adjustment programs (SAP). Menten shows that all of the associated problems of these externally imposed SAPs eventually hit Cameroon—unemployment, depressed local industry due to intensive privatization, crime, *inter alia*. In short, the promise and peril of SAP left Cameroon again beholden to the interests and whims of the western allies to which it was linked.

The chapter on sport is an exemplary exposition of another arena in which Cameroon has attained international acclaim—football. But it is more than that. It also is revelatory of local politics, ethnicity and the possibilities for state integration. The problem explored in the chapter is inherent in its opening story—a football fan who seeks to attribute an unappealing loss in a contest to the actions of a Bamileke official. The fan's explanation that attributes the loss to the actions of a notably powerful ethnic entity in politics speaks volumes about the role that ethnic subjectivities play in the society. But the resolution of the story wherein the fan maintains loyalty to a team whose members reflect the polyglot nature of the society, suggests the possibilities for the emergence of a national identity among Cameroonians.

Indeed, the football analysis may serve as a summary of the promise of Cameroon that this larger volume shows to have so far been betrayed. It reveals the existence of raw materials that may usefully be exploited for effective government and accountability by leaders and an unbounded citizenry in this diverse nation. Professor Gros' volume thus sketches the problems and the promise in bold relief.

Preface

Jean-Germain Gros

The Republic of Cameroon has been called many things: Africa in minia-ture, Africa's crossroads, Africa in one triangle, Mecca of African foot-ball, etc. These monikers are certainly well deserved. Sandwiched between West and Central Africa, Cameroon sits in at least three ecologi-cal zones: the dry Sahel to the north, the rainforest to the east and south and the volcanic mountains and high grasslands to the west. With over 250 ethnic groups, Cameroon is one of the most ethnically pluralistic and balanced countries in Africa. Cameroon is the only African country to have been under the tutelage of two (even three) colonial powers at the same time. As a result, different colonial legacies can be observed inside its borders. But Cameroon's microcosmic status is a double-edged sword. Like the continent, Cameroon is well endowed with natural resources, yet has fallen on hard times in recent years. Like the continent, Cameroon embraced democratization in 1990–91, yet the political system continues to evince authoritarian tendencies. Most decisions are made in the presi-dency, legislative power is limited, the judiciary is not independent and elections in the 1990s have been deeply flawed and seemingly engineered to thwart democracy. And, even though Cameroon has been stable for much of its history, political instability and violent conflicts with seces-sion overtones remain distinct possibilities, as they are in the rest of Af-rica. An apparent (and still unexplained) explosion at an army base in

Yaoundé in 2000 rattled the civilian government led by President Paul Biya, who undoubtedly remembered how close he came to losing power in 1984. Anglophones in the southwest are still restless, and pro-independence sentiments among sub-elites there may be gaining ground. Cameroon's dispute with Nigeria over the Bakassi peninsula has yet to be resolved, in spite of a recent court ruling in favor of Cameroon. This festering low-level intensity conflict could turn into full-scale war, if suspicions of significant deposits of oil in the disputed region are confirmed, if Nigeria itself begins to disintegrate, or if international arbitration, rather than settles the dispute for good, arouses nationalist sentiments on the losing side. A Nigeria-Cameroon war could, in turn, drag outside powers such as France, although not necessarily on the side of the protagonist that most analysts would predict.

In sum, Cameroon is more than a country with cute nicknames. Cameroon should be taken seriously because, as stated previously, all of Africa's problems and potentials are miniaturized therein, hence this volume. *Cameroon: Politics and Society in Critical Perspective* raises broad questions about underdevelopment amidst plenty, government corruption, Structural Adjustment Programs (SAPs) and poverty, the flawed nature of Cameroon's democratic transition as evidenced in its elections, and the challenges of managing ethnic, regional and language differences in a young state, especially in a context in which even leisure activities, such as football and popular music, are politicized. These topics are explored by a group of experts who tell it like it is, or at least tell it as they see it. And what the contributors see, many, not least Cameroon authorities, will not like.

ORGANIZATION AND OVERVIEW OF THE BOOK

The organization of the book is very straightforward. The book is divided into two (unmarked) sections. Following a synopsis of Cameroon in chapter one, which is intended to introduce the country to the uninitiated reader, formal politics is discussed in chapters two through six; society is explored in chapters seven and eight. Formal politics in Cameroon is examined from the angles of political history, political economy and election analysis. During the first two decades of independence Cameroon politics was dominated Ahmadou Ahidjo, the country's first president. Many adjectives have been used to describe the Ahidjo regime, from elitist to ethnocidal. Yet not much is known about Ahidjo himself, and what is known is shrouded in inconsistency and polemic. Chapter two by Victor Le Vine does much to answer the questions: who was Ahidjo and what was the nature of his regime? The chapter traces the genesis of the Ahidjo regime to the politics of decolonization in the 1950s. In so doing, Le Vine makes a convincing case that Ahidjo was neither the convenient idiot nor the political genius that his distracters and biographers, respectively, say he was. I agree with him. Fortuitous circumstances and Ahidjo's "native intelligence" explain his ascendance in a crowed field of power seekers, according to Le Vine. With respect to the nature of the regime constructed by Ahidjo (and maintained by Biya), Le Vine rejects the notion that it was (is) hegemonic in the Gramscian sense. Instead, he ascribes authoritarianism under Ahidjo and later Biya to a simple strategy of political survival by "an elite whose membership has varied en *gros* (wholesale) with the single change of president, en *detail* (retail) positionally as the president and his closest associates change policy lines, seek to bring new talent into the fold, reward the faithful, punish the 'disloyal' or grossly incompetent or excessively greedy, or clean house after a crisis or debacle like the April 1984 coup attempt" (Le Vine, p. 48). In the end, what the reader gets from chapter two is an exposé on political leadership and regime type.

Chapter three by Tatah Simon Ngenge continues the historical inquiry into post-colonial Cameroon by focusing on one single event and its aftermath: the abolition of the federal system on May 20th, 1972. Once again, Ahidjo was left, front and center of this decision; indeed, it is no exaggeration to say that he was the primary architect of the transformation. The shift from the Federal Republic of Cameroon to the United Republic of Cameroon eliminated power sharing between the elites of Anglophone and Francophone Cameroon. After 1972 formal power in Cameroon was indivisible, and in the new dispensation Ahidjo's leadership was institutionally uncontested, whereas before he had to contend with the premier and the assembly of West Cameroon. This would seem to confirm Bayart's—as opposed to Le Vine's assertion that the history of politics in post-colonial Cameroon is the history of an emerging state elite seeking to impose its hegemony. The chairman of the board of this "hegemonic project" was Ahidjo from 1960 to 1982, until he was succeeded by Biya in that year. Thus, chapter three provides an alternative interpretation of Cameroon politics in the first two decades of independence, even though Ngenge's discussion of hegemony is more implicit than explicit. Further, argues Ngenge, the "hegemonic project" that has seen the transformation of the Cameroon state from a federation to a unified republic and finally to a republic *tout court* has had debilitating effects on Anglophone interests.

Rightly or wrongly, Anglophones in Cameroon today, or at least their elite, feel that they are second-class citizens of a country dominated by Francophones. Ngenge, who hails from an Anglophone province (northwest), makes this point forcefully in chapter three but he is not alone. Nantang Jua makes a similar argument in chapter four. The works of these contributors may be seen as part of a literature and an art genre of protest developed by Anglophone intellectuals to counter what they see as the dominant (Francophone) elite's attempt to achieve hegemony through the lie of unity. It might even be called nationalist. Students of Cameroon ignore this emergent literature at their own peril. It is given prominence in this volume, although I believe that Anglophone nationalists (or at least the more ardent among them) miss several points about the Francophone-Anglophone divide.

First, the division of Cameroon between "Francophones" and "Anglophones" is more historical and geographic than linguistic. A Mbororo (a member of the Peul ethnic group) cattle raiser, who has difficulties communicating even with her fellow Foulbé brethren in Fulfuldé, might be quite surprised to learn that she is "Francophone." The label simply has no meaning at the grassroots level. Indeed, I suspect that a majority of Cameroonians on either side of the Mungo are completely fluent in neither the tongue of Molière nor that of Shakespeare. For the average Cameroonian ethnicity is of much greater currency than identification with this or that colonial experience. The cleavage is sustained mainly by intellectuals and politicians and does not correspond to reality on the ground, but then again myths and distortions are the stuff of politics. The invention and (or) sharpening of differences is the first step toward legitimizing claims and gaining followers. It is also important in the creation of a culture of "victims," especially when claims go unheeded by the dominant elite.

Second, Francophones in Cameroon are not a monolith nor are Anglophones. What does a tout-pourri in Kousseri (extreme-north province) and a pygmy in Bertoua (eastern province) have in common, other than their "Francophoneness?" Does anybody believe Francophonie means anything to either? What of Bamilékés and Bassas, who straddle between Francophonie and "Anglophonie," which side of their identity should be given currency, the linguistic or the ethnic?

Third, nationalist Anglophone writers have exaggerated how much Francophones have benefited from the Ahidjo-Biya dyad. The Biya regime in particular is a corrupt, manipulative, equal-opportunity violator of the public trust hell-bent in remaining in power, even if this means driving the country into abject penury. Cameroonians of all stripes have suffered from its malfeasance. Anglophones do not have the right of way in the maze of misdeeds drawn up by Biya and his acolytes, which is not to say that they have no valid claims. Cameroon is overcentralized and in dire need of honest government. Decentralization, as a return to federalism would make manifest, and better management of public resources would benefit everyone, not just Anglophones. On the other hand, outright secession, as advocated by some Anglophones, would likely contribute to the further Balkanization of the continent without any apparent benefit that could not be had from a less drastic measure and with much risk of further secession claims possibly inside the Anglophone community itself (southwest versus northwest). Biya has not even been all that benevolent toward his "home" province of center-south, which may explain why symbolic opposition to him there may be on the rise (see chapter eight).

Fourth, Anglophone nationalists have idealized West Cameroon's experience under colonial rule, when in fact the region was far from pristine. So little the British apparently thought of West Cameroon—or so much that they thought of the administrative skills of Lord Lugard—that they did not bother to send in a governor, preferring instead to rule the territory as an appendage to Nigeria. This may well explain why in 1961 independence for West Cameroon was not on the referendum menu. In the current atmosphere glorification of the colonial past may make for good political strategy but it is bad history. In addition, Anglophones are not being consistent when they mock their counterparts across the Mungo for claiming Gauls as their ancestors when they themselves base their identity on the British colonial experience to argue for changes in the architecture of state power and allocation of resources.

In the end, however, it matters not whether Anglophone feelings of marginalization in contemporary Cameroon and, by contrast, how good they had it under British rule, are rooted in myth or reality. The point is, such feelings may give (and have given) way to political action (such as the call by the Southern Cameroons National Council, SCNC, for secession) that could potentially alter the Cameroon landscape and (or) lead to violence. The "Anglophone problem" is the most burning issue in Cameroon politics today, not least because it is articulated by talented counter elite intellectuals, and how well (or poorly) it is handled by the ruling elite may well determine whether Cameroon continues to be an oasis of stability in an unstable region or joins the maelstrom of state disintegration in Central Africa.

Chapter five by Tatah Mentan examines underdevelopment and its primary manifestation, i.e., poverty, in Cameroon. Mentan uses a political economy approach to show the connection between the behavior of government officials and their allies and underdevelopment. In his view, four causes of state-sponsored underdevelopment can be identified: the existence of a self-interest-seeking network of political cronies and other actors, who control the allocation of public resources and use the latter to further their narrow interests, incompetent administrators who lack essential understanding of economics and business operations, lack of transparency in the functioning of government and the concentration of power in the presidency, which leaves no room for the other two principal branches of government (the legislature and judiciary) to play their check-and-balance role.

Further, Mentan shows how specific government policies have had a deleterious effect on ordinary people, especially the poor, in Cameroon. In particular, economic liberalization policies, such as privatization of former state-owned enterprises, reduction in state payroll through salary cuts and layoffs, cost recovery for government-provided services in health and education, trade liberalization and the devaluation of the CFA franc in 1994 have been accompanied by declining school enrollment among school-age children, increasing malnutrition among children, who, unfortunately, tend to be disproportionately represented among the poor all over the world, and a modest rise in infant mortality, which fell from the 1970s through 1989 but rose in 1997 at the height of the implementation of SAP (Structural Adjustment Program). Even though aggregate statistics point to a recovery and Cameroon is slated for debt relief, Mentan doubts that the lot of Cameroon's poor will improve.

Chapter six by Gros and Mentan examines the transition to democratic rule in Cameroon, using elections in the 1990s as its assessment tools. Why a chapter on elections? Although clearly not synonymous with democracy, elections, as G. Bingham Powell points out, are important instruments of democracy. Indeed, it may be (re)stated, as a matter of general principle: no election, no (representative) democracy. The politics of elections in contemporary Cameroon seems designed more to "modernize" autocracy than advance democracy. At least, that is the conclusion of chapter six. The chapter catalogues electoral abuses at all levels in Cameroon in the 1990s. Because these abuses are embedded in election laws and practices, the chapter focuses on the rules governing elections as well as their impact on election outcomes or results.

Chapters seven and eight depart from the focus on formal politics to examine society. Specifically, the chapters focus on football and popular music. The decision to include these seemingly banal subjects in a book aimed primarily at an academic audience is based on the editor's belief that mass culture has much to inform scholars, who have often been accused of being disconnected because they have allegedly taken refuge in the ivory tower. Mass culture is, in fact, a window on society, although obviously not the only one. One cannot understand modern society without understanding how most of its members—or at least those who matter in the political dispensation (i.e., urbanites)—"play."

Sports and music are key ingredients of local mass culture, and, through the electronic media (first radio, then television, now the internet), are helping in the creation of a global mass culture, especially among young people (30 and under). However, sports and popular music do more than create a curious—i.e., an age and largely gender and entertainment-based—*civilisation de l'universel.* In some countries, they are vehicles of expression of discontent toward power and the human condition in general. Popular music does this more directly and effectively than sports, because musicians often use the spoken word (the vernacular at that, so everyone can understand), whereas athletes impress with their physical prowess. However, it must not be assumed that sports is completely devoid of political expression; modern athletes are often spokespersons for various causes, and even if they choose to remain silent, fans can convey the message for them, sometimes in less than socially acceptable ways (e.g., riots and other expressions of "deviancy"). Furthermore, athletes, through their body "language" and performance on the field, can express themselves. One recalls the stir that the clenched fists of some African-American athletes at the 1968 Summer Olympics in Mexico City caused in the United States and throughout the world. One may also recall the violent reaction of the late Ivorian military dictator, Robert Guei, to the poor performance of his country's national football team in 2000, which he felt was deliberately engineered, thereby warranting jail time for some of the players. The point is, sports, nearly as much as popular music, and politics cross in modern society; no book that purports to examine politics and society in any country can afford to ignore either.

In Cameroon, football (or soccer in the North American context) is a national obsession, so much so it nearly triggered a war with neighboring Gabon in 1981. It is both a source of discord and concord. No other activity, save perhaps popular music, which is also examined in this volume, takes the pulse of Cameroon society as well as football. According to Bea

Vidacs (chapter seven), football is a two-edged sword. While it can be both ethnic and nationalist, even when it is nationalist it can be divisive. Thus Cameroonians have used football to emphasize their separateness from each other, as when local matches pit one team from one part of the country against another. They have also shown their nationalism by their support for the national team, the Indomitable Lions, especially in World Cup competition and the African Cup of Nations. These may be the only occasions when Cameroonians of all stripes show unity, and this is so for at least two reasons. Football matches in Cameroon are watched in *circuits* (informal restaurants), bars and street corners. Even when the experience of watching football takes place in a private setting, e.g., a living room, it is likely, says Vidacs, that the individual fan shares space with extended family members, friends and neighbors. In addition, the media provides extensive analysis of matches before and after they have taken place and people congregate around newspaper stands and television sets to comment freely about football matters. By watching football together in one setting and cheering the national team when it is playing and knowing that their compatriots elsewhere are doing the same, Cameroonians, through football and however temporarily, are able to construct an imagined community in the way expounded by Benedict Anderson.

The government has tried to capitalize on the unifying effect of football by sponsoring tournaments and providing financial support to the Cameroon Football Federation (FECAFOOT in its French acronym). In addition, it has associated itself to the success of the national team in international competition in recent years by appropriating the team's logo, the lion, and using it, along with President Biya's picture, on campaign posters, television commercials, postage stamps, etc. In this way, football has become a vehicle for rallying Cameroonians and, from the government's standpoint, repair its image. The efficacy of the latter strategy obviously depends on how well the national team does. Thus, the government was blamed when the Indomitable Lions took an early exit during the 1994 World Cup. By including a chapter on football the editor had hoped to underscore the importance of the "non-political" in the study of politics in Cameroon. It is scarcely an exaggeration to observe that football policy has been part of the Biya regime's governing strategy. It has paid far more attention to football than other matters, and Cameroonians, because of the fortune of the national team in recent years, have not been as critical of the government's football policy as they might otherwise be. This may well have taken the edges off Cameroon politics.

Popular music is another important vehicle of popular expression in Cameroon and throughout Africa. Post-colonial African leaders recognized the power of music soon after independence. They attempted to enlist the support of popular musicians in the construction of national identities (so did the US State Department, to shore up popular support for US policy toward the continent, when it sent jazz great Louis Armstrong on tours). In chapter eight Francis Nyamnjoh and Jude Fokwang explore the connection between music and politics in Cameroon in the 1990s. Cameroon politicians, including Ahidjo and Biya, have sought to coopt musicians into support them. In return, those who cooperated were given much airtime on the state-owned Cameroon Radio and Television (CRTV). Popular music has been politicized (some would say "ethnicized") in another way. Whereas under Ahidjo Makossa, which was popularized by Manu Dibango in the 1970s with the hit *Soul Makossa*, was considered the de facto national genre of popular music in Cameroon and enjoyed much airtime, under Biya there has been, some have argued, a deliberate attempt to downgrade Makossa in favor of Bikutsi, the fast-paced, almost frenetic, genre preferred by the Bétis, Biya's ethnic group. This has been one of the ways, critics of President Biya expound, the regime has sought to solidify support in its home base while pursuing cultural hegemony for Bétis nationally. This strategy, say Nyamnjoh and Fokwang, has not borne the expected fruits; it may even have backfired, for there is an emerging sub-genre of protest music among rural Bikutsi musicians, which may be a reaction to the government's indifference to the plight of farmers in "Bétiland." In the cities, musicians have been just as vocal, none more so than Lapiro de Mbanga in the early 1990s, whose case the authors explore in detail at the end of chapter eight.

The contributors to this volume represent a cross section of disciplines. In addition, they are based in Cameroon, Africa, Europe and North America but all are seasoned students of Cameroon. The slant taken in this volume is of the critical genre, that is to say, the contributors tend to be critical of the status quo in Cameroon without being unfair. Where Cameroon is placed in the larger context of globalization the critical stance is maintained. Thus, the book is skeptical of structural adjustment and debt relief as strategies for getting Cameroon out of its morass. At the same time, it does not see liberal democracy as a sufficient condition for rescuing Cameroon politics. In any event, Cameroon's transition to democracy is deeply flawed, as demonstrated in the elections of the 1990s. As long as the current clique remains in power, significant positive changes, either in the economy or politics, are unlikely. By the same token, the longer Paul Biya remains in power, the bleaker a post-Biya Cameroon looks. On the other hand, students of Cameroon and Cameroonians should not despair. Cameroon society has shown remarkable resilience in the face of hard times, as has Africa in general. *Cameroon: Politics and Society* is clearly on the left of the ideological spectrum but it is not dogmatic; its locality should in no way impugn its fairness, nor the intellectual rigor with which the contributors approached their topic. In the end, the reader will decide whether *Cameroon: Politics and Society* has helped to bring clarity to Africa's crossroads or increase its opacity.

ACKNOWLEDGMENTS

This book benefited from the contributions of many individuals, in fact, too many to be listed here. Therefore, I shall have to be very selective, in spite of the risk of leaving out some people who perhaps should not be left out. I would like to thank the editors of *Culture, Sport, Society*, a Frank Cass journal, for allowing the reprinting of chapter 7 by Professor Bea Vidacs. I would like to thank Joel Glassman, Director of the Center for International Studies at UM-St. Louis, for providing financial support for the project. My colleague, Ruth Iyob, provided valuable advice and, as usual, much encouragement. My colleague, Minion K. C. Morrison, was kind enough to read the manuscript in its entirety and write the Foreword section, in spite of being informed of his role on extraordinarily short notice. My research assistant in Cameroon during the summer of 2000, Patience Ngwa, was very diligent in identifying and contacting potential contributors. As usual, Ms. Deborah Whitford did an excellent job typesetting the manuscript and putting it in camera-ready format in almost record time. Above all, I thank my wife, Titilola, for granting me the freedom on some weekends to take leave of family responsibilities to perform the more tedious work of editing. The importance of these people to the completion of this book does not invalidate the usual caveat: the editor and contributors are ultimately responsible for the content of this volume.

Chapter 1

Cameroon in Synopsis

Jean-Germain Gros

In name Cameroon is a by-product of European exploration and expansion in the 15th and 16th centuries, which is not to say that it has no pre-European history. Cameroon is probably derived from the Portuguese *Rio dos Camaròes* (River of Prawns) in reference to the abundance of prawns in the Wouri River, which crosses the port city of Douala before emptying in the Atlantic. For the Portuguese, led by Fernão do Pó, were the first known Europeans to have explored coastal Cameroon, probably to exchange slaves for the European trinkets that African slave raiders thought valuable at the time. Cameroon, however, seems to have largely escaped the kind of carnage created by the Transatlantic slave trade. The country does not seem to have been a major center of slavery activities in the same mold as, say, Benin (formerly Dahomey) and Cape Coast to the west and Angola to the south. This may have been due to the absence of a strong coastal state, which could be used as a beachhead to invade and capture weaker groups in the interior.[1]

The strongest pre-colonial states were hundreds of miles away in the north, dominated by Muslim lamidos (statesmen) and marabous (clerics) and separated from the south by mosquito and tsé-tsé fly-infested rainforests and savannahs. Perhaps for the same reason Cameroon, during the period of the Scramble for Africa, was not considered a "prime real estate" by the major colonial powers. Indeed, technically and legally Cameroon was never a colony. The country came to be under German tutelage

on July 16, 1884, when Gustav Nachtigal, Bismark's envoy to Cameroon
(or Kamerun in German) signed a treaty with African kings Akwa and
Bell officially establishing the territory as a German protectorate. This
was a veritable coup for the Germans as they succeeded in outmaneuver-
ing the British envoy, consul Edward Hyde-Hewett, who was sent by
London to sign a similar treaty with the African kings, but who unfortunately (or fortunately, depending on one's viewpoint) arrived in Douala
five days too late for the task. Had Hyde-Hewett not stopped in Lagos en
route to Douala, there might not be a German Kamerun.[2]

German rule was limited to developing the agricultural potentials of the
protectorate through large commercial plantations.[3] Bismarck's unwillingness (or inability) to establish Kamerun as a full-blown colony, and thus
commit German taxpayers' money for the purpose, meant that the exploitation of the hinterland was to be gradual and financed by German merchant houses on the coast—something they were not prepared to do despite
their support for German occupation of the territory. By the beginning of
this century, however, German merchants did succeed in supplanting their
British counterparts not only on the coast but in the hinterland as well. Expanding trade and German religious missions around Mount Kamerun and
Victoria (now Limbe) helped to consolidate German control over
Kamerun. Thus, German capital and missionaries, not the old Prussian
army, set the path to German colonialism in Kamerun. Administration in
German Kamerun was initially indirect, especially in the north where centralized authority predated the European onslaught. As they expanded into
the interior, the Germans, with forced African labor, greatly improved the
infrastructure mainly to facilitate the transport of cash crops (e.g., cocoa,
rubber, palm oil) to the coast for export.

In sum, even though Kamerun enjoyed de jure protectorate status, de
facto it was a colony of Germany with all the visible imprints of early colonial rule: forced labor, dependence on a limited number of cash crops
grown on large plantations, expropriation of African land, single-track
railroads running from production centers in the interior to export points
on the coast, dominance of German capital, etc. Not surprisingly, Africans sometimes reacted angrily to German colonial policy, which then
led to severe repression. From 1884 to 1914 there were several violent
clashes between Africans and German troops over conscripted labor,
head taxes, and German attempts to expropriate African-owned land
around Douala (Delancey, 1989).[4] The latter issue was especially poi-
gnant, for the Dualas (the dominant *ethnie* in the area bearing the same
name) were one of the coastal groups to have developed relatively cen-

tralized political institutions. The Dualas were ruled by an *akwa* (king), assisted by a royal court. Some Duala entrepreneurs were successful in commerce before the arrival of the Germans and had even formed a chamber of commerce to protect their interest; they did not look too kindly on competition from German merchants, much less the confiscation of their property.

The outbreak of World War I in 1914 put an end to German domination in Kamerun, As it turned out, Lord Hyde-Hewett's lateness in arriving in Douala was only a partial setback for the British, for in March 1916 roughly 10 percent of non-contiguous territory of the former Kamerun was turned over to London while the French found themselves in charge of the remaining 90 percent. The Cameroons, composed of French East Cameroun and British West Cameroons, became an official League of Nations mandate under French and British stewardship in 1922. It has always been a mystery to this writer as to why the British settled for so little of the Cameroons cake—to paraphrase King Leopold of Belgium—when they could have had a much larger slice. A possible explanation of British "modesty" is that they were much more interested in southern and eastern Africa, where the takeover of erstwhile German-ruled Tanganyika (Tanzania) gave the British a swath of contiguous territory from Egypt to Rhodesia (Zimbabwe). Further, Britain was in possession of nearby Nigeria, which was larger and much more populous than the Cameroons. Significant British expansion in the Cameroons was likely to (a) stretch the limits of the resources available to Lord Lugard, and (b) cause conflict with the politically organized polities of the north. So averse the British seemed to have been to ruling British West Cameroons directly that they opted, in British Cameroons Order-in-Council of June 26, 1923, to divide the territory into northern and southern sections. The former was to be administered as part of northern Nigeria while the latter was ruled from Lagos as part of the British southern colonies of Nigeria. Finally, what the British failed to gain in quantity they gained in quality; British West Cameroons contained most of the German plantations, including those that grew bananas, rubber, palms and cocoa.

For their part, the French resisted the designation of French East Cameroun as a League of Nations mandate, for this opened their stewardship to international scrutiny and sometime in the future, even a distant one, the loss of the territory to independence. In their eagerness to lay the foundations of an empire from Dunkirk to Oubangui, the French were not prepared to submit "their" hard-fought territory to the League's rules. High expansionist sentiments favored outright colonial annexation. Despite France's agreement to Article 22 of the Treaty of Versailles, which spelled out the rules for territories administered as League mandates, East Cameroun was for all intents and purposes a French colony, distinguished from other territories of the French empire only by the platitudes and the nebulous language normally enshrined in international treaties. The French sought to take maximum advantage of the wealth of the territory by expanding banana and cocoa (and later coffee) production into hitherto virgin areas, using the practice previously adopted by the Germans: forced African labor. However, unlike the Germans, the French did not limit their involvement to commercial agriculture. As early as 1920, they made headway into livestock by creating one of the first cooperatives in central Africa. The *Cooperative Agricole et d'Elevage* in Dschang in 1924 represents France's early attempt to develop a viable livestock sector in Cameroun. This effort was undermined by the fact that Dschang was a predominantly Bamiléké agricultural area with little room for large-scale livestock production.[5] The north, with its open savannahs and a tradition of nomadic cattle raising, was more suited for this endeavor. Once again, because political institutions were stronger in the north, French colonial officials had to wait a few more years until advances could be made there, and even then success was limited. For example, French interest in building a railroad linking Lake Chad to the coast never materialized.

British involvement in British West Cameroons during the interwar period was limited and indirect. As the territory was never technically a colony and with a much larger and richer Nigeria next door, the British invested little in the Cameroons, to the bitter complaints of their subjects who remembered the "good old days" of German colonialism. They did expand cocoa production for export, but, according to Le Vine, compared to French investment in East Cameroun or British investment in Nigeria, British investment in West Cameroons was negligible.[6] However, the British did have a significant impact in the areas of language, education and administration. The distinct culture of English-speaking Cameroons has its roots in this early period of British domination, and the tension that exists to this day between predominantly French-speaking East Cameroun and English-speaking West Cameroons can be attributed to the multiple colonial influences that Cameroon has come under since 1884.

The thrust of British economic policy during the interwar period seems to have been on taking over formerly German-owned plantations and developing them to produce cash crops for the international market.

The Cameroon Development Corporation (CDC), which was to play a visible role in the economic development of post-colonial Cameroon, was created in 1937 to carry out this task. What should be noticed from the narrative so far is that no matter who the colonial power was, economic policy was the same. The underlying logic of German, British, and French colonialism was to integrate Cameroon (or, for that matter, the rest of Africa) into the world economy as a producer of cash crops. The "innovation" made toward this endeavor in Cameroon was the establishment of large commercial plantations, whereas in the rest of West Africa this mode of production was relatively rare (except in Liberia). There were (are) commercial plantations for almost every major crop produced in Cameroon: rubber, palm, cotton, banana, cocoa, coffee, tobacco, etc. As a result, state-owned, agro-industrial companies mushroomed in the post-colonial period, which would later have financial consequences on the Cameroon state when economic growth became stagnant (see chapter by Mentan).

World War II changed the territory's legal status from a League of Nations mandate to a United Nations trusteeship under French and British rule. The post-war era also saw much larger French and British investment in the Cameroons, although the former continued to invest much more than the latter. French investment in French East Cameroun was encapsulated into two five-year development plans. Supported by the Investment Fund for Economic and Social Development (FIDES in French), these plans focused primarily on developing East Cameroun's infrastructure to facilitate the shipment of goods in and out of the country.

From 1947 to 1953, French investment in East Cameroun amounted to $80 million French francs, a sum greater than what was spent on France's other central African colonies of Chad, Congo-Brazzaville, Gabon and Oubangui-Chari (now CAR) combined. However, investment was highly skewed: 83 percent of the funds in the first five-year plan were spent to modernize the port of Douala, expand the railways and build more landing strips and storage facilities.[7] In the mid-1950s, in other words, toward the very end of colonialism, French authorities made a more concerted effort to raise living standards through greater investment in health care, education, and other social endeavors. In the countryside, rural credits were made available, although the emphasis appears to have been on improving techniques to increase the production of cash rather than food crops. Increased social spending by France during the 1950s may have been intended to appease nationalist sentiments for independence, which by this time were being expressed most vocally by *l'Union des Popula-*

tions du Cameroun (UPC) created in 1946. Indeed, French officials banned the UPC in 1955, and this led to outbreaks of violence in Mungo, Wuri, Bassa and other areas where support for the party was strong.

In 1956 the National Assembly in France passed the Loi-Cadre—dubbed *loi cadre de fer* by the masses—in parts of Francophone Africa. This law set out to restructure the relationship between metropolitan France and the colonies. The Loi-Cadre was in furtherance of the informal understanding between De Gaulle and African supporters of Free France against the Vichy government, and by extension Nazi Germany, by which France would reconsider the status of the colonies, although not necessarily grant them independence, after the war. Before the Loi-Cadre the 1946 constitution of France had established the French Union, within which French East Cameroon had the status of an "Associated Territory" rather than a colony. Nevertheless, Cameroon was represented in the Assembly of the French Union (to which Ahidjo was elected in 1953) as well as in the French National Assembly, although Cameroonians were not granted French citizenship. In addition, a Representative Assembly (ARCAM) was created, although its powers were subservient to those of French authorities. In 1952 ARCAM was replaced by a Territorial Assembly (ATCAM), which had greater African representation and powers. ATCAM quickly became a tribune for Cameroon's most ambitious politicians. France's grip on Cameroon was further loosened in 1957 when Decree No. 57-501 created a Cameroons Legislative Assembly—in place of ATCAM, dissolved in November 1956—and government with unparallel control over internal affairs. André-Marie Mbida became the first prime minister of (Francophone) Cameroon in May of 1957. He resigned less than a year later and was replaced by Ahmadou Ahidjo (chapter two provides greater detail on the circumstances surrounding Ahidjo's accession).[8]

As an overseer of a UN trust, France was bound by Article 76 of the organization's charter, which stated that all trust territories were to be administered in such a manner as to move them toward self-government or independence. Ahidjo seized on this clause to steer Cameroon to independence. He led the Assembly to adopt a resolution that called for independence at the end of the trusteeship. In addition, the resolution calls for the reunification of the two Cameroons (i.e., French East Cameroun and British Cameroons). Negotiations between Ahidjo and French authorities resulted in Ordinance No. 58-1375 on December 30, 1958, by which the Cameroon government and legislature, beginning on January 1, 1959, were to have full autonomy over most internal matters, with monetary and security policies remaining in French hands. Ordinance No. 58-1375 was "the last stage in the evolution of the Cameroon institutions before the termination of the trusteeship"[9] (Blaustein and Flanz, 1987). And so it was until January 1, 1960, when Cameroon, officially *République du Cameroun*, became independent. But this victory for Cameroon state builders was only partial; there remained the matter of reunification, or, depending on one's point of view, unification, with British Cameroons to which I will turn shortly. For now, a brief diversion from the narrative is necessary to avoid a potential misunderstanding.

The uninitiated reader may be under the impression that the transformation of French Cameroon from a UN trust to an independent state was orderly and peaceful. I wish to dispel this notion. Led by the *Union des Populations du Cameroun* (UPC), there was a brief but violent opposition to the way Cameroon was being "decolonized" in the 1950s. The brutal suppression of this movement by French officials and their Cameroon allies has even prompted accusations of genocide in recent years (see next chapter by Le Vine). This makes Cameroon unique among "French-speaking" countries in sub-Saharan Africa in that its independence was not achieved entirely peacefully. In fact, it can be argued that there has never been a completely peaceful transfer of power in modern Cameroon, as violence as either preceded or followed such events. The radical expression of Cameroon nationalism has been explored in depth elsewhere and will not receive extensive coverage in this chapter.[10] It will suffice to say that the way radical nationalism was handled—i.e., through brutal suppression of UPC guerrillas by the French and their Cameroon allies, the physical isolation of areas of the country thought to be guerrilla strongholds and the concentration of political power in one institution, if not to say one man—has shaped politics in post-colonial Cameroon. Inflexibility, prevarication, obstruction, secrecy and violence have been the typical responses of Cameroon's elite to popular demand for greater democracy, transparency, equitable wealth distribution and independence vis-à-vis France. From the beginning the state in independent Cameroon was imbued with a security ethos, while other concerns have been given short thrift. Under the cover of security and stability Cameroon heads of state—there have only been two in forty years—have stifled democracy and undermined transparency in the management of the country's resources. Thus, no one, except perhaps the World Bank, the International Monetary Fund (IMF) and the French government (all outside actors), really knows how much revenue Cameroon earns from oil sales, for the authorities in charge of oil-related transactions answer only to the head of state and oil revenue is *hors budget* (off budget).

It should be recalled at this point that British Cameroons was divided between a northern section and a southern one. Events in former French East Cameroun would have an impact on British Cameroons, if only because the latter too was a UN trust. On March 13, 1959, the UN General Assembly adopted two resolutions that would prove fateful to British Cameroons. The first stated that on January 1, 1960, when independence for French East Cameroon was to be proclaimed, UN trusteeship over British Cameroons would also end. The second resolved that separate referenda be held in the northern and southern parts of British Cameroons, so the people there would decide their future. This was done on February 11, 1961, when British-ruled Cameroonians were asked to decide whether to join Nigeria, which became independent on October 1, 1960, or the *République du Cameroun*. Absent from the ballot were continued UN tutelage or independence. The international community seemed to have agreed that partition was undesirable in this instance, and, to the best of the writer's knowledge, pro-independence voices were faint inside the territory. The results were Solomonic, perhaps not accidentally, in their effect: British northern Cameroon voted to become part of the Federation of Nigeria while British southern Cameroon opted to join the *République du Cameroun* in a federation, which was formally constituted on October 1, 1961.

The Federal Republic of Cameroon consisted of the Federated State of East Cameroon (Francophone) and the Federated State of West Cameroon (Anglophone), which, to the edification of the reader, was the southern portion of British Cameroon that had voted against joining Nigeria. (In today's Cameroon West Cameroon is split between northwest and southwest provinces, with Bamenda and Buea as their respective capital). There is no question that Ahidjo was the prime mover behind unification, as he was behind the drive for independence. There is also no question that for Ahidjo the federation was a necessary, but temporary, arrangement. A close reading of the deliberations of the Foumban constitutional conference in July of 1961 clearly shows Ahidjo's preference for a strong central government. After all, the 1960 constitution of the Republic of Cameroon was patterned after the 1958 constitution of France, and Ahidjo's personality had little room for sharing power with anyone including John Foncha, then premier of West Cameroon. Federation was the price to pay for unifying a divided Cameroon but Ahidjo would reclaim his money in 1972. In that year, in the type of sham "elections" and referenda that would be repeated all over Africa as post-colonial incumbent rulers tried to consolidate their power, 99.9 percent of Cameroon voters said yes to a new constitution that abolished the federal republic and its institutions and declared Cameroon a unitary state (formally named *République Unie du Cameroun* and United Republic of Cameroon). This event, which followed the formation of a *de facto* one party-system in 1966 (the Cameroon National Union), consecrated Ahidjo as the only cock that could crow in Africa's crossroads. Coercive apparatuses were developed in support of Ahidjo's authoritarian design, including detention camps (e.g., at Tchillore), intelligence gathering agencies (e.g., CEDOC), secret trials, etc. These were supplemented by the extensive powers of the president in the management of the country's resources. Thus the economy too (examined later) would become a governing tool, in other words, politicized to reward supporters and punish enemies. Ahidjo ruled Cameroon until 1982 when concern about his failing health apparently forced him to resign. He was succeeded by Paul Biya, who has been governing Cameroon ever since.

ASSESSING AHIDJO

How does one assess Cameroon during the first two decades of independence? In the same vein, how does one assess Ahidjo's stewardship? Much has been written about the man, including in this volume (see next chapter by Le Vine). Some revile him; others, especially among middle class Cameroonians of all ethnic stripes, have bestowed a measure of respect upon him in recent years. In northern Cameroon (Adamawa, north and extreme-north provinces), as well as in the overwhelmingly Muslim neighborhood of Briquiterie in Yaoundé, Ahidjo is extremely popular. Posters of him have reappeared, as have tapes of some of his speeches from which this chapter greatly benefits. Even the government occasionally jumps into the fray—usually in times of elections—by promising to allow Ahidjo's body reentry into Cameroon for proper burial. It is not hard to understand Ahidjo's quasi rehabilitation among ordinary Cameroonians. His tenure is now remembered as a time of prosperity, when primary commodity prices were relatively stable, oil prices were high and the crime rate low (see next section and chapter five by Tatah Mentan). This is in sharp contrast to the Biya era, which many associate with stagnation, corruption and banditry. However, it is important not to get carried away by the current wave of revisionism sweeping Cameroon. Ahidjo must be put into proper perspective. This requires intellectual sobriety and objectivity. In probing Ahidjo I realize I am anticipating somewhat the chapters that are to follow, especially the next chapter by Le

Vine, but no editor worth his (or her) salt can fail to say something about the "founding father" of Cameroon in a major study of the country. Whatever Cameroon is (or is not) today is due, in no small part, to what Ahidjo did or did not do.[11] In this regard, he is simply *incontournable*. It is a measure of the weight of Ahidjo in contemporary Cameroon history that all of the chapters in this volume, even those that are not directly connected to politics, mention his name.

Ahmadou Ahidjo was neither the ogre that his critics say he was nor the genius that nostalgists have made him out to be. Ahidjo was very much in the mold of the first generation of post-colonial African leaders upon whom all kinds of paternalistic titles were bestowed, sometimes with some justification sometimes not (e.g., Father of the Nation, Osagyefo, Mwalimu, Mwenze, Nana, etc.). In this pantheon Ahidjo could be compared with Jomo Kenyata and Houphouet Boigny. If he lacked the Mau Mau pedigree of the former and the avuncular joviality of the latter, he was just as substantive and successful as they were. But substantive and successful in terms of what? Ahidjo has a long record of domestic accomplishments, which include formal independence (achieved in 1960), territorial consolidation (achieved in 1961), political hegemony for his party (achieved in 1966 with the formation of the Cameroon National Union) and for himself (achieved in 1972 when the Cameroon federation gave way to a unitary state) and economic development (Cameroon was considered a success story until the mid 1980s, around the time Ahidjo resigned). Ahidjo could have failed at any of these efforts but did not, and his success cannot simply be attributed to luck. In foreign policy, Ahidjo kept Cameroon out of conflagration in Nigeria (1966–1970), and quickly resolved a dispute with Gabon in 1981, when Cameroon airlifted 10,000 of its nationals out of that country in an impressive display of military discipline and organization by an African country. Ahidjo clearly valued Cameroon's relations with France, perhaps above all other relations, but he was not France's lackey by any means. A nationalist, he showed independence on several occasions. He broke with France over Biafra (see section on foreign policy), paid at least lip service to African unity and publicly supported the non-aligned movement.

Ahidjo used the entire repertoire of state coercion and diplomacy to craft a unified Cameroon with a strong center. This makes him a state maker, a centralizer, precisely what Cameroon (and much of Africa) needed at the time of independence and even now. He went astray by concentrating power around his person and the ruling CNU, thereby ignoring the rudiments of democratic rule (i.e., separation of powers, checks-and-balances, multipartyism, a free press, etc.) and local sentiments for autonomy, especially among Anglophones. Personal rule, in turn, required the detention camps, the secret trials and the intelligence networks for which Ahidjo became infamous among scholarly critics and human rights activists.

In sum, a democrat Ahidjo was not, nor, however, was he a tyrant. Without belittling the abuses committed under Ahidjo, let it be remarked, in the name of fairness, that Cameroon never descended into the abyss of Uganda under Idi Amin or Equatorial Guinea under Macias Nguema, which it could easily have under a more brutal dictator. Again, Ahidjo's regime was authoritarian, but so too were at least 90 percent of the regimes that ruled Africa during this time. Ahidjo's excesses were moderated somewhat by his penchant for reconciliation, which he pursued through a policy of *equilibre* or ethnic balance in the bureaucracy. In this dispensation northerners were clearly privileged—as reflected in murmurs of *Garoua d'abord* (Garoua first) by deputies in the National Assembly during debates over the national budget—but other groups were represented as well via "their" ministers, secretaries of state, director generals of parastatals, etc.

Ahidjo's regime was an authoritarian regime of the administrative-hegemonic type described by Chazan et al.[12] The president clearly epitomized state power and used coercion to enforce his will, but he was assisted in the task of state making by a bureaucracy in which technical competence was given some currency and ethnic balance perhaps just as much. That Biya, a technocrat and a southerner, was Ahidjo's prime minister for years before succeeding him as president gives much credence to the assertion. Also, massive corruption is not associated with the Ahidjo era, which is what would be expected of an administrative-hegemonic regime. Although more powerful than anyone, *Grand Patron* Ahidjo (that was one of his nicknames) did not always have his way. He had to move more slowly on some issues than he probably would have liked (the transformation from a federal state to a unitary one took 11 years) and may have even retreated on others in the face of growing opposition (i.e., whether SONARA, the oil refining parastatal, should be located in Limbe, southwest province, or Douala).

The administrative-hegemonic regime in the African context, although clearly authoritarian, represents an advancement in statecraft, for it comes closer to Weber's legal-rational model than its competitors (the party-mobilizing or the military regimes) save perhaps "demoracy." Where Cameroon is concerned, there is a point that is absolutely crucial:

by labeling the regime led by Ahidjo administrative-hegemonic I do not mean to suggest that it did not exhibit any other traits. All I am saying is that regime behavior or orientation tended more toward the administrative-hegemonic than the other regime types. In other words, Ahidjo's regime was overwhelmingly administrative-hegemonic but not exclusively so. The ruling party, the CNU (later CPDM), was not exactly a nonentity. It mattered whether local party bosses could churn out 100 percent support for Ahidjo at "election" times, which required a certain amount of mass mobilization (and cheating); and *Grand Patron's* penchant for secrecy at times made Cameroon look like a military camp, with movements to parts of the country (e.g., the west) severely circumscribed long after *maquisard* activity had ceased. Ironically, the passing of the baton from Ahidjo to Biya may have resulted in a decline of political modernization in Cameroon (ironic because Biya was supposed to be the modernizing technocrat and Ahidjo the despotic *petit Peul*). Regime behavior under Biya, especially since the aborted coup of 1984, has displayed the characteristics of patronage rather than those of legal rationalism, of which I consider the African administrative-hegemonic regime a deformed hybrid.[13]

Where the economy was concerned (see next section), Ahidjo was a *dirigiste*, meaning that in his "modernization" scheme the state was given a key role in sectors deemed strategic by the president.[14] This does not mean that Ahidjo was a socialist. Cameroon's investment code emphasized partnership between private (mainly foreign) capital and state capital. When the former was not forthcoming, the state, through *Société Nationale d'Investissement* (SNI), became the sole operator in much of the industrial sector. Earnings from oil and a tight-fisted fiscal policy gave Cameroon plenty of money, which it could invest in the priority sectors (e.g., metallurgy, textile, agro-business, etc.). Here too Ahidjo was neither outside of the mainstream nor a genius. Raoul Prebisch had written the gospel on the virtues and necessity of state-led industrialization and import substitution in the Third World, the Bretton Woods institutions had helped to spread it with their financing, and African leaders, in the name of nationalism, were willing to sell it as sound economic policy. Critics of President Biya often accuse him of using state assets in the private economy for political ends; they forget that statism was begun under Ahidjo. Biya, who, as Le Vine points out in chapter two, has turned out to be a much more astute student of Ahidjo than he would care to admit in public, has merely continued what his predecessor started. Biya cannot be blamed for having run the Cameroon economy into the ground because of his statist policies when Ahidjo is lauded for the same. There is a disconnect and an inconsistency here that can only be explained by the type of convenient collective amnesia that people engage in when they want to discredit living opponents and rehabilitate dead ones.

ECONOMY AND POLITICAL REFORM

Until the mid-1980s, Cameroon was recognized by many as one of the few "economic successes" in Africa. Blessed with adequate natural resources and a competent bureaucracy, Cameroon consistently achieved respectable levels of growth (over 5 percent) and a positive trade balance. Indeed, it is still one of a handful of countries in Africa to be self-sufficient in food production. Ahmadou Ahidjo followed a policy of economic development which emphasized agriculture, foreign investment, albeit with majority shares held by the state, and relatively prudent spending of oil revenues to avoid inflation. However, despite its "success" Cameroon was no different from other African and Third World countries. Dependence on primary commodities, especially oil, made the country very vulnerable to external shocks. Moreover, the *dirigiste* approach to economic development, which entails state participation in key sectors of the economy, eventually overburdened the state as many of the state-owned enterprises were money-losing ventures. Even privately-owned firms came to cause headache to the state. Many had been created by pseudo entrepreneurs connected to the regime, which gave them access to bank loans. These loans would never be collected, since the businesses that served as collaterals to them were either non-existent or had worthless assets.

State spending excesses could be tolerated as long as oil revenue was on the rise, but that trend came to an end in 1981–82. The worldwide recession of the early 1980s, combined with sharp drops in cocoa and coffee prices throughout the decade, sent Cameroon's economy into a downward spiral from which it has yet to completely recover. External shocks had significant repercussions on Cameroon because oil revenue represented a major source of foreign exchange for the government. In 1965, fuel, mineral and metal exports accounted for 17 percent of merchandise exports, by 1983–84 these commodities accounted for 68 percent of Cameroon's exports. At the same time, the share of agricultural commodity exports fell from 77 percent in 1965 to 27 percent in 1983–84.[15] In sum, the Cameroon economy was rocked by falling prices for oil and cash crops. Government debt, caused not only by declining foreign exchange earnings but also an expanding bureaucracy and poor performance of state-owned enterprises, rose. The economy was further destabilized by an overvalued currency—the Central Africa CFA franc—and the near-collapse of the banking system in the wake of the scandalous collapse of BCCI in 1989 and the bad debts made by Cameroon banks to politically well-connected "entrepreneurs."

Popular frustration with the economy, President Paul Biya's failure to bring about *le libéralisme communautaire* (communitarian liberalism) promised in his magnum ocpus of the same name, the fall of the Berlin Wall and the increasing vocality of civil society sparked political reform in Cameroon. In chronological terms, the drive toward multiparty rule began in 1989, when prominent attorney and Douala chief Yondo Black attempted to create a political party, which was not explicitly illegal even under the restrictive Cameroon constitution. In February 1990, Black and some of his collaborators were arrested for their organizing work and charged with attempting to destabilize the government by fomenting ethnic tension. Cameroonian artists and intellectuals protested; the international community soon joined them. Stirred to action by the Black affair, John Fru Ndi, a librarian from English-speaking Nortwest Province, announced the launching of the Social Democratic Front in May 1990. Government security forces used violence to break up the SDF's first public rally in the western town of Bamenda, killing between four and a dozen people. A law officially permitting the formation of political parties was adopted in December 1990; shortly thereafter, opposition parties formed the National Coordination Committee of Opposition Parties (NCCOP), largely in response to what some opposition leaders saw as government maneuvering to control the outcome of the democratic game by unilaterally making up its rules.[16]

The NCCOP's three main components were the Social Democratic Front (SDF), the Union National pour le Dévelopement et le Progrès (UNDP), and the now-legal but seriously divided Union des Populations du Cameroun (UPC). In addition, there was a swarm of smaller parties, many of which had no more than a leader and a few activists. These parties tended to be less antagonistic toward the ruling Cameroon Peoples Democratic Movement (CPDM) than the three main ones, and at least one minor party, the Mouvement Démocratique pour la République, was known to be an offshoot of the ruling party organized as part of a scheme to draw support away from the UNDP in the northern provinces, its stronghold. Like its counterparts in other "French- speaking" African countries, the opposition in Cameroon demanded that the government convene a sovereign national conference whose first (but by no means last) order of business would be to devise rules and procedures for holding the upcoming local and national elections. The Biya government refused, arguing that the democratization process in Cameroon was already well underway, thus obviating the need for a national conference. The government further contended that the 1972 constitution, following the example of the French Fifth Republic, clearly placed all elections in the hands of the minister of territorial administration, who was ostensibly independent and thus immune from political pressure applied by either side. In sum, the government responded to popular calls for political reform by using the tactics identified earlier: first violence followed by half-hearted measures designed to give the incumbent clear advantages in the new (ostensibly liberalized) dispensation.

The opposition responded to the government's obstinacy by calling in June 1991 for a general strike, dubbed *Opération Villes Mortes* (Operation Ghost Town), designed to shut down every city and town in the country from Monday through Friday until the government agreed to its call for a sovereign national conference. In addition, Operation Ghost Town called for citizens to withhold taxes from the state. At the end of October 1991, after the government had demonstrated its ability to withstand the pressure of this campaign, the opposition came to the bargaining table. The trilateral talks brought together representatives of the government, the opposition, and the so-called *forces vives* of Cameroonian society: local entrepreneurs, the media, religious bodies, workers' and students' unions, and so on. Although the fanfare that preceded these talks misled some opposition leaders into thinking that they were getting the substance of a national conference under a different name, it quickly became clear that the government's agenda fell far short of their hopes. To begin with, President Biya brushed aside calls for his personal participation and sent his prime minister, Sadou Hayatou, instead. Next Biya succeeded in restricting the main agenda to constitutional questions; in other French-speaking African countries, the scope of such national conferences had been much broader. Third and perhaps most important, while the government led everyone to believe that constitutional reform would take place before the upcoming legislative and presidential elections, this did not happen.

Instead, the first presidential election since one-party rule was abandoned in 1990 took place on October 11, 1992, under the old rules and with the minister of territorial administration in charge of the process. These rules could hardly be said to have created a "level playing field" for the competing parties. The following irregularities are noteworthy. First, the campaign period began on September 17, making it a full six days shorter than the 30-day run-up mandated by Article 51 of the 1972 constitution. Many of the opposition parties, the SDF in particular, had no experience in running for office and simply did not have enough time to organize. Moreover, the important work of voter registration and education could not be properly done within such a short period of time, in spite of the willingness of foreign organizations such as the US-based National Democratic Institute to provide assistance. Not surprisingly, many voters were turned away on election day because they lacked the needed identification papers or found their names mysteriously omitted from the rolls. Second, the minister of territorial administration, far from being the paragon of neutrality and fairness touted by the regime, was in fact a close ethnic kindred of President Biya and an unabashed CPDM partisan. Putting the minister of territorial administration in charge of the electoral process guaranteed, at a minimum, widespread suspicion of foul play. The opposition had pushed for an independent electoral commission to run the election, but had to settle for a National Commission of the Final Counting of Votes. This body had 19 members, of whom 13 were appointed by the government, with 11 of these coming from Biya's strongholds of south and center provinces. Third, the government enjoyed an overwhelming advantage in resources. State-run Cameroon Radio and Television (CRTV), the most pervasive source of news and information in the country, gave Biya much greater coverage (all of it favorable) than it gave to the opposition. Events that were really government-staged political propaganda were reported on CRTV as "news."

Numerous irregularities were noted by international and domestic observers on election day, including stuffed ballot boxes, the inclusion of "votes" from nonexistent or "ghost precincts," physical intimidation of opposition supporters, and, as stated earlier unexplained omissions of voters from voting lists. Finally, the investigation and resolution of election disputes were left to the Cameroon supreme court, which in its final report admitted the possibility of widespread fraud. In the same report, however, the court also made it clear that, since it lacked the power to annul the election, it had no choice but to declare President Biya the winner. Indeed, the impotence of the judiciary was vividly underscored four days after the election when, with only 20 percent of the votes counted, the minister of territorial administration unilaterally declared Biya the winner without waiting for the supreme court to investigate charges of fraud and pronounce its findings.

In 1997, his five-year term having expired, President Biya ran again and won what was largely a dispirited election in which the outcome was known in advance. All of the advantages that the president had enjoyed in 1992 were in play in 1997, and the regime used the full arsenal of its machinations to remain in power. In 1997, there was also a semblance of return to economic growth. The devaluation of the CFA franc in 1994, increased export earnings (made possible in part by currency devaluation), IMF and World-Bank mandated cuts in government expenditures and earnings from the sales of former state-owned enterprises made the economic environment at the end of the decade less volatile than it was at the beginning. In sum, political apathy combined with somewhat brighter economic prospects helped Biya in 1997. Also, it has to be said that the Cameroon government has learned to better "handle" the opposition. Even though the presidency continues to be "off limit" to the opposition, it is well represented in the legislature.[17] Further, the cabinet contains ministers from the opposition, including Bello Bouba Maigari, Biya's old nemesis, who was appointed minister of commerce and industry. Further, by the end of the 1990s the government had lifted many of the restrictions on the press. The net result of Cameroon's clumsy march toward democracy is a regime that is not as authoritarian as it once was but not as democratic as it should be. In other words, politically speaking Cameroon is neither fish nor fowl.

FOREIGN POLICY

Since independence Cameroon foreign policy has been decidedly pro-western, even though some of Ahidjo's early speeches made allusion to "African socialism" and Cameroon maintained diplomatic relations with the former USSR and some eastern bloc countries during the Cold War. The state did play an important role in the economy, but this was a reflection of the economic orthodoxy of the time (import substitution, protectionism, state-led industrialization, etc.) and the clientelistic nature of the Cameroon state, not rigid adherence to socialist dogma. Cameroon leaders have been decidedly non-ideological in their foreign and economic policy. In spite of its location between West and Central Africa, Cameroon has not played a visible role in regional, much less continental, politics, although it is a member of all the major African organizations. Unlike the smaller Gabon, for example, Cameroon has not tried to negotiate an end to the conflagrations that have engulfed Congo-Brazzaville, the Central African Republic and Chad, in spite of sharing a common bor-

der with these states. Non-interference in the affairs of sister African
states has been a cornerstone of Cameroon foreign policy for reason(s)
that will be discussed later. Cameroon has been very close to France, but
it is too simplistic to argue, as disgruntled Anglophones are wont to do,
that Cameroon diplomacy is hostage to France's. France may still be
Cameroon's most important partner but French interests and Cameroon's
are not identical. This reality has at times created foreign policy differences between the two states. As in the other African countries that make
up the historical *pré carré*, Franco-Cameroon relations are developed
through and shaped by personal contact between the heads of state and
the politico-economic elites of the two countries, the monetary union
linking the Central Africa CFA franc and the French franc (replaced by
the Euro), development aid and security concerns.[18] These factors shall
be examined in turn.

Close ties between Cameroon and France were assured at independence. In 1960 there were more experienced and talented political, business
and civic leaders than Ahidjo, men such as Douala Manga Bell and Paul
Soppo Priso in Francophone Cameroon and Foncha in West Cameroon.
However, Ahidjo, hailing from the north and less educated than many of
his urbane compatriots, was thought to be malleable and conservative (see
next chapter). Further, even as a relatively low-level official in the colonial
administration, he had strong ties to French officials. These attributes (if
they can be called that) made him a safe choice. Further, the French played
a key role in the defeat of the UPC counterinsurgents. They contributed
mightily in terms of humanpower, materiel (i.e., weapons), intelligence
and training. The French did not exactly handpick Ahmadou Ahidjo to be
Cameroon's first president, who, as stated earlier, was his own man in
many respects, but there is no question that their maneuvers facilitated his
ascension to power in 1960 and their continued support after that contributed, at least in part, to the longevity of his tenure.

Close ties between Cameroon and France remained under Paul Biya,
who was educated in France and had been Ahidjo's prime minister for
seven years before becoming president. Thus Biya knew his way around
French power before ascending Cameroon's highest office. Cameroon's
membership in the CFA franc zone has meant that it has had to surrender
its autonomy in monetary matters. Representatives of the Bank of France
sit on the governing board of the zone's central bank. France is Cameroon's biggest provider of bilateral economic aid and its principal interlocutor before the international financial institutions (i.e., World Bank,
IMF, EU, etc.). Perhaps above all, France provides military assistance to

Cameroon. French officers provide training to their Cameroon counterparts in Cameroon as well as in France. There have long been rumors of a "secret pact" between the countries, whereby France would intervene militarily in case of a coup d'état, as it has in other "Francophone" African countries. In sum, the relationship between France and Cameroon is clearly asymmetrical and points to the dependency of the latter on the former. However, as stated earlier, it is an error to view Cameroon foreign policy only through one lense.

The foreign policy of nations is shaped as much by domestic factors as it is by international ones. Indeed, foreign policy is but domestic policy writ large. State elites often use foreign policy to pursue domestic goals, which in young states include securing their border, raising living standards and gaining the allegiance of their citizens—in sum, consolidating state power through security, prosperity and stability. Cameroon is no exception. There are at least two instances where domestic considerations weighed far more heavily in Cameroon foreign policy than the country's dependent relationship with France. During the Biafra War French support for the rebels were well known. They provided weapons to the Biafrans and encouraged their former colonies to do the same. Ahidjo, on the other hand, was steadfast in his support for the federal government of general Gowon. In all likelihood this had nothing to do with ethnic affinity, for Gowon, although from the north, was neither Hausa-Fulani nor Muslim, as Ahidjo was. Ahidjo's decision was probably based on his interpretation of what was in Cameroon's national interest at the time. He had formed a federation between the southern portion of the former British West Cameroons and French East Cameroun in 1961, six years before the outbreak of the Biafra War. If he supported the cause of the Biafrans, what was to prevent Nigeria from retaliating by supporting future Anglophone demands for secession from Cameroon? This was an instance in which French and Cameroon interests clashed. While the French were looking at the partition of Nigeria as a way of gaining greater influence in West Africa, Cameroon was paying greater attention to the implication that supporting the breakup of its neighbor would have on its state-making efforts, specifically as they relate to the Cameroon federation. Anglophones in Cameroon had no less of a claim to sovereignty than Biafrans in Nigeria. Consolidation of the Cameroon federation at the time meant supporting a similar arrangement across the border, even if this was not the policy of the former colonial power.

Cameroon's decision to seek membership in the Commonwealth under President Paul Biya provides further evidence that the country's foreign policy is not hostage to France's. By some indications French officials were not keen on the idea when they got wind of it, but the Biya government went ahead and Cameroon was eventually admitted into the group, thus becoming the only country in Black Africa (indeed, in the world) to have dual membership in the *Francophonie* and Commonwealth. Cameroon's decision to join the Commonwealth was driven by the fact that the Biya government wanted to appease Anglophone sentiment of estrangement from the rest of Cameroon. By joining the Commonwealth Cameroon could claim balance in its foreign policy, for it was now a member of both the *Francophonie* and the Commonwealth. The Anglophones could no longer claim that Cameroon's foreign policy did not reflect "their" interest in the wider, non-French-speaking, world. Anglophone noise in favor of secession could thus be more easily drowned out. Further, Cameroon membership in the Commonwealth may have been intended to "diversify" the country's foreign policy portfolio. It meant possibly more aid from Britain, more scholarships for Cameroon students and greater cultural contact. Keeping Cameroon intact—in other words, preventing secession—has been at the core of Cameroon foreign policy since 1961. To the extent that close ties with France help this goal, Cameroon leaders have no interest in challenging the former metropole. But where French policy in Africa seems to contravene state making in Cameroon, Cameroon rulers have shown a willingness to exert independence. The neutral stance that Cameroon has adopted toward the conflicts in the Great Lakes, Congo-Brazzaville, the Central African Republic and Chad, conflicts in which France has been involved lock, stock and barrel, shows a determination by Cameroon to stay out of its neighbors' problems, perhaps in the hope that that they will refrain from inserting themselves in its.

This brief incursion into Cameroon history, politics, economy, society and foreign policy shall be transformed into a full-blown invasion in the subsequent chapters. For now, I would like to draw the reader's attention to the "fault lines" of Cameroon politics and society in the 21st century.

The Fractured Society Versus the Centralization-Obsessed State

Cameroon, Africa's crossroads, is an ethnic melting pot perched vicariously on a fire of regional and linguistic differences. By the same token, Cameroon is perhaps the most effectively centralized state in Africa. Cameroon was born a republic in 1960, was named a federation in 1961, and became a unified republic in 1972, only to be declared a republic *tout court* a second time in 1984. It is scarcely an exaggeration to say that the story of post-colonial Cameroon is the story of centralized authority in Yaoundé trying to impose itself on the rest of the country, sometimes by force sometimes by inducement, and using foreign policy to consolidate domestic power. This attempt has been largely successful. One does not travel from one part of Cameroon to another without encountering evidence of centralized authority, whether in the person of the gendarme, préfet or ministerial délégué. The failed state syndrome experienced by many African countries in the last two decades of the 20th century missed Cameroon, where "Gaullism" is alive and well. However, it is precisely the hyperconcentration of formal power not only in the capital city (Yaoundé) but especially in the presidency, two features of "Gaullism" in Africa, that is undermining the legitimacy of the state in the hinterland.[19]

The sources of tension between state and society in Cameroon today are two-fold. First, as stated earlier, Cameroon is one of the most ethnically plural countries in Black Africa; further, it is the only one with three colonial legacies, two of which continue to shape politics. The diversity of Cameroon society and the perception of politics as a zero-sum game naturally create strong sentiments for regional, even local, autonomy. On the other hand, the need of state elites in Yaoundé to achieve hegemony, in other words, to control this fragmented policy, puts severe limits on how far they are willing to go to share power with sub-elites in the provinces. Thus in Cameroon power sharing typically means power delegation, not its wholesale transfer; and administrative reform tends to be of the deconcentration, rather than decentralization, type, even though the latter is sanctioned by the 1996 constitution. Both reforms leave real power in the presidency and reinforce the patron-client ties that so characterize the Cameroon political system.

In addition, the resources of Cameroon are not evenly distributed. Oil, Cameroon's number one foreign exchange earner, is exploited on the coast of southwest province and wood in the south and center provinces. Two of these provinces (southwest and south) are populated by groups that feel estranged from the state and are not willing to let it exploit "their" resources without their input. The call for autonomy at the periphery, even independence in the case of southwest province, is undergirded in part by poor management of natural resources by the center, and, more seriously, the belief that mismanagement is a deliberate and systematic attempt to marginalize one group (i.e., Anglophones in the southwest) by stripping it of its assets and enrich another (i.e., Francophones in general, and Bétis in particular since they ostensibly control the state). The future of Cameroon may well depend on how well ethnic, regional and language cleavages, as well as the economy, are handled in (and by) a state that has always given priority to its goals: security, law and order and control of the citizenry.

Transition Frustration: The Authoritarian Wall Versus the Democratic Tide

The Biya regime was severely tested in the 1990s. The wind of political change that swept through the African continent then did not bypass Cameroon territory; however, it did not wipe out authoritarian rule. The transition to multipartyism in Cameroon has been tightly controlled by the ruling Cameroon Peoples Democratic Movement (CPDM) party, which successfully resisted calls for a sovereign national conference that would have set the rules of the democratic game before the first transition presidential election was held in October 1992. Indeed, a pattern may be discerned in the behavior of the Cameroon government vis-à-vis democratization that may be described as intimidation, extemporization, acceleration and continuation through adjustment. When calls for political opening were first made, the government responded by labeling pro-democracy activists seditious and arresting a number of them. This was to buy time to see whether pressure for change would stop and to determine how to respond in case it did not, in other words, the regime extemporized. When the strategy did not work, the regime quickly passed a series of laws in favor of democratization and established timetables for elections. The advantages conferred by incumbency plus actions by the government designed to destabilize the opposition (e.g., financing the creation of splinter parties inside the opposition) resulted in President Paul Biya winning not one but two multiparty elections in the 1990s. Since then the biggest change in political governance in Cameroon has taken place in parliament, which has representatives from all the major parties: CPDM, UNDP, SDF, etc. But since the legislature has no power to initiate laws and the discretionary powers of the executive are extensive, the president continues to dominate national affairs as much as before the transition. There is greater freedom of the press in Cameroon than there was before 1990. However, censorship still exists and the government alone decides when criticism of its actions has crossed the line.

In sum, democracy in Cameroon is in a state of suspended animation. As stated earlier, the political system is neither democratic all the time nor authoritarian all the time. Cameroonians appear to have resigned themselves to this confusion, although tensions continue to simmer under the surface and occasionally break into the open at election time. Daily resistance to authoritarianism takes other, more subtle, forms. In theater, plays criticizing one or the other aspect of Cameroon life have been performed. For example, Victor Ngome's *What God Has Put Asunder* is widely thought to be about the Francophone-Anglophone rift. Bate Besong's *Requiem for the Last Kaiser* explores the same theme: the alleged victimization of Anglophones in the Cameroon political dispensation (see chapter by Nantang Jua in this volume). The popularity of *Mapouka* among young Cameroonians, which originated in Ivory Coast, may have been a direct challenge to authorities, some of whom deemed the dance so "obscene" that they banned it in some areas. Even football, which superficially binds Cameroonians to one another, provides an occasion for dissent. Be it the composition of the national team, who coaches it, and how many goals the Indomitable Lions score in international competition, Cameroonians look for every opportunity to attribute team performance to issues of social, even foreign, policy.

Succession or Secession Question: After Paul Biya, Who or What?

Among students of Cameroon this is the great imponderable. Of course, the question would be immediately answered if Biya were to be forced from office either by way of a coup d'état or electoral defeat. Although the possibility of a coup can never be discounted in African politics, in the short term it seems implausible in Cameroon.[20] The Cameroon armed forces, perhaps more than any other in Francophone Africa, have generally shown respect for republican government (except in 1984). Further, Biya has taken great care to put loyalists in key military posts while rotating and retiring others whose allegiance is suspect. Finally, military support from France could be expected in case of a coup attempt, although this is not guaranteed (unless long-standing rumors of a secret pact between Cameroon and France sanctioning French intervention in case of a coup attempt turned out to be true). It seems just as implausible that Biya would ever be forced from power by an election, for the evidence thus far suggests that he is a man who is willing to do anything to win. Incumbency in Africa confers tremendous advantages, as it does everywhere, and President Biya has not been bashful in using it to guarantee electoral victories.[21]

The biggest precipitator of a succession crisis in Cameroon is death. Paul Biya is not a young man, although in appearance he seems reasonably vigorous. A septuagenarian, he is by now one of the oldest and longest serving heads of state in Africa. Sooner or later he too shall pass, and then what? Unlike Ahidjo, Biya has not visibly groomed anyone to replace him. Part of his governing strategy has been to rotate personnel around the ministries, embassies and parastatals while he reigns at Etoudi unperturbed. Thus, there is not one minister who has been in the cabinet continuously since Biya took power. The way in which some ministers have been dismissed (e.g., Akame Mfoumou, former minister of defense and so-called super minister of finance), in fact, points to a strategy of humiliation, perhaps intended to remind everyone who is boss in Cameroon. The net result of keeping friends and foes guessing by bringing them in and out of power is a dearth of identifiable successors capable of immediately filling any void created by Nature. In addition, the flawed nature of the transition to democratic rule makes it unlikely that constitutional provisions toward succession would be respected. A more likely scenario is that Biya's passing would be seen as an opportunity for disaffected groups to exercise what Hirschman calls the exit option. In this vein, Anglophones might be the first to say good riddance to Cameroon, or at least insist on fundamental changes in the structure of the state (e.g., a return to federalism). In sum, a leadership succession crisis might lead to a secession crisis with violence accompanying both.

Economic Malaise + Administrative Malfeasance = Crisis of Poverty and State Legitimacy

Regardless of aggregate figures provided by the World Bank that point to a recovery, Cameroon is a country in crisis. Unemployment is at least 40 percent, attendance among school age children is 80 percent (down from nearly 100 percent in the 1980s), and crime is a major problem in the cities. The root causes of economic malperformance are two-fold. In the first instance, Cameroon is overly dependent on primary commodities, such as cocoa, cotton, coffee, rubber and palm oil, whose prices have been stagnant. The commercial plantations where some of these products are exploited have either been privatized or should be "soon," but there is no evidence of a significant infusion of private capital in the commercial agriculture sub-sector as promised by structural adjustment advocates. This is unlikely to occur, as long as primary commodity prices remain low. Small to medium-scale cocoa and coffee farmers are unlikely to capitalize their holdings for the same reason. Cameroon has oil, but the offshore area in which the "black gold" is exploited—Rio del Rey—is expected to be depleted in a few years' time (2010). Oil is suspected near Kribi (south province) and in the Lake Chad basin (extreme north province), but commercial exploration, much less exploitation, had not started as of the time of writing (although Cameroon is expected to earn millions in fees from a pipeline that will take oil in Chad to Kribi for export).

In recent years, logging has played a significant role in the Cameroon economy. However, Cameroon is not taking full advantage of its forests since it mainly exports wood, thereby foregoing the value added that comes with the forward and backward linkage industries, such as paper and plywood. The finished products derived from wood are mainly for local consumption (e.g., furniture). Much of the exploitation of timber seems to be informal, meaning that the government is not extracting its "fair share" of the proceeds in the form of taxes. Further, without forest conservation and regeneration logging is likely to be of transient economic benefit (mostly for loggers and their associates). The long-term effects, however, could be devastating: loss of valuable habitat to humans and animals, decreased rainfall, soil erosion and the spread to population centers of diseases hitherto confined to the forests.

The devaluation of the CFA franc in 1994 was supposed to stimulate export and reduce import, and to some extent it has. However, the decision, plus government cut in salaries mandated by the World Bank, has had its downsides. It has pauperized thousands of middle class Cameroonians, who no longer have the purchasing power to stimulate a moribund economy. It goes beyond cynicism that poor countries like Cameroon are often asked to tighten their belt when faced with economic crises but rich ones are allowed to resort to stimulus packages (i.e., higher spending and deficits) to accelerate recovery. Graft and corruption have exacerbated Cameroon's economic problems. In 2000 Transparency International, whose methods, if not motives, one must admit, are suspect, ranked Cameroon the most corrupt country in the world, "outperforming" Nigeria to which the dubious distinction had hitherto belonged. The kind of corruption that has beset the Cameroon state is not the familiar bribery of government officials that inspired Jean-François Bayart's *La politique du ventre*.[22]

Although bribery as a form of government corruption surely exists in Cameroon, as it does throughout Africa and elsewhere, we are talking about corruption on such a massive scale as to pose a threat to economic, socio-political and environmental order. Specifically, we are referring to asset stripping on a national scale in the agricultural, industrial, forest and banking sectors by barons of the regime, not all of whom are necessarily in government or even Cameroonians. The fraternity of corruption in Cameroon—or for that matter, much of Francophone Africa—is multifarious; it includes current government officials as well as those *en réserve de la république* (waiting to serve the republic), private local entrepreneurs with ethnic affinity to the regime (the so-called Béti lobby), French entrepreneurs and politicians, international arms dealers, cross-border smugglers, especially of Nigerian origins, in connivance with Cameroon soldiers, etc.[23] Above all, corruption is embedded in the prebendal nature of the Cameroon state; it is the lifeblood of the Biya regime.

The primary casualty of economic stagnation and government graft has been the Cameroonian people. The statistics cited earlier support this assertion; more evidence is presented in the chapter by Tatah Mentan in this volume. Fortunately, the effects of the economic crisis and poor governance have been mitigated by Cameroon's self-sufficiency in food production. The peasant farmer is one of the unsung heroes of Cameroon society today. Thanks to her staple foods—e.g., banana plantains, rice, maize (corn), macabo (a type of yam) and salt fish—are available in most parts of Cameroon, although the dry *grand nord* (comprised of extreme-north, north and Adamawa provinces) has had bouts of famine in recent years. The other factor that has prevented a social explosion in Cameroon relates to what might called the Cameroon national character. Although the concept itself is ill defined and using it in a multicultural context carries obvious risks of overgeneralization, I believe that to deny the existence of a national character in Cameroon is to deny that Cameroon society exists. Here I will simply outline the broad contours of the Cameroon national character after defining it.

National character refers to certain traits shared by the overwhelming majority of a political community in contradistinction to another, which traits may be artificially constructed (usually by elites) for the purpose of so-called nation-building, or organically developed in the course of common experiences with the physical and social environment. That Cameroon is Africa's crossroads does not mean that it lacks a core essence, a *gestält*. National character does not require ethnic, language and religious homogeneity. Indeed, the very heterogeneity of Cameroon may have favored the development of a national character that is essentially vocal without being violent. Because no group is large enough to forcibly impose its will upon all the others, conflicts tend to be handled vocally rather than violently. Language is used to communicate with, or otherwise denigrate, opponents, rather than the bayonet to exterminate them. The Babel nature of Cameroon society, on top of its multicolonial past, makes for a very rich lexicon on everyday reality. Ordinary Cameroonians have developed a formidable arsenal of epithets to describe the Biya regime and its ethnic support base, but it is worth observing that there have been few violent acts against established authority and no intercommunal strife since the early 1990s. Government forces have, in fact, committed most of the violent acts.

Cameroonians have consistently used dialogue, as opposed to armed struggle, to resolve political differences. The Sovereign National Conference, whose antecedent was perhaps the Third Estates General on the eve of the French Revolution, was the opposition's main demand in the early 1990s. This was to be a gathering of the *forces vives* of the Cameroon "nation," which was intended to set a new path for governing the country. When the Cameroon government balked at a Sovereign National Conference *à la beninoise*, deeming it *sans objet pour le Cameroun* (pointless for Cameroon), the opposition proceeded to Operation Ghost Town (discussed earlier). The key elements of Operation Ghost Town were withholding taxes and refraining from normal activities from Monday through Friday (e.g., going to work and market). One may see this method of protest, i.e., boycott, as the opposite of dialogue but it is in fact a different side of the same coin. Silence is as integral a part of communication (and hence language) as vocality, and Cameroonians have employed both in their resistance to authoritarianism. In their struggle to alter the current structure of the Cameroon (unitary) state, Anglophones have used legal arguments to bolster their case. They have taken their cause to international bodies, such as the United Nations, the Commonwealth, the Organization of African Unity and the World Court. They have not blown up bridges, electrical power plants and the like. In contrast to Nigeria to the west, Chad to the north and the Central African Republic (CAR) and Congo-Brazzaville to the east, Cameroon politics seems remarkably civil although by no means dull. The rebellion led by the UPC in the 1950s and 1960s was an aberration. Political culture in Cameroon combines French verbal grandiloquence and administrative centralism, British legalism and African humanism, but the latter is born not of pseudo-biological, or *négritudiste*, factors but of the kind of pragmatism the configuration of ethnic groups necessitates.

Another trait of the Cameroon character, which may be coterminous with the rest of Central Africa, is the capacity to make adjustment and even thrive against long odds. In Congo (ex-Zaire) individuals have reacted to state and economic collapse through *débrouillardisme* or hustling (others, though, have resorted to more predatory behavior, which takes the form of warlordism and wholesale stripping of national assets); in Cameroon, where decay is less complete, hustling certainly does take place but it is complemented by beer, music and football. Simply put, Cameroonians are economic *débrouillards* and social *bon vivants*. These attributes have helped to contain crises of economy and state legitimacy. Any study of Cameroon would be incomplete if it focused on formal politics alone, for the vibrancy of Cameroon, and that of Africa as a whole, lies outside of the state, specifically in the web of societal institutions, some of which, in fact, predate colonialism (e.g., secret societies, witchcraft, etc.). Sensitive to this reality, this book combines history, political economy and sociology to create as complete a profile of contemporary Cameroon as possible.

NOTES

1. It is possible that the Dualas had already crafted a city-state with centralized authority vested in a king, but it may have been too small to engage in wars of conquest, especially over long distance. Also, Dualas in modern-day Cameroon are not exactly known as warriors. It is highly instructive that one of the most illustrious books on African history, whose two editions are nearly 20 years apart, says very little about Cameroon during the slave trade; I was no luckier examining others. See Philip Curtin, Steven Feierman, Leonard Thompson and Jan Vansina, *African History, From Earliest Times to Independence*, New York: Longman Group Limited, 1998.

2. Victor Le Vine, *The Cameroons: From Mandate to Independence*, Berkeley, CA:University of California Press, 1964.

3. Throughout this chapter I will use Kamerun, Cameroons, Cameroon, and Cameroun, depending on the time period and territory in question, to underscore the country's mixed colonial legacy, although I realize this cacophony can create confusion. I will use the English name Cameroon to refer to the country after 1961.

4. Mark Delancey, *Cameroon: Dependence and Independence*, San Francisco: Westview Press, 1989.

5. Jean-Germain Gros, *The Privatization of Livestock Services in Cameroun*, Anne Harbor, MI: UMI Dissertation Servives, 1994.

6. Le Vine, op. cit.

7. République du Cameroun, Ministère des Finances et du Plan, *Premier Plan Quinquennal*, 1961.

8. For this period of the narrative—i.e., from 1947 to 1961—I rely heavily on the chronology developed by Salacuse, Cohen and Blaustein. See Jeswald Salacuse, Susan Cohen and Albert Blaustein, "Republic of Cameroon" in Albert Blaustein and Gisbert Flanz (eds), *Constitutions of the Countries of the World*, Sidney and London: Oceana Publications, Inc., 1987.

9. Ibid., p. vi.

10. See Richard Joseph, *Radical Nationalism in Cameroon*, Oxford: Oxford University Press, 1977.

11. Just about every major issue in post-colonial Cameroon bears Ahidjo's imprint. Anglophone dissatisfaction may be traced to his decision to abrogate the federation in 1972; the obstinacy of the Biya regime in addressing popular demand for democracy may be attributed to the legacy of authoritarian rule inherited from Ahidjo (and he from the French); and the preponderant role of the state in the economy is a direct result of Ahidjo's *liberalisme planifié*. This is not an argument for political and economic determinism. Nor is it an apology for the mistakes of the Biya regime. It is merely a recognition of the importance of the past as prologue. On a related note, I do not consider myself a student of Ahidjo. I shall defer to my colleague Le Vine, who writes much more extensively about him in the next chapter than I do in this chapter. Although I lack Le Vine's personal experience with Ahidjo, I stayed in northern Cameroon in 1991 and came to know some of Ahidjo's closest aides, including one of his most powerful ministers, whose name shall remain anonymous for obvious reasons.

12. Naomi Chazan, Robert Mortimer, John Ravenhill and Donal Rothchild, *Politics and Society in Contemporary Africa*, Boulder, CO: Lynne Rienner Publishers, 1992, pp. 137–140. The authors identified five regime types in post-colonial Africa: administrative-hegemonic, party mobilizing, military, tyrannical and democratic. Further, they explicitly placed Cameroon under Ahidjo in the first category, as do I in this chapter with some qualification.

13. Biya may have started with a commitment to maintain the administrative system bequeathed him and perhaps improve upon it through "communitarian liberalism." Indeed, only modest personnel changes were made when he first took office. The aborted coup of 1984, and Ahidjo's alleged role in it, canceled all bets. The coup laid bare Biya's vulnerability. Security and survival became paramount, and there was a retreat from political modernization. The social base of the regime became more restricted as the policy of ethnic balance was abandoned. This resulted in an intensification of so-called tribal politics and corruption. Had it remained administrative-hegemonic with a commitment to economic development and social (read: ethnic) balance, as had been the case under Ahidjo, Cameroon might have an easier time making the transition from authoritarianism. Alas, in 1990, the year of timid political liberalization, decay had already set in, making it difficult for architects of the regime to craft even modest changes. The profundity of the hole they had dug for themselves explains their intransigence then and now.

14. Ahidjo never used the term *dirigiste* to describe his economic philosophy; he preferred *libéralisme planifié* (planned liberalism), which suggests the same thing.

15. See *World Bank Development Report,* Washington, D.C.: World Bank, 1986.

16. This part of the narrative relies heavily on a previously published article. See Jean-Germain Gros, "The Hard Lessons of Cameroon," *Journal of Democracy,* vol. 6, number 3, July 1995, pp. 112–127.

17. In the mid 1990s, there were 60 UNDP representatives in the 180-member National Assembly (Cameroon has a unicameral legislature). The CPDM, the ruling party, was forced into an alliance with smaller parties (and eventually the UNDP) known as the presidential majority. As of the time of writing (May 2002), opposition representation in the legislature was on the decline as a number of legislators from the major opposition parties (UNDP, SDF) had defected after they had failed to receive their respective party's nomination. In my view, the strength of opposition parties in Cameroon, and therefore democracy itself, is greatly undermined by how parties are run and elections financed (i.e., by the government). Party loyalty seems to decline with each election cycle. This is because at election times the government can danggle money before candidates, which many find irresistible regardless of exhortation by party leaders. Moreover, party leaders, such as John Fru Ndi of SDF and Bello Bouba Maigari of UNDP, have been heavy-handed in the way they run their organization. If democracy is to endure in Cameroon, parties must become more democratic internally and financially self-sustaining. And if elections must be publicly financed, the authority in charge of doling out money must, at minimum, be an entity other than the government (e.g., an independent electoral commission), and the rules should be transparent to all. Election financing cannot be left entirely to the whims of the government and its ruling party, thereby forcing opposition candidates to become political strip teasers.

18. I do not believe that France ever had the kind of control over Francophone Africa that French leaders during the Cold War liked to convey, or the West, especially the United States, was willing to grant the hexagon. For one thing, while most African leaders in the *pays du champ* or *pré carré* welcomed French economic aid and military protection (not to mention easy access to the boutiques of Paris for themselves and their mistresses), many resented French interference in their domestic affairs and sought to maintain at least the appearance of independence. It is worth remembering that the first generation of African leaders consecrated their career on the altar of nationalism. This was in direct conflict with the kind of tutelage that many thought was essential for their personal survival but suicidal to their public posture. Consequently, many Francophone leaders in Africa during the Cold War were political acrobats; they yielded to French pressure on some issues while resisting it on others. They had to keep French aid flowing while looking tough and independent at home. Also, the relationship was not always asymmetrical in favor of France. African leaders, especially those in oil-rich states (e.g., Gabon) or with proven intellect (Senghor of Senegal) could influence French politics and policy in surprising ways. In sum, Franco-African relations were much more complex (and therefore unpredictable) than conventional writing on the subject, especially by English-speaking writers, has let on. In making the case, I realize I am making a partial retreat from previously held

views. The autobiography of Jacques Foccart, for years the *eminence grise* of French policy toward Africa, has convinced me of the necessity of this *volte face*.

19. This concept—i.e., Gaullism—is not particularly useful, for presidential regimes cut across colonial legacies in Africa. If Gaullism is as ubiquitous in Anglophone and Lusophone Africa as it is in the *pré carré*, then one must look beyond the administrative style of particular colonialists. In my view, the root cause of presidentialism in Africa is two-fold: colonialism, which was everywhere authoritarian regardless of the colonial power in question, and the patriarchal nature of most African societies, which first gave us decentralized despotism at the local level—to borrow from Mahmood Mamdani—and neo-patrimonialism on a national scale later.

20. The 1999 coup d'état in Ivory Coast—hitherto the citadel of political stability in Francophone Africa—should have thrown cold water on any talk of "democratic consolidation" in the sub-region. There is no country in Africa, with the exception of South Africa (perhaps), that is immune from coups, but their occurence is more plausible in some places than in others. Cameroon, it seems to me, is in the coup implausible category, at least in the foreseable future, but, as always, the volatility of African politics makes forecasting a most unreliable profession.

21. Former president Mobutu Sese Seko is said to have remarked to an unfortunate incumbent that one does not hold elections to lose them, which may well explain why Congo's transition to democracy stalled and he had to be pushed out of office.

22. It should be abundantly clear that how corrupt a country is deemed to be is largely a function of how corruption itself is defined, which means that politics cannot be separated from the exercise. In this connection, organizations like Transparency International, whose cadres are mostly former World Bank and IMF officials, have been all too quick to define corruption in ways that exacerbate the prevalence of the phenomenon in the South, leaving rich countries largely unscathed or looking very good on the corruption scale. The bribing of government officials is, without question, a form of corruption, but what about the undue influence of private groups in the making of public policy, whether such influence is gained through lobbying, which is legal in many countries, or the more nebulous act of campaign donations without explicit quid pro quos? As recent revelations about the younger Bush administration's energy taskforce show, corruption, if broadly defined, may be just as widespread in the North as it is in the South. It really depends on what ingredients get thrown into the stew.

23. Bayart, op. cit.

Chapter 2

Ahmadou Ahidjo Revisited

Victor T. Le Vine

For the better part of the latter half of the twentieth century, Ahmadou Ahidjo dominated the political landscape of Cameroon, first from 1958 to 1960 as Prime Minister, then from 1960 to 1982 as President, and then for the next seven years until his death in 1989, first as his successor's nemesis and then (according to the regime), as a continuously malevolent presence in the political background. When Ahidjo finally died, (or so the story goes) Paul Biya breathed a sigh of relief, wished his predecessor's soul a speedy journey to hell, and immediately commissioned an appropriate eulogy to be read when the occasion presented itself. Nevertheless, with all that presence, in and out of office, Ahidjo remained something of an enigma to both outsider and Cameroonian insiders: no one ever quite knew what to make of him, or what he thought, or what he really wanted. This essay is unapologetically intended as yet another attempt to assess—and here reassess—Ahidjo and his legacy, although thirty years watching him from near and afar should provide me some cover for the effort. I have no ideological axes to grind, neither hated nor admired the man, and though for a time I was *persona non grata* in Cameroon (but unaware of it),[1] bore him no grudge and strove to be fair in my judgments about him.

PERSONALITY AND POLITICAL STYLE

Ahmadou Ahidjo, President of Cameroon from May 5, 1960, until his resignation on November 6, 1982, died of a heart attack on November 30, 1989, in Dakar, Senegal. As of midyear 2001, notwithstanding the efforts of his family and some former friends in Cameroon, his remains had not been repatriated and reburied. (An Ahidjo chronology is appended to this essay.) Ahidjo was not an easy man to know. Publicly reserved, sparing of word and gesture, he admitted few people into his private world though he could be an agreeable companion and smoked, drank alcohol, and chewed kola in the company of his closest confidants. He shunned small talk, avoided social conversation if possible, and admitted that he disliked public debate and argumentation.[2] He rarely laughed in public, and though he was known to have used humor, irony, and sarcasm in some of his early speeches as a legislator in Cameroon, once he became President he maintained a grave and relatively humorless demeanor. Though a Muslim from the Muslim north, his Koranic education was shallow, and though he did undertake the Hajj in 1966 (and thus qualified for the title "Alhaji"), he avoided public displays of piety and had little to say on religious matters. At all events, whatever the other reasons he usually displayed this particular public face, there is little doubt but that he cultivated both his reserve and aloofness, since that gave him an air of imperturbability and impenetrability and undoubtedly heightened whatever fears people might have had in his presence. What it also did, of course, was to make him very difficult to read and to leave open the question, "Who was Ahmadou Ahidjo?"

The facts about his origins, upbringing, and education are sparse, and what we know about these matters is in some dispute. We are fairly sure that he was born in August 1924 (Victor Kamga says 1922; exact day unknown) of a Fulani Muslim mother, Astagabdo Ada Kano Garoua, who died in Garoua on February 16, 1983. The identity of Ahidjo's father is uncertain; he may have been one Youssoufou, and Ahidjo may have known him briefly inasmuch as Youssoufou is supposed to have died in 1929, when Ahidjo was five. Some who write about him claim Ahidjo was illegitimate, and argue that this fact in part accounts for his seeming social reticence; perhaps so, but since there isn't enough known about Ahidjo's paternity, suggestions about its effect are pure speculation. Abel Eyinga states (but without providing a name or corroboration) that Ahidjo's father was a Sierra Leonean, a former soldier in Britain's colonial army, who passed through Cameroon shortly after the end of the First World War.[3]

At all events, the young Ahmadou apparently was reared by his mother and in 1939—aged fifteen—was finally admitted to the Ecole Primaire Supérieure (EPS) in Yaoundé (Kamga claims he failed the entrance exams on his first try in 1937) from which he graduated in 1942 by the "little door."[4] That, in turn, led to a civil service position as radio operator (his official biographers later claimed "electrical engineer") for the posts and telegraph (PTT) service and postings in Douala, Yaoundé, and Garoua. One of Ahidjo's oldest foes, the author Mongo Beti (the *nom de plume* of Alexandre Biyidi), characterized Ahidjo as "illiterate" and ridiculed his lack of formal education beyond the EPS. The innocent stranger, argued Mongo Beti, could hardly imagine that every one of the President's silences, his studied hesitations, his lowered voice, his almost formulaic responses were due not to the wisdom of deliberation, but simply to his lack of education and the verbal poverty resulting from it. Embarrassed by his poor education, (according to Mongo Beti), he covered up; thus, his famous, much-admired reserve and dignity were little more than thin pretense.[5] This made him easily manipulable and thereafter, say Mongo Beti and Eyinga, all his important public statements and declarations were composed by others—first by the French, later by his smarter, better educated colleagues—and he only read the texts, usually badly. Ahidjo the puppet?

The accusation is hard to sustain, though it is true that initially, he was very much a creature of the French, especially the veteran Dr. Aujoulat who took him under his wing and helped get him up the political ladder (see below). But Ahidjo was not stupid, but cunning, and once in power, increasingly threw off the French traces. He was not well educated, and no master of the French language, and it is hardly surprising that he let others write his speeches for him—but so do most prominent politicians anyway. Mongo Beti overly ridicules Ahidjo for his lack of education, and it is difficult not to see a measure of intellectual snobbery mixed in with Beti's dislike of the man. In my own conversations with Ahidjo I certainly found the reserve to be there, as well as obvious care in choosing words. But he was articulate, appeared to enjoy our conversation, and quite forthcoming in response to the questions I posed. And the intelligence was there, as well as mastery of detail and argument. On balance, I think Philippe Gaillard got it right:

> . . . in a Fulani milieu where it paid to have connections to the nobility, a modest, even introverted postal employee had little weight besides the political leaders of the South, all better educated, older and already

veterans of political or trade union activity, (as well as) brilliant orators. These scandal-mongers played a losing hand. They forgot that coming from an educationally impoverished region, of his age cohort, the little Fulani [Ahidjo] was the most highly educated child of the North. And that the filter of the colonial school—to which the little or big feudal grandees, by refusing to send their own children and nephews, in effect sent Ahidjo—was an admirable instrument of selection.[6]

Jean-François Bayart, no admirer of either Ahidjo or his regime, may have come closest to characterizing his personality and style of ruling:

In the unanimous opinion of those who have worked with him, M. Ahidjo fully assumes the responsibility of power and governs alone. He never seems to have an unofficial counselor, an eminence grise. Before making a decision, he multiplies his audiences and contacts, gathers the maximum differing points of view from his close advisors: (this is) a process which delays his choices and leaves him open to (charges of adopting) wait-and-see attitudes. This impression is accentuated by his preference for unspectacular results and the care he takes to avoid creating a stir. From which (arises) a certain preoccupation with managing his enemies and not crushing them when they are defeated—a (kind of) restraint that sometimes irritates his companions. As one of his partisans was supposed to have declared to the Head of State, "Better to be your enemy than your friend!" When he disgraces someone, he does so brutally, but such disgrace is generally of short term: M. Ahidjo uses men, casts them aside when they are no longer useful, and recalls them when they have been reformed (to his satisfaction). He is neither a nepotist nor a tribalist, and does not encumber the apparatus of state with his friendships. Difficult to influence, patient, cunning, secretive: M. Ahidjo's personality facilitated the regime's orientation to presidentialism.[7]

To which can be added the observation that when Ahidjo did make up his mind, he usually did forcefully, again, usually carefully preparing his ground beforehand and leaving little to chance. For example, when, in September 1966, he decreed the formation of the *Union Nationale Camerounaise* (UNC) as the country's sole legal party, he left the other parties' chiefs no choice but to join; they'd been warned (some of them already had been jailed earlier in 1962 for being politically recalcitrant), and thus immediately fell into line. Equally, in 1972, when he decided that the federation had run its course, he left Anglophone leaders no choice but to endorse his referendum which, to no one's surprise, adopted the proposed unitary state by 99.97% of the votes.[8] The one major political decision that did not run true to form may well have been his last: to resign his office. I have elsewhere argued that he carefully prepared his departure,[9] and I still think so. However, I now think that he may also have thought a compliant Biya would allow him (Ahidjo), as titular head of the party, to pull strings from behind the scenes. What Ahidjo had misjudged was Biya himself: the man he (Ahidjo) thought a foil and easily manipulable had ambitions of his own, with visions of a future in which Ahidjo played no part. Ahidjo apparently admitted as much in 1983.[10] At any rate, perhaps it was something Ahidjo could not have foreseen or understood; he had always played his subordinates with great skill, including an almost unfailing ability, year after year, to mix workable dosages—ethnic and regional balances—in his governing circle. Ahijdo, to all intents and purposes, had created Biya, and probably could not imagine that Biya the disciple would, or could, cross his master, nor probably, was it any consolation to Ahidjo that Biya had well and truly learned from his example.

Ahidjo could and often did act brutally, particularly against his political opponents and those who crossed him, and during his rule Cameroon's prisons housed a sizeable number of political detainees. Political murder has been put at his door, as has torture, and he has been accused of aiding and abetting a Cameroonian ethnocide. We will return to these matters later, when we consider the nature of "his" regime.

WHY AHIDJO?

Philippe Gaillard was right: when Ahidjo entered Cameroonian politics it was dominated by the clever, better educated, even sometimes, "brilliant" men of the south. There was the redoutable Louis-Paul Aujoulat, a French medical doctor deeply involved in Cameroon politics almost from the day he arrived in the colony in 1936 and Secretary of State for Overseas France in two French governments, the "Antillais" (West Indian) Jules Ninine, plus a phalanx of talented Cameroonians including Leopold Moume-Etia, Charles Assald, Daniel Kemajou, Charles Okala, Paul Soppo Priso, and above all, the extraordinary Prince Alexandre Ndoumbe Douala Manga Bell, German- and French-educated, *Chef superieur* (paramount chief) of the Douala, once a fervent opponent of colonialism and now, after World War II, become a member of the 1946 French Constituent Assembly and other local and metropolitan legislative and constitutive bodies.[11] How then did *le petit Peul* ("the little Fulani," a mocking title already used by his detractors in 1952), this taciturn, poorly educated northern mediocrity" come to rise so high, so quickly, in Cameroon politics?

The characterization "mediocre" is Bayart's: he explains that Ahidjo became prime minister on February 18, 1958 because the French, who had engineered the rise and then the fall of the hapless Andre-Marie Mbida, saw Ahidjo as a second-rank politician, someone who could easily be manipulated, blamed if things went badly and then replaced without second thoughts. (Richard Joseph even contends that High Commissioner Jean Ramadier was brought in [from Guinea] in early February 1958—as replacement for Pierre Messmer—*specifically* to remove Mbida and usher in Ahidjo.[12] Having done so, Ramadier was recalled three months later.) Besides, given the crisis which brought Mbida down, plus the ongoing UPC violence in the countryside (which, as Mbida's Minister of the Interior, Ahidjo had been left to manage), no one rushed to volunteer himself for Mbida's job.[13] By that view, then, Ahidjo, already marked by his "apparent" mediocrity, was propelled upward by his French patrons, most likely as a temporary expedient, to be easily sacrificed later if the need arose.

George Chaffard went Bayart one better: he argued that Mbida had been designated Prime Minister in 1956 precisely so that he would prove incapable of handling the job, and thereby advance Ahidjo's cause. Bayart, who appears to like conspiracy theories, did not buy this one. "It is possible," wrote Bayart, "that the colonial administration had noticed since 1956 the talents of the young deputy Ahidjo, but improbable that the long-term strategy of Paris would be based on so marginal a political figure."[14] Chaffard also mentions that at the time, there was also the so-called "Ahidjo option," by which Ahidjo (as temporary expedient) would have prepared the way for the later accession of Paul Soppo Priso. Soppo, says Bayart, at the time President of the Cameroon Assembly, figured in the (French?) calculus as the future leader of an independent Cameroon—as had Douala Manga Bell before him—but lost that footing when his attempts to reconcile the UPC and the French administration failed.[15] The "Ahidjo option" seems as improbable as the "Mbida option," if it can be called that, not because of Ahidjo's alleged "mediocrity," but because at the time it would have been much more politically economical to have moved Soppo directly from the Assembly to the Prime Ministry, thereby eliminating any unpredictable moves by Ahidjo.

Ahidjo's main critics—Chaffard, Bayart, Mongo Beti, and his opponents of the Left—all choose to explain Ahidjo's rise as due either to chance/force of circumstance or French manipulation, but not to Ahidjo himself though, to be fair, Bayart does acknowledge that the man had visible "talents" and some intelligence. In any case, in their view, whatever it was that propelled Ahidjo, it did not come from Ahidjo. Unfortunately, Ahidjo's official biographers and political hagiographers leaned all the way in the other direction, ascribing his rise to power, and his later "successful" Presidency, entirely to Ahidjo and to traits of intelligence and character that appeared entirely to have escaped the notice of his detractors. In the effulgent praise language appropriate to royal griots, he was described (for example) as "Father of the Nation, Pioneer of Negritude, Prophet of Pan-Africanism, Defender of African Dignity,"[16] as well as the "[*sic*] quasi-charismatic . . . personification of the national ideal . . . [whose] boundless love for his country and noble sense of justice and the national interest predestined him . . . for this exalting but difficult role of leading men."[17] This "pioneer of modern Africa," according to another authorized biographer, became an "enlightened guide for Africa."[18] (If "quasi-charismatic" sounds odd, it should, as it appears to be an awkward way by which Ahidjo's praise-singers dealt with the fact that Ahidjo was never genuinely popular, or inspired popular love, or really "connected" with his people. He was certainly feared and viewed with apprehension by friend and foe alike, respected by some, but was never, as far as I can recall, regarded with affection.) So if Ahidjo was neither the manipulable mediocrity, or illiterate puppet, or country bumpkin, of his detractors, nor the towering political genius and idealist portrayed by his griots, his rapid rise to the top of the Cameroonian political heap remains to be explained.

First of all, I think it must be conceded, as does Bayart backhandedly, that Ahidjo in 1946 had political talent (albeit still raw and untested), plus considerable native intelligence, and that the combination must have made an impression on the experienced politicians of the Cameroon south. During our first conversation, in 1959, I asked Ahidjo about the early part of his career in politics, and he said he had been much impressed by the skill and self-assurance with which the politicians of the day conducted themselves. I should have asked him if this in fact inspired him to enter politics, but I did not, but if Bayart is right it was Pierre Rocaglia (together with Ahidjo, delegate to the new Cameroon Representative Assembly—ARCAM), who urged the young Ahidjo to take his first political steps in 1946, though his interest in politics already may have been aroused in 1945. (Abel Eyinga disagrees, quoting a Guy Georgy, the chief French colonial administrator in north-

ern Cameroon from 1951 to 1955: Ahidjo had to be pushed into politics.[19])

Small wonder that Ahidjo's interest was aroused (if that is what happened), since there was in fact a good deal about which to become excited, and the young Ahidjo, already marked because of his education,
probably did not require much additional prompting: by the end of 1945
Cameroonians had already tasted the excitement of both wartime and
post-war politics. During mid-1940, there was the tussle of divided loyalties (Vichy vs. Free France), won by De Gaulle's followers, and for a
time—between August 1940 and recapture of Paris in 1944—Cameroon
was at the very center of De Gaulle's Free France and Gaullist politics.
On October 8, 1940 De Gaulle himself landed in Douala, and before long
the colony became the launching pad for General Leclerc's brilliant military expedition across the Sahara into Libya and the Italian rear. In January 1944 De Gaulle convoked the Brazzaville Conference, and six month
later, the French Communist-dominated trade union, the Confederation
Générale du Travail (CGT) established a Cameroonian affiliate. In September 1944, strikes and violent demonstrations swept Douala, put down
with force by the French administration.

So it is that in October 1947 Ahidjo is elected delegate to the ARCAM,
and that same year, is defeated in a closed race for a seat in the Assembly
of the French Union (created by the 1946 French Constitution), both can-
didacies benefiting from French endorsement and encouragement. He
also begins to get acquainted with the big men of Cameroon politics:
Aujoulat, Ninine, Mbida, Okala, Douala Manga Bell. In 1948, in Garoua
(which he represents in ARCAM) he delivers his first public speech. In
Vol. 2 (p. 78) of the Cameroon Encyclopedia, there is picture of the
young Ahidjo giving that speech; he looks to be no more than a teen-ager
(though he was, in fact, 26 at the time), and visibly uncomfortable.[20] At
any event, in April, he is credited with founding ASSABENOUE (Association Amicale de Benoue), a Garoua-based social/political club for educated northerners. In 1953 he is designated a member of the Assembly
of the French Union, and in 1954, he becomes a Secretary to the Assembly, inscribed as a member of the Indépendants d'Outre-Mer along with
Senghor and L.-P. Aujoulat. In May 1955 he is Vice-President of the Territorial Assembly (ex-ARCAM), and in December 1956, heading another
of his creations, the Union for the Growth of North-Cameroon (UENC—
Union Nord-Cameroun) he contests Jules Ninine's seat to the French National Assembly and is soundly beaten. Back in the Cameroon Legislature (the ATCAM, reconstituted as a Legislative Assembly later) in

January 1957, he is elected President of the Assembly by acclamation. And, in the first Cameroon government under the *Loi Cadre* in May 1957, he is named Minister of the Interior in Mbida's cabinet, and then, nine months later in February 1958, prime minister. From ATCAM backbencher in 1947 to prime minister in 1958: a vault from bottom to top in ten years is a pretty impressive political ascent in anybody's book. But did he do it on his own or was he pushed (catapulted?) or pulled up? As usual, the answer lies somewhere between the extremes. At various points Ahidjo certainly had help, and guidance, and good counsel, and most important, the intercession of people who counted and could further his career. The French were there, though at the beginning it was the local Frenchmen and southern-based "évolué" Cameroonians involved in the territory's politics, like Aujoulat and Rocaglia and the "Antillais" Jules Ninine and Mbida who perhaps saw in him the core of a manageable future northern Cameroonian leadership. But there was also ambition, and an eye for opportunity, and native intelligence. Sometimes he overreached himself, as he did when he challenged Jules Ninine for the latter's French National Assembly seat in the north; I think it a measure of "the little Fulani's" resilience that the experience of defeat only derailed him briefly, going on as he did within a month to become the local assembly's president.

Finally, his stepping into Mbida's prime ministerial shoes in 1958 was neither the result of an "Ahidjo option" nor an "Mbida option," as I suggested earlier. What did happen was that at the beginning of 1958, Ahidjo was so positioned that he was able to take advantage of the opportunity presented by Mbida's inability to deal with the UPC uprising, the consequent impatience of France's Minister of Overseas France, Gerard Jaquet, and the actions of Jaquet's replacement for (Cameroon High Commissioner) Pierre Messmer, Jean Ramadier. I think that, of all those who have searched this history for ways of detracting or adding to Ahidjo's repute, Robert Mortimer, who sought neither, got it more right than anyone.

Mortimer recounts how the UPC's terror campaign mounted in intensity during 1957, and after Mbida gave a fiery speech in Reuben Um Nyobe's home village of Boumnyebel denouncing the UPC as a "clique of liars and demagogues" and threatening further repressive measures, the rebellion spread to the Bamiléké region where, on the night of December 13–14, a Bamiléké member of the territory's Legislative Assembly, Samuel Wanko, was murdered along with six others. Mbida flew to Paris to seek military reinforcements, but met resistance from both

French politicians and Cameroonian leaders who still hoped for reconciliation with the UPC. However, not even the Bishop of Douala, Thomas Mongo, who had managed to see Um Nyobe in person, could persuade him to accept a cease-fire. According to Mortimer:

> Jaquet, Minister of France d'Outre-Mer, took a personal dislike to Mbida and began to think his government was the principal obstacle to peace. But Mbida was backed up by the High Commissioner, Messmer, who, like Roland Pre before him had been converted by the course of events from leniency to a tardy and heavy-handed repression. Like Buron in 1954 and Deferre in 1956, Jaquet decided that a new High Commissioner would stand a better chance. At the end of 1957 he promoted Messmer to be High Commissioner for AEF, and replaced him in Cameroon with Jean Ramadier, who had just come back from Guinea He instructed Ramadier to sound out the political possibilities and then report back. Ramadier exceeded these instructions spectacularly. Virtually his first action on arrival in Yaoundé was to persuade Ahidjo's *Union Camerounaise* to desert Mbida's government. Left without a majority, Mbida resigned, and on 18 February Ahidjo was elected prime minister in his place. Mbida flew again to Paris, and filled the lobbies of the Palais Bourbon with his complaints.[21]

If Mortimer has it right, and I think he does, the key to Ahidjo's accession to power was first and foremost Ramadier who, had he obeyed Jaquet, would have left Mbiya in place. Mortimer interviewed Jaquet, and the phrase about Ramadier exceeding his instructions clearly came from Jaquet, not Mortimer. Even given Jaquet's dislike of Mbida and conceding that he might well have wished Mbida out of office, Jaquet would not have acted until Ramadier had reported back to him as instructed. Moreover, there was Ahidjo, Mbida's Vice-PM in charge of the Interior, to take the fall if needed, and if the mediocrity thesis holds, then he could have been easily sacrificed. But Ramadier either thought he had been charged with bringing Mbida down,[22] or took it upon himself to do what he thought Jaquet would have wanted, or he simply did what he thought necessary under the circumstances. I think the second and third interpretations equally credible, and in any case, absent additional evidence there is no warrant for interpreting Jaquet's dislike of Mbida as an order to remove Mbida and substitute Ahidjo for him. A 1964 letter from Ramadier to Abel Eyinga, cited by by Eyinga and later, by Victor Julius Ngoh, reinforces my impression but does not resolve the issue. However, it does confirm that Ahidjo did not like Ramadier or his appointment, that he (Ramadier) thought he had approval to remove Mbida, and that he saw an Ahidjo government as a transitional operation (transitional to what?) designed to pursue negotiations with Um Nyobe:

> At the end of 1957 everybody understood that Mbida hung on only because of us [the French government] and that all solutions to the Cameroonian problem had to start with his elimination [from office]. . . . I must admit that, before my departure [for Cameroon], I'd considered looking into the possibility of having Mbida depart without delay, and that that was approved. The choice of Ahidjo had been, in a way, imposed on me. I met him in Paris; our first contact was rather brutal. Ahidjo did not conceal the fact that he opposed my appointment solely because I was a socialist, and I made it clear to him that there were socialists and socialists. But to be more precise, the solution that I envisaged, absent an immediate detente with Um [Nyobe], was to put in place a transitional Ahidjo-Assale tandem . . . a transitional government whose only role would be to enter into negotiations with Um and the internal opposition.[23]

And so Ahidjo moved stage front and center in Cameroon on February 18, 1958, and there he stayed for the next 24 years, impelled (both before and after that year) in part by those who helped set him on his way, in part by his own talents and intelligence, and in part by opportunities presented by the circumstances in which he found himself. Ahidjo, as it turned out, was in the right place at the right time, and despite their mutual dislike of one another, took the opportunity offered by the new High Commissioner. As for Ramadier's "transition," he was not around long enough to oversee either a transition to another government (perhaps even one led by Soppo Priso, which is what he may have had in mind in the first place) or, as it turned out, Cameroon's transition to independence.

A third conundrum that needs revisiting, along with my own revisit of Ahidjo's political style and rise to power, is the nature of the regime that bore his name, and it is to that I now turn.

THE AHIDJO REGIME

It is probably no compliment to the Biya regime to point out that in a great many ways, it was at first and still is much like the Ahidjo regime, in fact more so in the former's bad aspects than in its good ones.[24] I admit the judgment is mine, but happily, here I am seconded by Philippe Gaillard, Victor Kamga, Mark Delancey, and most recently, by Joseph Takougang and Milton Krieger.[25] The UPC, which had always denounced the Ahidjo regime as a neo-colonial creation with Ahidjo in the role of *fanioche* (puppet) of France and French interests, predictably saw Biya's as no less compromised and ultimately, just as malign.[26] The reflexive judgment of the UPC aside, this much is certain: that after the abortive coup of 1984, the Biya regime shelved its early moves at political reform and a more relaxed overall political atmosphere, adopting many of the most authoritarian methods of Ahidjo's rule including heavy-handed police operations, physical assault on opponents, imprisonment without trial, extra judicial punishments including torture and death. However, to say that Biya used pieces of the Ahidjo template in constructing his own regime does not reveal much about Ahidjo's construct except to remind us of its repressive ways. So what kind of a regime was it, in fact? Was it a Gramscian "hegemonic project," as Bayart claims? Was it a "ruling elite," or ruling class, per Pierre Ngayap? Was its example so persuasive that Biya could find one no better or more useful? Or was it, above all, a wholly murderous, evil, and perhaps even genocidal regime, as (most recently) Frangois-Xavier Verschave strongly suggests?

The last charge needs to be addressed first because, if true, it should color all subsequent judgments and analysis about the regime, and because, being of recent vintage, it has gained currency and wide dissemination. And it is not a new charge, since the UPC and its friends have described the Ahidjo regime in such terms since 1958. At all events, put briefly, Verschave, in reviewing the 1958–1963 French-Cameroonian campaign against the UPC rebellion in the country's Bamiléké area, approvingly quotes a French helicopter pilot, Max Bardet, to the effect that they (the combined French-Cameroonian forces) "massacred between 300,000 and 400,000 persons. A true genocide. They practically annihilated the race. (It was) spears against automatic weapons. The Bamiléké didn't have a chance. . . . Their villages were razed, a bit like Attila."[27]

Verschave offers no corroboration for these figures, but accepts them implicitly as he argues (in a chapter entitled "Massacres en pays Bamiléké"—massacres in Bamiléké-land) the common complicity and guilt of the new Ahidjo regime, the French government and its colonial military, all organized and directed from Paris by Verschave's *bête noire*, Jacques Foccart. Foccart, who apparently met Ahidjo when both served in the Assembly of the French Union, also becomes, in Verschave's account, one of Ahidjo's chief puppeteers. There's little question about the ferocity with which both the rebellion and the military campaign to suppress it were waged, and that in the process, thousands were killed,

wounded, or rendered homeless. Verschave calls it a rehearsal for Viet-
nam, and I can offer eye-witness testimony to the brutality of both sides.[28]
However, I'm convinced the counter-insurgency campaign never attained the Vietnam-like intensity or scope claimed by Verschave, nor (as
my own research indicated) did the casualty count exceed 1,000 military
and somewhere between 10,000 to 20,000 civilian casualties sustained
between 1955 and 1962. In fact, Verschave even undermines his own argument in a cryptic footnote:

> The number cited by Max Bardet remains hypothetical inasmuch as the
> survivors, with the support of Cameroonian and foreign historians, are
> themselves reluctant to evoke the horror [of the massacres]. This cast of
> mind, which has lasted a third of a century, by itself testifies to the scope of
> the massacre.[29]

Suffice it to point out that this is classic illogic: the claim that the absence of evidence about something is the best proof of its existence. Further, Verschave need not have gone to such lengths to make the case for an
Ahidjo-Foccart collaboration, and in his zeal to assign guilt for the horrors
of the rebellion and exculpate the U.P.C., he went overboard. And, in any
case, admittedly bloody as was the rebellion and its suppression, the facts
about the counterinsurgency campaign do not also warrant a charge of
genocide, or wholesale massacre, against the Ahidjo regime. It was brutal,
but not genocidal. (I also wonder who those "Cameroonian and foreign his-
torians" are/were who helped "the survivors" repress their memories.)

As I suggested earlier, it was clear that after 1984, and including the
events before and after the 1992 presidential elections, the Biya regime
was not prepared to surrender power even by constitutional means, or
permit deviation from the pattern of rule established by the Ahidjo regime in the early 1960s.

Of that pattern, at least this much is certain: it took shape with the decision by the Ahidjo government in 1962 to convert the country to a single
party system, in the process forcibly integrating the opposition parties
and imprisoning its leaders on various, transparently trumped up conspiracy charges. On September 1, 1966, with the dissolution of the main parties of West Cameroon, the newly renamed *Union Camerounaise (UC)*
became the country's *parti unifié* (unified party), the *Union Nationale
Camerounaise*. Bayart has argued that this was all part of the emerging
ruling class' "hegemonic project," that is, the attempt to give itself per-
manence by creating its own stable economic and political base.[30]

The point of this Gramscian "project," of course, was to do any-thing—or virtually anything—to preserve power in the hands of Ahidjo, his confederates, clients, and constituents, that is, the regime's nascent ruling class. This meant not only avoiding the uncertainties of electoral competition, but arranging periodic staged symbolic demonstrations of popular support ("elections," referenda, party holidays, public manifesta-tions of thanks, etc.) and creating (among other things) an elaborate sys-tem of patronage that rewarded loyalty to the regime, and maintaining the political supremacy of Ahidjo's so-called "northern barons" while bal-ancing the competing demands of various competing regional interests.[31] All this Ahidjo did with a mixture of political savvy, guile, and where necessary, brutality.

Biya certainly turned out to be no Ahidjo, but (to pursue the Gramscian argument) the hegemonic project begun by Ahidjo was so well along by 1984 that it benefited Biya—first by giving him a 99.98% vote in a January referendum on his Presidency and, even more impor-tant, by providing him with critical regular Army support during the vio-lent attempted coup of April 6–7, one that, ironically enough, appeared to have Ahidjo's support. Biya, in turn, took several pages from his men-tor's book and perpetuated Ahidjo's pattern by being the sole candidate for the 1988 presidential elections, and by replacing Ahidjo's "northern barons" with his own (co-ethnic) group of "Beti barons" and a new North-South, East-West network of clientelistic relationships. Seen in this context, the flawed 1992 and 1997 elections came as no surprise: Biya was only protecting his class and its hegemonic project. Perhaps, had Biya been more politically astute, he might have—as did Senghor in Senegal—brought about a Gramscian "passive revolution," creating a narrow-spectrum multiparty system and the semblance of liberal democ-racy in which the ruling class could continue to hold the levers of power with popular approval.[32] (I do not know if Ahidjo thought of the possibil-ity in 1982 when he was about to turn power over to Biya, but I doubt it.)

Bayart's Gramscian analysis is intuitively attractive because it does incorporate most of the salient elements in a persuasive description and analysis of the Ahidjo regime's pattern of rule. There is no need here to argue against the Gramscian pattern—I had not intended, in any case, to use it as a straw man—save to point out that its Achilles heel is the prem-ise of class. A credible case can be made, à la Pierre Ngayap, that how-ever mutable its composition, Cameroon has a ruling elite, but that is far cry from demonstrating empirically that this elite is the core of a ruling class bent on its own "hegemonic project." My point is, that premise cannot, without considerable distortion, encompass the role of Cameroon's very powerful ethno-cultural solidarities, themselves at the very heart of the country's recurrent oppositional crises. The Bamilékés, the left ventricle of the heart of the old UPC resistance, remain uneasy and restive in the embrace of the regime, and it was Anglophone Cameroon and its long-standing grievances that originally animated the opposition from which John Fru Ndi and his party sprang. In recent years, many dissatisfied Bamilékés have made common cause with the Anglophones' political projects.[33] Consequently, if there was a "hegemonic project," as Bayart contends, the regime and its problematic nascent ruling class never successfully incorporated, or neutralized, some of the significant forces which, during the 1960s, stood hesitantly at the periphery of the Cameroonian polity: the Bamilékés, the Anglophones, the radicalized intelligentsia, and the Christian communities of the south and center-south. (Not even having a Catholic and former seminarian as President has done the trick for Biya, as witness the angry exchanges between Cardinal Tumi and Biya's regime. And if Cameroon has a nascent ruling class, it stands to reason that it should have been able to muster, or mobilize, enough electoral strength to give Biya, its evident champion, overwhelming support at its first open test of electoral strength in 1992.) Moreover, the class solidarity, much less its hegemonic project, was seriously compromised by the Ahidjo-Biya succession crisis. The logic of Bayart's argument would have predicted a seamless, peaceful transition, since it was simply a matter of one part of the same team passing the baton to another. Not so, of course: the succession not only witnessed mutual charges of "betrayal" by the principals of one another, but also re-exposed the system's older north-south, Anglophone-Francophone, Muslim-Christian rifts, fault lines that Ahidjo had more or less kept covered up.

In this perspective, another, perhaps simpler pattern of regime rule can be argued. Put bluntly, my reading of the events, personalities, and actions of Cameroon's political elite over the past forty years suggests that (a) the Ahidjo regime, having held at bay, and eventually defeating, its pre-independence UPC opposition, as well as wresting independence from the French, saw itself as the legitimate successor to the colonial state and thus, (b) entitled to rule and enjoy the fruits of its victories, something which naturally included tight control over all the levers of power in the system—personnel, the structures and institutions of rule-making, coercion, persuasion, and symbolic output—at all levels from the village to Yaoundé. It had, after all, the example of the Fifth Republic, inaugurated in 1958 and crafted as something new for France, a Presidential system with a subordinate, not sovereign, legislature. By that example and the logic of the independence transition, which took place under the auspices of the Fifth Republic, the single "unified" party made sense, as did the personalization of power and a muscular presidentialism. So too did minimum tolerance of opposition, and (in a perversion of the French system) the creation of a structure of official repression, complete with its own secret police (SEDOC and its successors), eminence grise (Jean Fochivé), prisons for political criminals, and non judicial punishments (for details, see special and annual reports of Amnesty International, Human Rights Watch, and the US Department of State).[34] It made sense for Ahidjo and his regime, and it appears to have made equal sense to Biya and his.

In sum, the Ahidjo-Biya regime pattern is less a "hegemonic project" than it has been a political strategy to hold and maintain power not so much for a class, but for an elite whose membership has varied *en gros* (wholesale) with the single change of president, *en detail* (retail) positionally as the president and his closest associates change policy lines, seek to bring new talent into the fold, reward the faithful, punish the "disloyal" or grossly incompetent or excessively greedy, or clean house after a crisis or debacle like the April 1984 coup attempt. Always, the aim is to preserve, and if possible, to enhance the power of the regime and/or its head. Ahidjo succeeded quite well in this strategy during the almost twenty years he remained in power. Biya, now in power for almost as long, has tried to emulate his predecessor (at least since 1984), but for reasons I do not rehearse here nearly wrecked the whole system so carefully crafted by Ahidjo—and may still do so if he keeps increasing opposition to him and his policies.

CONCLUSIONS

My revisit of Ahidjo has been, of necessity, narrowly focused and unfortunately, limited in scope. What has hampered the revisit is that it has been difficult to get an objective view of the man and his works, given the ideological lenses through which most of those who have written about him have done so. There are still all too few published, authoritative works on the Ahidjo era, and those of us who are interested in it, keep finding (and citing) each other's work in our own. In this revisit, I sought to emphasize points which I think are frequently overlooked or neglected: that the Ahidjo "enigma" was not so much the product of his shortcomings than of his calculations; that Ahidjo was much more his own man than he is usually credited with being; that his rise to power was not French-propelled, but in considerable part his own, as well as the product of circumstance; and that the Ahidjo regime was not so much an "hegemonic project" than an ongoing effort by Ahidjo (and his successor) to keep political power and its attendant prerogatives for themselves and their clients, kinsmen, and supporters. These are not, admittedly, earth-shaking revelations, but I offer them to help clear analytical space for the other essays in this volume.

NOTES

1. I only learned of this in 1971, when I returned to Cameroon to deliver a lecture at the University of Yaoundé. Apparently, someone in the Presidency had got hold of a copy of the first French version of my first book on Cameroon (*Le Cameroon du mandat à l'independance),* took offence at something I had written about Ahidjo, and had me declared *persona non grata* for defaming the President. The Librairie Clé in Yaoundé, which sold my book, was ordered to remove all copies from its shelves, which was done, and the books consigned to storage. My "p.n.g." only lasted several months, and I was rehabilitated after cooler heads prevailed. My book was put back on sale, all of this happening without anyone informing me of it. I never found out just what it was that offended, or why I and my book were rehabilitated, or perhaps, forgiven?

2. I met President Ahidjo three times, and on each occasion engaged him in extended conversation. The first time was in 1959, during my first visit to Cameroon, when I sought and obtained an interview with him in his office. The second time was during Ahidjo's state visit to the United States in 1966, when I sat next to him at a White House luncheon arranged by President Lyndon Baines Johnson. Johnson, who spoke no French (Ahidjo spoke no English), ignored his visitor for much of the lunch, preferring instead to talk with Sen. George Smathers (D., Florida); as a consequence, Ahidjo, who appeared glad to see me ("Aha! A friendly face!"), turned to me for conversation. The third time was in June 1971, a visit arranged by Solomon Tandeng Muna, then Vice-President of the Federation. Ahidjo's admission about public debate and argument occurred during our third meeting. I should also add a somewhat embarrassed confession at this point: the research for this essay proved more difficult than I had anticipated. I have been writing about Cameroon for more than forty years, and I kept running into my own published work in many of the sources (both Cameroonian and non-Cameroonian) where I hoped I might find new insight into Ahidjo's rule and personality. If this essay, then, has a déjà-vu quality about it, I apologize, and can only claim that I tried as much as possible to avoid stumbling over my own footsteps.

3. Abel Eyinga, *Introduction à la politique camerounaise* (Paris: l'Harmattan, 1984), p. 161. Eyinga, whom I first met in Paris in 1959, was a steadfast opponent and vehement critic of Ahidjo, and has now become a critic of the Biya regime.

4. Z Victor Kamga, "Ahidjo et le mythe populaire," p. 17, in Kamga's *Duel camerounais: democratic ou barbaric* (Paris: l'Harmattan, 1985). Philippe Gaillard, *Le Cameroun, Tome 2* (Paris: l'Harmattan, 1989), p. 11, explains that "the little door" (la petite porte) was a terminal departure out to work or whatever; "the big door, a narrow one, led to the Health School at Ayos, and thence, to the Medical school in Dakar." Gaillard adds that the paths to the Catholic seminary (in Yaoundé) or to the Protestant teachers' school were not open to Muslims.

5. Mongo Beti, *Main basse sur le Cameroun* (Rouen: Editions peuples noirs, 1984), p. 73.

6. Philippe Gaillard, op. cit., p. 11. My translation.

7. Jean-Francois Bayart, *L'Etat au Cameroun* (Paris: Presses de la Fondation Nationale des Sciences Politiques, 1979): 172–173. The translation is mine.

8. Of the latter decision, Bayart noted:

> It is not necessary for the President to order the manipulation of the voting in any election. Administrative authorities, party officials, and the police make it their business to understand from his declarations the results needed and then to achieve them by whatever means necessary. The abrupt and arbitrary announcement by the Head of State on 2 May 1972 that within two weeks a referendum would be held on the question of abolishing a federal state . . . meant, in effect, that within three weeks a Unitary State would be established with an overwhelming "Yes" vote.

Ch. 5, "The Structure of Political Power," in Richard Joseph, *Gaullist Africa: Cameroon Under Ahmadou Ahidjo* (Enugu, Nigeria: Fourth Dimension Press, 1978), pp. 80–81. The coming of the single-party system in Cameroon and the events of the 1966 transition are described, inter alia, in Bayart's *L'Etat au Cameroun*, op. cit., pp. 109–140, in Willard Johnson's *T he Cameroon Federation* (Princeton, NJ: Princeton University Press, 1970), pp. 243–256, 278–285, and in my *Cameroon Federal Republic* (Ithaca: Cornell University Press, 1971), pp. 110–113.

9. "Cameroon: The Politics of Presidential Succession," *Africa Report* 1983, 28: 22–26.

10. "Je me suis trompé. J'ai fait un mauvais choix. C'est un échec." (I made a mistake. I made a bad choice. It's a setback.) Quoted by Victor Kamga, op.cit. p. 24.

11. Richard Joseph offers a telling vignette of Prince Alexandre in *Radical Nationalism in Cameroun* (New York: Oxford University Press, 1977), pp. 79–84. Leopold Moume-Etia, one of the first trade union leaders of post-war Cameroun, has an unflattering portrait of the Prince in his *Cameroun, les années ardentes* (Paris: Jeune Afrique Livres, 1991), pp. 72–74. "If he'd had the will and the tenacity," wrote Moume-Etia, "really to give himself to politics and create a political party, he would have made Cameroun into a monarchy." I met Prince Alexandre in Douala in 1959 and found him frail, apparently literally drinking himself into the grave, but still gracious, generous, and articulate (in four of the

seven languages he claimed to know). After our meeting, I could well understand why, at one time, he might well have been considered a likely candidate to become president of Cameroon; I could also understand why he had so many passionate supporters, as well as enemies.

12. Richard Joseph, *Radical Nationalism in Cameroun* (New York: Oxford University Press, 1977), p. 343. Though Joseph offers no corroborative evidence for his proposition, it has found currency among Cameroon scholars. I have my doubts that it was all as stark as Joseph implies: I think it likely that Ramadier was sent because Messmer and Mbida proved unable to master the UPC rebellion and a more conciliatory line was seen necessary by Paris. Ahidjo, already in place as Vice-Premier and Minister of the Interior, was deemed ready to take on the job—or he may have so represented himself. Also, Joseph says that Ramadier came to Cameroun in 1957; not so: he was still in Guinea in early January 1958.

13. Bayart, *L'Etat au Cameroun*, op. cit., p. 49: "L'apparente médiocrité du personnage entra beaucoup dans sa fortune, et, si l'on peut dire, nul n'aurait donné très cher sa peau politique en ce mois de fevrier." (The apparent mediocrity of the man had much to do with his fate, and, it can be said, during that month of February, his political skin was not worth much.) The translation was modified by the editor.

14. Ibid., p. 47. The reference is to Georges Chaffard, *Les carnets secrets de la décolonisation*, vol. 1 (Paris: Calmann-Levy, 1967), p. 302.

15. Bayart, note 46, in Joseph, *Gaullist Africa*, op. cit., pp. 46–47.

16. The quote is a translation from Mongo Beti's Main *Basse sur Cameroun*, cited in Joseph, *Gaullist Africa*, op. cit., p. 95. Beti does not exaggerate: I heard these terms myself in Cameroon.

17. From the "Introduction" to *The Political Philosophy of Ahmadou Ahidjo* (Monte/Monte Carlo: Political Bureau of the Cameroon National Union/Paul Bory, 1968), pp. 11–12.

18. From the dedication to Beat Baeschlin-Raspail, *Ahmadou Ahidjo, pionnier de l'Afrique moderne* (Monte Carlo [Yaoundé: Paul Bory, 1968), unpaginated.

19. Abel Eyinga, "Historique de la françafrique en 5 dates" (suite), *Le Messager*, bftp://wagne.net/messager/0101/10histoire.httn, p. 3, sourced 3/23/01:

> I held him (Ahidjo) in the highest esteem. I knew him since his beginnings. . . . He dreamed of becoming the chief of the postal service in the region, maybe even of the whole country, but above all, he didn't want to enter politics. But I kept pushing him into politics. . . . I got him elected to the Territorial Assembly. One almost had to get him votes by stuffing the ballot boxes! But it was for a good cause. . . . He was the natural son of a Fulani of modest origins . . .

Jeune Afrique, no. 1410, 11 December 289. My translation.

20. *Encyclopédie de la République Unie du Cameroun.* Four Volumes, boxed (Douala: Nouvelles Editions Africaines, 1981). I hope I didn't misread Ahidjo's look: Arouna Njoya, one of Ahidjo's oldest friends and advisors, once told me that at least until 1951, Ahidjo was always very nervous when speaking publicly. The caption does say that it was Ahidjo's first public speech, and Arouna had a pretty good memory. [Note: The Encyclopedia became available in a limited edition to subscribers in the national party, the legislature, the higher ranks of the administration, and the community of foreigners. Needless to say, failure to subscribe could be interpreted as mark of disloyalty and/or lack of friendship toward the regime. I own set no. #678, which includes a bronze medallion with Ahidjo's likeness on the cover of Vol. I. Since the subscription cost about US $200, I was willing to risk being thought both disloyal and unfriendly and obtained my set through informal channels for US $40.00. A note in Vol. I says that 10,300 sets were printed. If all the sets had been subscribed, the take would have been over $2.0 million. I was told at the time that the edition had been "oversubscribed."]

21. Robert Mortimer, *France and the Africans, 1944–1960, a Political History* (London: Faber and Faber, 1969), p. 300. Bayart's account of these events ("L'Accession au pouvoir de M. Ahidjo") is on pp. 23–52 in his *L'Etat au Cameroun*, op. cit; Richard Joseph's version is on pp. 342–350 in his *Radical Nationalism in Cameroun*, op. cit.; and in my book, *The Cameroons from Mandate to Independence* (Berkeley: University of California Press, 1964), pp. 162–171. Ramadier was recalled three months after he'd been sent not because he had accomplished the task of putting Ahidjo in place, as even Mortimer hints, but because he'd exceeded his instructions and because he became insubordinate thereafter. What saved him from disgrace were his Socialist credentials, which included being the son of the distinguished Socialist Paul Ramadier.

22. Jean Ramadier's biographers, Jacques Larrue and Jean-Marie Payen, argue the former alternative. See their book, *Jean Ramadier: Gouverneur de la décolonisation* (Paris: Karthala, 2000).

23. In 1964 Eyinga and Ramadier corresponded, and the letter in question was dated 15 October 1964. It is reproduced in full in Abel Eyinga's *Mandat d'arrêt pour cause d'élections* (Paris: Harmattan, 1978), pp. 104–105. The translation is mine. A poor and hence misleading translation (e.g. "entente" instead of detente of parts of the letter appears in Victor Julius Ngoh, *Cameroon 1884–1955: A Hundred Years of History* (Yaoundé: Navi group, 1987), p. 154. It has been suggested to me that the letter is a fraud, authored by Eyinga, not Ramadier. I think not; having met Eyinga and thought him an honest person, I give him the benefit of the doubt.

24. Part of this section is derived from my paper on "Crisis and Democratic Succession in Cameroon," presented to the panel on "Succession in Africa" at the annual meeting of the African Studies Association held in Seattle, Washington, November 20–23, 1992.

25. Gaillard, op. cit.; Kamga, op. cit., Mark W. Delancey, *Cameroon: Dependence and Independence* (Boulder, CO: Westview/Dartmouth, 1989), p. 70; Joseph Takougang and Milton Krieger, *African State and Society in the 1990s: Cameroon's Political Crossroads* (Boulder, CO: Westview, 1998), pp. 62–85, passim.

26. See, for example, the special issue of *Peuples noirs, peuples africains* (Nos. 55, 56, 57, and 58, together; Jan.–Aug, 1987) on "Le Cameroun de Paul Biya: autopsie d'un chaos annoncé." Mongo Beti was editor of this journal. [Among other items, the issue contains an odd piece intimating that an Israeli neutron bomb was responsible for the 1986 deaths of over 1,200 farmers living on or near the shores of Lake Nyos, in west Cameroon, all of whom had in fact died from a poisonous gas emitted by the lake.] See also the *Cahiers Upécistes*, Jan.–March 1985, no. 21, and the article on the 1984 attempted coup d'état (pp. 6–120).

27. Max Bardet and Nina Thellier, OX *Cargo!* (Paris: Grasset, 1988), quoted without page reference by François-Xavier Verschave, *La françafrique: Le plus long scandale de la République* (Paris: Stock, 1998), p. 91. My translation. The latter book gained additional currency because of the international publicity given a suit—by three incumbent African Presidents—against Verschave and his publisher for alleged defamatory statements made in his latest book, *Noire silence* (Paris: les arènes, 2000). In May 2001 the French court before which the case was being heard threw out the suit, deciding that the old 1871 law on which it was based, was now itself in contravention of the Statutes of the European Union.

28. I was in Cameroon in October 1959, and visited a Bamiléké village that had just been "liberated" by the UPC's *Armée de liberation nationale kamerunaise* (ALNK). The villagers had been accused of collaboration with the authorities, and for that sin, over 150 men, women, and children had been hacked to pieces. Two days later, I was shown the fresh corpses of several dozen alleged "terrorists" shot by the French-Cameroonian forces: a number of women were included, as were several children barely over ten years old. For whatever it's worth, I traveled around in the Bamiléké and Cameroon highland areas of western Cameroon during the years 1960 and 1961 and found few traces of the rebellion, much less people who described it in Verschave's terms. The rebellion had pretty much died down by 1961, being reduced to sporadic outbreaks, what with Um Nyobe's death and the splits within the UPC itself in which several of its leaders had changed sides and "rallied" to the Government in 1960 and 1961.

29. Verschave, op. cit., p. 91 (footnote #2). My translation. My own figures are drawn from my chapter "Cameroon (1955–1962)" in D. M.Condit, Bert H. Cooper, Jr., et al., *Challenge and Response in Internal Conflict,* Vol. III (Washington D.C.: American University, Center for Research in Social Systems, April 1968), pp. 239–267.

30. Bayart, *L'Etat au Cameroun*, op. cit.

31. Bayart, ibid., pp. 185–235, passim.

32. This is the thesis advanced by Robert Fatton, Jr., in *The Making of a Liberal Democracy: Senegal's Passive Revolution* (Boulder, CO: Lynne Rienner, 1987).

33. For details of the Anglophones' dissatisfaction and the Fru Ndi phenomenon, see Takoungang and Krieger, op. cit. I offer anecdotal support for the stories of the Bamilékés' political troubles: a dozen of over thirty Cameroonian asylum cases (brought before the US immigration courts) in which I've been involved as an expert consultant or witness have had to do with Bamiléké who fled political prosecution in which their identity as Bamiléké played a role.

34. The essays in the book edited by Richard Joseph, *Gaullist Africa: Cameroon under Ahmadou Ahidjo* (Enugu: Fourth Dimension Publishing, 1978) all accept the premise that Cameroon under Ahidjo was a part of France's "indirect colonialism," replicating the worst aspects of the De Gaulle regime including its neo-colonial designs. Joseph's essay on "The Gaullist legacy," pp. 12–27, is to the point.

AN AHIDJO CHRONOLOGY

Date	Ahidjo	Cameroon	French/ International Context
1924, August?	Born in Garoua of Astagabdo Ada Kano Garoua, father unknown (?)	Cameroon is League of Nations Mandate	
1925, ?	Death of Yousouffou, putative father. Enters koranic school in Garoua directed by Mal Oumarou		
1932, ?	Enters regional (elementary) school in Garoua		
1937, February	Fails CEPE, entrance exam for Yaoundé Ecole Primaire Supérieure (E.P.S.)	Mandessi Bell founds *Union Camerounaise*	
1938, February	Passes CEPE and entrance exam for Yaoundé E.P.S.	Paul Soppo Priso founds *Jeucafra*, 1st legal Cameroon political org.	
1940, October 8	Studies at E.P.S.	De Gaulle debarks at Douala; Free French rule	France under German occupation, Vichy rule
1942, ?	Graduates from Yaoundé E.P.S., probation period at Douala		
1943	Posted to Yaoundé Beroua, Mokolo		
1944, January	Posted to Garoua		Brazzaville Conference
1945, July	Becomes interested in politics (?)	Trade union protests UN Trusteeship for Cam.	W.W. II ends
1946	Enters politics	Houphouet et al. create RDA	Nov., League of Nations ends; Cold War begins

Date	Ahidjo	Cameroon	French/ International Context
Jan. 1947 (–1952)	Delegate to Cam. Rep. Ass'y (ARCAM) from Benoue district		
1948, April	Founds ASSABENOUE (Assoc. Amicale de Benoue)	UPC founded by Um Nyobe, et al.	
Mar. 1952, Dec. 1956	Re-elected to Cam. Terr. Ass'y (ATCAM); VP ATCAM,1955–'57		
1953	Designated Councillor to Assembly of French Union		
1954	Sec'y to Ass'y of Fr. Union; becomes member of I.O.M. group		
1955, May	V.P., ATCAM	UPC rebellion begins	
1956, December	Creates UENC (Union pour l'Evolution du Nord-Cameroun); beaten by J. Ninine for seat in Fr. Nat'l Ass'y		June: Loi Cadre grants partial self-gov't to 'colonies
1957 May 9	(Jan.) Elected Pres. ALCAM; Vice-PM, Min. of Interior in Mbida gov't	"Etat sous tutelle;" (Feb.) J.Ramadier arrives; First Cameroon gov't (Mbida)	
1958, February May September 13	Resigns from Mbida govt; Invested as PM by ALCAM *Union Camerounaise* founded	(Feb.) Mbida resigns; Ramadier replaced by X. Tore Um Nyobe killed	French constitutional crisis: DeGaulle & 5th Republic arrives
1959, March July	Meets Foncha in Buea		UN votes independence for Cameroon
1960, Jan. 1 May 5	Sworn in as 1st Pres. of Cam	Cam. becomes independent (Feb.) Const. adopted	

Date	Ahidjo	Cameroon	French/ International Context
1961, Feb. 11 October 1 October 1 November 11	Granted *pleins pouvoirs* Pres. of Cam. Federal Rep. Press conf. on "great national unified party"	(Feb.) UN plebiscite in Brit. Cam.: So. Cam votes to join Cam. Rep., N. Cam. votes to join Nigeria. (Oct.) Reunification: Cam. Federal Republic	
1962	Moves toward single party system	June: Main opposition leaders reject "national unified party," are jailed. E. Ouandie returns to lead UPC guerrilla struggle	
1965	Re-elected President Reconciles w/ Archbishop Zoa, received by Pope in Rome		
1966	Heads "unified" party, *Union Nationale Camerounaise*	Single-party state inaugurated	Ahidjo state visit to US
1970, March	Re-elected President; moves toward "reinforced" presidential regime	July: E. Ouandie arrested; Aug: Bishop Ndongmo arrested—"Holy Cross Plot"; in prison until '75	Georges Pompidou, president of France (1969)
1971, Jan. 13		Ouandie, 3 others executed; UPC rebellion dissipates	

Date	Ahidjo	Cameroon	French/ International Context
1972, May 20 June 2 July 24	Supports ending federation Decrees division of Cam. into 7 provinces	(May) Referendum on ending federal state (June) Const. of United Cam Rep. promulgated	
1975, June	Names Paul Biya 1st PM of United Cameroon Republic		Valry Giscard d'Estaing, Pres. of France (1974)
1979, June	Reconfirms Biya as PM, names him constitutional successor		
1982, Nov. 2 Nov. 6 December 11	Resigns as Pres.of Rep., but elected VP of UNC Central Com. Retires to Nice-Grasse (France) Returns from Nice; meets w/ Pol. Bureau of UNC	 (Nov. 6) Biya takes oath as President	François Mitterand, Pres. of France (1981)
1983 Jan. 23–30 February 16 March 3 May 14 June 18 July 19 August 23 November 1	 Tour of provinces Death of Ahidjo's mother Awarded Dag Hammarskjold peace prize Radio address angers Biya Meets w/ northern ministers, asks them to resign; maybe plot to retake power? Leaves by ordinary AF flight Resigns as President of UNC Named as co-conspirator in plot v. Biya (along w. Salatou & Ibrahim)	(Jan.) Biya announces mottoes of his admin.: rigor and morality; tours provinces, Feb.–June '83. (June 20) Biya meets w/ French Pres. Mitterand, gets blessing (Aug. 8, 18) arrests of Capt. Salatou & Cmdt. Ibrahim; Biya claims plot vs. him & state	

Date	Ahidjo	Cameroon	French/ International Context
1984, Feb. 23–Apr. 5 Apr. 6–8 April 14	Trial of plotters, incl. Ahidjo (Apr. 6) Broadcast from Monte Carlo blaming Cameroonians. Abidjo charged as instigator of attempted coup, issues denial, asks to be left in peace	(Jan. 14) Biya elected President of Republic (Apr. 6–8) Attempted military coup vs. Biya. (Apr. 27–May 10) trial of accused coupmakers.	
1984–89	Exile (Nice, Spain, Senegal)	1988, Biya elected Pres.	Mitterrand re-elected (1988)
1989, Nov. 20	Death in Dakar, Senegal		
1991	Presidential decree rehabilitating political opponents who died in exile, including Ahidjo		
1992		Biya re-elected President in tarnished & disputed election	
1997	Gov't comission agrees to return property confisctaed from Ahidjo in 1984; Ahidjo's son, Mohamadou, signed to receive it. Remains remain in Senegal.	Biya re-elected President in elections bycotted by opposition	Jacques Chirac, Pres. of France (1995)

Chapter 3

The Institutional Roots of the "Anglophone Problem" in Cameroon

Tata Simon Ngenge

Without question, the transformation of Cameroon from a federal to a unitary state was one of the most significant political developments in the country's post-colonial history. Almost overnight the change put an end to what former president Ahidjo himself called a unique and most interesting experiment, i.e., the merger of French and British colonialism, which was intended to show that Africans from diverse background could live and prosper together. Alas, the federation lasted little more than 10 years. This chapter examines the causes and effects of Cameroon's political transformation in 1972. Its main argument is that the roots of the "Anglophone problem" in Cameroon are fundamentally institutional and economic, having to do with how state power is exercised in a fractured polity and how the same (i.e., state power) is used to benefit one group at the detriment of the other. Thus, institutions, specifically those of state and the economy, are at the heart of the analysis. But first, what are institutions?

As used in this chapter, institutions are the sum total of rules, both formal and informal, norms, and customs that govern a society. This definition is close to that provided by economic historian Douglas North. According to North, "Institutions are a set of rules, compliance procedures, and moral and ethical behavioral norms designed to constrain the behavior of individuals in the interest of maximizing the wealth or utility of principals."[1] A taxonomy of institutions include the following: constitutional order, institutional arrangements, and a normative-cognitive map.The constitutional order refers to the body of rules that govern all rules within the society, or, as Feder and Feeny put it, "the rules for making rules."[2] From the constitutional order—the mother of all rules—emerges "lesser" rules, which are designed to structure the terms of specific transactions among society's members; these include laws, regulations, contracts, property rights, and so forth. Finally, the normative-cognitive map refers to the norms and values that have been internalized, usually over long periods of time, by members of the polity. The legitimizing and self-restraining role of this cognitive map is so vital that no society can survive without it for long. When there is dissonance between the formal rules and the informal normative codes, there results a corresponding breakdown in the willingness of people to "play by the rules" on their own, because they no longer believe in the latter.

Institutions are to be differentiated from organizations, which are purpose-specific. Much of the confusion amongst social scientists emanates from the tendency to use institutions and organizations interchangeably, Organizations, according to North, exist to take advantage of the opportunities created by institutions. To use a sport analogy, if institutions are the rules of the game, organizations are teams whose purpose is to win; they do so sometimes by playing by the rules and sometimes by transcending them either by accident or on purpose. There is therefore a symbiotic relationship between institutions and organizations: while the types of organizations that come into being are shaped by the institutional framework; organizations, in the pursuit of their goals, help the process of institutional change by, amongst other things, constantly stretching the rules and boundaries set by institutions. Again, part of the confusion surrounding organizations and institutions may well stem from the nature of the relationship between the two.

Broadly speaking, the state is an organization, or a set of hierarchically ordered organizations, whose aim is to exercise exclusive authority over a given territory and the people therein through persuasion and (or) force. But state authority is not exercised in a vacuum, instead, it is shaped by the institutional environment, among other factors. Since the French and American Revolutions, institutional constraints have been put on the state. These are usually spelled out in constitutions, which have at least two components—one dealing with rulers (i.e., who is eligible to rule and for how long, what is the connection between different types of rulers, etc.) and the other, the ruled. In the latter connection constitutions generally make certain civil liberty commitments enshrined in so-called bills of rights (often borrowed from the Americans). Both components are intended to prevent the abuse of power, in other words, to minimize its discretionary application so as to make the relationship between rulers and ruled predictable. Thus constitutions, and more generally the laws that exist within their ambit, are at the top of the totem pole of formal institutions essential to making or organizing a state. By the same token, how well, and indeed whether, constitutional strictures are respected depend on (a) how strong the state is, (b) the willingness of state makers to abide by the rules they set, and (c) civil society. In other words, values matter for what is in a constitution as well as what is out; moreover, values determine whether what is in is taken seriously. Seen from this prism, constitutions are not value-neutral, nor are they crystallized in stones.

In Africa constitutional manipulation is part of the game that post-colonial rulers play to buttress regime survival and state hegemony over other institutional, and in some cases pre-colonial, contenders (e.g., traditional chieftaincies). The arsenal of constitutional dirty tricks in the post-colonial era contains a wide range of weapons, some more sinister than others, among them: amendments that allowed certain incumbents to become life presidents and thus avoid the prospect of electoral defeat, amendments that allowed incumbents to declare state of siege so they could rule by decree, the use of referenda orchestrated to achieve astronomical, in fact statistically impossible, victory margins, the imposition of one-party rule in the name of national unity, which thereby eliminated political pluralism, the imposition of unitary state over federal state structures for the same reason, the passing of sedition laws that permitted the jailing of dissidents indefinitely in clear violations of rights to due process and other constitutional guarantees, the passing of anti-diffamation laws whose true intent was to muzzle the press in spite of pledges guaranteeing its freedom, and, more recently, the calling into question of the citizenship of well-known figures to exclude them from political debates.

Naturally, Cameroon has not escaped the tendency of formal institutions in Africa, such as constitutions, to be manipulated by African leaders. As an organization, the state too has been used in fungible ways. This chapter is about the nexus between institutions and organizations and their elasticity in the Cameroon socio-political milieu. Specifically, Cameroon's two national leaders since independence, i.e., Ahmadou Ahidjo and Paul Biya, have used institutional (read: constitutional) means to transform Cameroon from a federal to a unitary state, and the paramount weight of the latter in the economy to perpetuate the hegemony of

Francophone over Anglophone Cameroonians. The persistence of the "Anglophone problem" in contemporary Cameroon, which has earned Anglophones the sobriquet *enemi dans la maison* (enemy within), attests to the partial failure of the exclusive use of ostensibly inclusive institutions and organizations and threatens the future of Cameroon. That future will be assured only when power-sharing and national resources are equitably distributed.

PRELUDE TO THE UNITARY STATE

The alarm bell announcing the death of federalism, or power sharing, in Cameroon should have sounded on September 1, 1966. The creation of the Cameroon National Union (UNC in French) on that date was a clear signal indicating the end of the Foumban constitution, which brought Southern Cameroons and the Cameroon Republic into a federal structure on October 1, 1961. The introduction of the single party structure marked the end of opposition politics in Cameroon; henceforth, conformity masked as "unity" would carry the day.[3] Politically speaking, nothing could have been better for Anglophone Cameroonians (and indeed for all Cameroonians) than the Foumban constitution, which divided power among a federal president, vice president, ministries, a national assembly and judiciary. Articles 5 and 6 specify the responsibilities of the federal government, with those not explicity granted by the document to federal authorities given to state authorities. The Foumban constitution contained extensive human rights guarantees and limited presidential terms to five years, which could be indefinitely renewed.[4]

After imposing the one-party system on September 1, 1966, the only obstacle to Ahidjo's project was the opposition which came from disgruntled members of the now-dissolved Kamerun National Democratic Party (KNDP), who included Dr. John Foncha, former vice-president of the federal republic and prime minister of West (Anglophone) Cameroon. To dislodge these elements and their entrenched positions, he appointed, in May 1968, Solomon Tandeng Muna to the post of prime minister of West Cameroon, replacing A.N. Jua, formerly KNDP vice president. Two years after Ahidjo surprised west Cameroonians with his appointment of Muna as their prime minister, he chose him as his running mate in the presidential election of 1970, which they easily won. Thus, in addition to being prime minister of West Cameroon, Muna was vice president of the federal republic. Ahidjo firmly believed, and rightly too, that Muna would not say no to his centralization project, since Muna owed his key positions to him.[5] However, while Ahidjo was busy setting the stage for the creation of the unitary system, Foncha was canvassing for internal and external support to launch a new political party, the Christian Democratic Alliance (CDA). The institutionalization of the unitary state in May 1972 cut him short.

The creation of the CNU in September 1, 1966, as the sole political party, the tactful appointment of Muna as prime minister of West Cameroon in 1968 and federal vice president in 1970 to undercut Jua, Foncha and other pro-federalism Anglophone leaders, and changes to the federal constitution by presidential decree (e.g., Law No. 69-LF-1 of November 10, 1969) rather than plebiscite, all show Ahidjo to be a manipulative and determined leader. The coup de grâce came on May 6, 1972, when Ahidjo, addressing a special session of the federal assembly, announced an impending change from the federal structure to a unitary state on May 20, 1972. According to the president, federalism was adopted in 1961 because Cameroon had not been "united" for at least 40 years. Cameroon could not claim to be a nation then. But in 1972 more than 10 years had elapsed since Cameroonians had been living together. Federalism threatened national harmony, which Cameroonians had fought so hard to achieve. The president also justified the unitary state on administrative ground: it would eliminate duplication of government services and make the bureaucracy accountable, for henceforth Cameroonians would know exactly to whom to turn (i.e., Yaoundé-based ministries) when in need.[6]

The May 20 referendum, described by politically minded Cameroonians as "Ahidjo's coup d'état," was described by the president as a "peaceful revolution" marking a turning point in Cameroon political history. The peoples of both states were not given room to discuss the project. The speed with which Ahidjo took to implement the unitary state became suspicious to many. Ahidjo's unilateral decision to effect this major change marked the beginning of "monarchical/presidential" rule. Parliament became a rubber stamp. At any time, the president could simply change the constitution without informing lawmakers, much less consulting the people. Just as the "consensus" to create the CNU marked the end of political pluralism in Cameroon in 1966, the advent of the unitary state began another new chapter: presidential dictatorship following the total dismantlement and (or) emasculation of countervailing institutions (i.e., the federal legislature, vice presidency, the judiciary, etc.).

Before the statement issued by the presidency mentioned above, people expected the president, according to Article 47 (III) of the federal constitution, to table the draft constitution before the federal house for debate. The president obviously feared his proposed constitution would be rejected by the federal national assembly. To bail himself out of embarrassment, he issued the famous decree (DE-72-270) of 2/6/1972 by which he abolished the federal constitution and instituted the constitution styled the "Constitution of the United Republic of Cameroon," which he, without consulting the people or their representatives, drew up secretly.[7]

In one stroke Ahidjo dissolved the East Cameroon House of Assembly and Government, the West Cameroon Assembly, the House of Chiefs and the Federal House. Also by decree, he instituted articles 50–60 of the Cameroon penal code. As Fongum Gorji-Dinka observed:

> He, Ahidjo, then installed his so-called United Republic of Cameroon and the system of government by which Cameroon, its people and resources became forfeited to whoever becomes the head of State. He also set up institutions and men to operate the system. And that is the system which we have today and which is now disintegrating our people. Instead of government by dialogue, we have government by terror. Instead of law and order by persuasion, we have law and order by banditry and piracy. He, Ahidjo, himself has since been referring to it as a "peaceful revolution." . . . Thus from 2nd June 1972, our country passed from the era of constitutional government to that of a junta. Today's government, today's institutions, today's system and today's style of leadership were installed by the junta. And that is the junta system we must destroy, otherwise it will destroy us.[8]

The unitary state came into legality on June 2, 1972, when President Ahidjo promulgated by decree the constitution governing its existence. Though the constitution was promulgated on this date, the working machinery of the unitary state was not yet in place and Cameroon momentarily became a one-man state. During this interval there existed no federal parliament and no state legislature. The president took time to re-orient the federal and state agencies to conform to the unitary state structure. During this transitional period all government work virtually came to a standstill, while people were being appointed to man the newly designed structures. Appointed officials were busy moving to Yaoundé to take up their new functions. Buea, the former headquarters of West Cameroon, was emptied of its top personnel as almost all of them were appointed to the various ministries in Yaoundé.[9] Files of West Cameroon civil servants were equally transferred to Yaoundé. It was quite an exciting wave of new movement eastward as if to Eldorado.

THE "CONSTITUTION OCTROYÉE" OF THE UNITED REPUBLIC

The 1961 Foumban constitution, dubbed *constitution évoluée*, and the 1972 constitution, dubbed *constitution octroyée*, bear witness to Cameroon's changing political reality.[10] The Foumban constitution emerged after a long struggle and compromise between the centralists led by Ahmadou Ahidjo and the federalists led by J.N. Foncha, who believed in power sharing. The outcome was that Foncha retained as much political autonomy as possible for the West Cameroonians he had reluctantly carried into the federal union following the UN-imposed two options in the plebiscite of February 11, 1961. In all respects Ahidjo's *constitution octroyée* was an illegal abrogation of the Foumban constitution approved by the UN for the former trusteeship territory of Southern Cameroons and the Cameroon Republic.[11] It made away with territorial and institutional provisions guaranteeing the minority rights of the West Cameroonian people. The one clause Ahidjo entrenched in the new constitution that appealed to the Anglophones was that of bilingualism, a unique blend of the two cultural groups.[12]

By creating the United Republic the president carefully shifted opposition to his rule in East Cameroon to the national problem of Anglophones and Francophones, whereby the two culturally diverse groups looked upon him as referee. Commenting on the *constitution octroyée* Victor T. Le Vine rightly observed: "To all intents and purposes there was no national debate on its provisions: the pre-referendum campaign was designed to secure an overwhelming turnout in its favor rather than to provoke discussion on its contents."[13] The 1972 *constitution octroyée* eliminated the office of the Vice President, which it considered superfluous. In line with those institutions that disappeared were: the prime minister and cabinets of the federated states, the state legislatures and the West Cameroon House of Chiefs. The *constitution octroyée*, which was a mockery of democratic principles, stated that "state authority shall be exercised by the President of the Republic and the National Assembly."[14] But in essence, most, if not all, powers resided in the president, including those previously exercised by the state governments, the federal legislature and the state assemblies. He was empowered to appoint and dismiss all ministers."[15] He alone could declare a state of emergency and a state of siege by decree, and "he shall inform the nation by message of his decision."[16]

The awesome power of the president was vividly in evidence in the way the constitution defined his relationship with the new unicameral legislature. As it is traditional with the one-party system, the president, as party chairman, was to draw up a single list of faithful militants, theoretically in consultation with the CNU central committee, to become members of the National Assembly. The institution had limited *real* legislative powers. It was to meet twice every year with a duration of 30 days for each session. The opening date of each session was to be decided by the assembly's steering committee after consultation with the president of the republic. Owing to the fact that the National Assembly was composed of members of a single party, who were themselves chosen by Ahidjo (more or less), its meetings were intended not to propose, debate, change and enact legislation but endorse the government's proposals. Where the judiciary was concerned, it was the president who appointed, by decree, the judges of the supreme court, as well as councilors in municipalities and their chairmen. He reserved the sole right to dismiss anyone who opposed him, be it inside the ruling party, the executive branch, the legislature or judiciary.[17] Elections became mere rituals as the electorate had no alternative but to endorse the list submitted to it by the party. After each ritual exercise the air was full of messages of support and congratulations to the president for the success of his list and reaffirmation of attachment to his ideology.

One important clause of the 1972 *constitution octroyée* was a holdover from a 1967 law dealing with the right to form political parties.[18] This law was adopted barely seven months after all the existing political parties were dissolved on September 1, 1966 to form the Cameroon National Union. Its legal purpose must have been to maintain de jure multipartyism, since the parties that formed the CNU were not allowed to maintain their individual identity. It therefore became imperative that this law be enacted so that those who became dissatisfied with the *parti unifié*, CNU, could break from it and form their own parties. This law became Article 3 of the 1972 constitution, which read thus:

> (I) Political parties and groups may take part in elections. They shall be formed and shall exercise activities in accordance with the law.
> (II) Such parties shall be bound to respect the principle of democracy and of national sovereignty and unity.[19]

The importance of Article 3 (I & II) was not recognized at the time but it became, almost two decades after its enactment, the basis for ending the one-party system in Cameroon. It is a matter of speculation as to why Ahidjo did not declare the CNU the sole party in Cameroon *in perpetuity* when he clearly had the power to do so. As head of state and party chairman, perhaps he inserted this clause in the 1972 constitution to give it a democratic character in the eyes of the free world. Perhaps he felt safe enough in his power to make the one concession, which he thought no one would ever call on him to honor. Indeed, the 1972 constitution can be seen as the personal document of the president; he could manipulate it at anytime and in any form, by issuing decrees without the endorsement of his own named assembly. The power of manipulation first surfaced three years after the enactment of the constitution, when at the Douala CNU Congress of Maturity President Ahidjo announced his plan to modify the constitution so as to introduce the post of prime minister,[20] who, he emphasized, was to be the president's constitutional successor.

It is rather ironic that Ahidjo once again recognized the need for a prime minister whose function he had earlier criticized as superfluous under the 1961 constitution that led to a reunified Cameroon. This game clearly indicated that his ultimate task was to eliminate the Anglophone who, by the 1961 Constitution, was his constitutional successor.[21] In the name of national unity the West Cameroon people lost the key post of premiership, which clearly demonstrated that, in the new arrangement, an Anglophone could never become president of Cameroon.[22] Still in the name of national unity, Ahidjo's constitutional successor (Paul Biya) carried out in the same manner the following unilateral amendments to the constitution. On February 4, 1984, the United Republic of Cameroon became the Republic of Cameroon (Law No. 84-001, Article 1), the name it had on January 1, 1960, when it became a sovereign state before reunification on October 1, 1961. This was nothing short of an acknowledgement that the assimilation process of the Anglophones was complete. The initiator of the project held as a defense that the word "United" indicated that the two cultural entities were still divided. (How united could really mean divided only Biya knew, but in Cameroon words are not beyond distortion to suit political action.)

By the same modification, the post of prime minister, which Biya held under Ahidjo, was once again abolished (Article 5 of the 1972 constitution). In case the president became temporarily disabled, he could appoint a minister to fulfill his duties. In case the vacancy was permanent, the president of the National Assembly would become president until new elections were held within 40 days.[23] According to the amendment, the president of the assembly cum provisional head of state could neither amend the constitution, organize a referendum, nor run for the presidency of the republic. The new president was perhaps just modest (due to the economic crisis) not to have called another referendum to endorse the

"New Deal" constitution. The eight amendments introduced between 1984 and 1985 rendered the *constitution octroyée* of 1972 a worthless document in many areas. The nonchalance with which major constitutional changes were made led the elite of the Anglophone provinces residing in Douala to address a powerful memorandum to President Paul Biya lamenting, amongst other things, that:

> We have over the years watched with increasing alarm the various unilateral manipulation of the Constitution to the extent that the English-speaking region of Cameroon is now being treated by the administration either as a conquered territory or as a buffer zone, and its citizens as foreigners. Because of this colonial status, which has been imposed on us both dictatorially and through political chicanery, we now find ourselves almost completely stripped of that cherished British cultural heritage to which some of us were born and nurtured. And while actively engaged in this cultural deprivation process our Francophone brothers have not only jealously preserved their French culture (our Francophone brothers regard France as their home), but have mobilized and unleashed a force for the total assimilation of their English-speaking "brothers." This force has been christened "INTEGRATION."[24]

THE POLITICAL AND ADMINISTRATIVE STRUCTURES OF THE UNITARY STATE

As stated earlier, the unitary state came into being on June 2, 1972. By this date the three governments had disappeared in favor of the unitary executive. The four legislative assemblies wound up forming the national assembly with a total of 120 members. The state protocol was altered at the top echelon following the elimination of the post of the vice president. In hierarchical order, the President of the United Republic was followed by the President of the National Assembly and third in the order was the President of the activated Economic and Social Council. When the post of premier was created in 1975, the protocol order changed as he became the No. 2 man in the pecking order.

The creation of the unitary state provided impetus for finishing the job of centralization Ahidjo all along was yearning for. With respect to local and regional institutions the presidential decree of July 24, 1972, carved out the former federated states of West and East Cameroon into seven provinces. West Cameroon was divided into two provinces: southwest (capital Buea) and northwest (capital Bamenda). Governors were appointed to man the provinces and the posts of Federal Inspectors of Administration were abolished. The governors, appointed by presidential decree, were answerable to the Minister of Territorial Administration, who was appointed by the president as well. The divisions, sub-divisions and districts were still under the command of a prefect, sub-prefect and district head. They, in turn, were subject to the orders of the governor of the province (appointed, once again, by the president). The unitary system saw the creation of new divisions, sub-divisions and districts with the ostensible aim of bringing the administration nearer to the people which, as the president indicated, "will enable us in the course of the day-to-day administration of the state, to take into account local peculiarities." It is hoped, he added, "that such measures would remedy some of the problems associated with centralization."[25]

In East Cameroon the advent of the unitary state ended a variant of the classic French prefectoral system that had been maintained from the colonial era to 1972. The classic French prefectoral system Cameroon adopted after independence operated jointly with another involving urban and rural communes and an array of major and minor chieftaincies, the latter legacies from the colonial period. In this sector again the relationship between the chiefs and the government's agents became one in which the chiefs were subordinate to the central administration. The administrative set up after May 20, 1972, preserved some older structures in the new arrangement. Thus former West Cameroon local councils continued to enjoy limited autonomy, while in former East Cameroon the communes continued to function in the same manner. This notwithstanding, the reality was that power did change. The center became stronger while regional, local and traditional governments considerably weaker. Further, the Francophone system of administration became prevalent throughout the nation as public and local administration fell under the jurisdiction of the Minister of Territorial Administration.

The first government of the United Republic was named on July 3, 1972, by presidential decree. It had a total of 28 members of government drawn from the 7 provinces as follows: Central South 7, East 1, Littoral 1, North 6, Northwest 4, West 6 and Southwest 3.[26] The provincial governors had no right to initiate and take any decision on any matter without authority from Yaoundé. This equally applied to the provincial delegates representing their various ministers in the provinces. Appointments, even those of primary school headmasters and office clerks, promotions and transfers, emanated only from the capital city. All workers in the public sector received their salaries directly from the ministry of finance, which became known as the "super market." All civil servants with a problem, for example, with their salary, be it non-payment or an error on their pay vouchers, had to go to Yaoundé to resolve it. This of course meant the suspension of work for an indefinite number of weeks or months while the worker is in Yaoundé running up and down, from the tutelage ministry to the public service and finally to finance, for rectification. The civil service became abysmally corrupt and inefficient, while appointments were based on ethnic favoritism.[27] An African magazine commentator noted that these were being encouraged by the president.[28] Because of the awkward bureaucratic structures established under the pretext of national unity, those charged with the task of processing dossiers preferred to wait until those affected left the extreme ends of the republic to chase them in Yaoundé. Of course, the physical presence of civil servants with problems in Yaoundé also facilitated bribery, which in fact became a sine qua non for moving dossiers forward. Even the national daily *Cameroon Tribune*, no muckraking newspaper, viewed with regret that "going to Yaoundé for this purpose you must be armed with 'cash' to tip at every table if the dossier is to be processed."[29]

The inefficiency and corruption of the bureaucratic system as spelled out above were further worsened by the two-shift system (again, borrowed from the French), which kept government workers busy struggling on bad city roads to get to their jobs. By the time they got to their destination they were usually so exhausted that they were not able to perform. Further, the two-shift system entailed significant expenditure on local transport, as a result, poorly paid workers were forced to take bribe to survive within the system. In time corruption, far from being a cog in the Cameroon administrative wheel, became its grease. Civil servants needed money to survive in Yaoundé, and owners of dossier needed their documents to move. Bribery served everyone's interests, as a social scientist, Mr N. Nfor, in the Political Directorate of the Ministry of Territorial Administration, keenly observed: "the citizens are forced to accept bribery and corruption as a norm of the society as one after the other comes to realize that, that is the only means by which one can survive, as each comes to realize that in the society there are no rights left for those at the bottom."[30]

The institutionalization of corruption and the legalization of favoritism and tribalism put Ahidjo's post-referendum Cameroon in question more so as it concerns the Anglophones. According to Huntington, corruption is a product of social and economic modernization.[31] If this is the case, modernization is a negative phenomenon for it ushers decay into the body politic. Corruption, from all empirical evidence, is a capitalist tendency. It is a dehumanized means of exploiting the masses without mercy or redress. Capitalism, says Walter Rodney, "did bring social services to European workers in Africa: firstly, as a by-product of providing such services for the bourgeoisie and the middle class, and later as a deliberate act of policy."[32] In the Ahidjo regime public servants, who were the privileged recipients of patronage, indulged in corruption, thereby becoming parasites.[33] Given these circumstances, the masses lost confidence in the existing political institutions, which the well-placed people used without pity in exploiting them. In retaliation to these acts of inhumanity, the masses became agitated, apathetic, frustrated and ultimately disloyal to the regime. The latter was manifested in many ways: from popular songs mocking the regime in the late 1980s and early 1990s to massive transfer of CFA francs from banks to *tontines* (i.e., informal savings associations) to the founding of the Social Democratic Front (SDF).

Public outcry over corruption, embezzlement, swindling, tribalism, nepotism, inefficiency, political blackmail and state terrorism vividly illustrates that the imposition of the unitary state in 1972 resulted in a fraudulent political system operating through a cumbersome and unaccountable bureaucracy. The unitary state, because of this structure, became very wasteful, expensive and more difficult to manage than the federal republic that had three governments and four assemblies. The unitary system had no public service commission that could objectively examine the performance of the bureaucracy. Nor were presidential appointments to government corporations subject to parliamentary scrutiny. The end result was that the system offered no reward for hard work. The fortunate ones, who happened to have entered the club of the ruling class, did so through the sponsorship of a member of government, or one who was in one way or the other close to the president.[34]

THE EFFECTS OF THE UNITARY STATE ON FORMER WEST (I.E., ANGLOPHONE) CAMEROON

The advent of the unitary system did not bring the glories West Cameroonians were told its creation would bring. Ahidjo, in his campaign for this vicious project that placed the people's destiny in the hands of an individual, propagated it using the political rhetoric "national unity, social justice and balanced development." In the creation of this deleterious structure he had reiterated "we are better equipped, FELLOW COUNTRYMEN, to face the future. A nation ever more united; a strong and democratic state; a party carrying out its role ever more effective; a plan clearly defining our objectives in the economic, social and cultural fields."[35]

While Francophone Cameroon has been reaping more and more the overall fruits of the creation of the unitary system, Anglophone Cameroon has become more desperate than it was under the federal system. Under the federal structure, as mentioned earlier, the region had her little share of the national cake by right and had determined what to do with it. With the unitary system it was Ahidjo (personified by his fans and the favored few in key positions as "father of national unity") in Yaoundé, who, by his benevolent good will, dished out what he wanted and to whom he wanted. The survival of Anglophone Cameroon depended on Ahidjo, consequently, he was looked upon as a tin-god. Soon after the unitary state came into effect, ex-West Cameroon began experiencing the worse moments of its history. The post-referendum era clearly showed a deliberate move to reduce Anglophone Cameroon into a mere economic periphery, supplying raw materials and cheap labor to the rest of the economy. The two seaports in West Cameroon, which, prior to reunification, ranked close to Nigeria's seaports (as regards foreign trade) were paralyzed and neglected (see table 3.1 below).

Table 3.1
Tonnage of Cargo Unloaded in Southern Nigeria and West Cameroons Ports in 1959 and 1960

Ports	Unloaded		Loaded	
	1959	**1960**	**1959**	**1960**
Lagos	1,795,179	2,171,749	1,142,181	955, 164
Sapele	64,023	104,316	293,477	345,025
Warri	57,283	66,434	52,850	51,303
Burutu	61,819	58,863	64,522	81,429
Degema	4,739	4,973	75,982	60,793
Port Harcourt	574,051	652,000	1,004,482	1,190,327
Calabar	43,089	35,601	127,130	95,302
*Victoria	31,908	40,177	42,380	159,676
*Tiko	15,074	14,544	193,380	154,812
Koko	--	69	—	563
Total	2,647,165	3,148,726	2,996,435	3,094,394

Source: Federation of Nigeria, Office of Statistics: Trade Report for the Year 1960. Federal Ministry of Information, Printing Division, Lagos, table no. 3, p. 8.
*Cameroon ports

The table shows that the Victoria and Tiko seaports contributed to the development of Southern Cameroons. In 1960 these seaports came 4th and 5th respectively in the tonnage of cargo loaded out of Nigeria ports. All imports and exports to West Cameroon passed through these two ports. But when the United Republic Cameroon was created in 1972, the two ports were neglected as the government made it a policy that all transactions should be through the river port of Douala. Imports and exports became concentrated in the Douala river port, which subsequently accounted for 92% of all maritime traffic. All customs clearing agencies in Tiko and Victoria ports had to move to Douala. While attention was paid to the seaports of Kribi, Campo and Garoua riverport, those of West Cameroon, including the Mamfe riverport, were abandoned. The move to reduce the ports of Tiko and Victoria into disuse or third class was publicized in the 1976–1981 Development Plan. In this Five-Year Development Plan, 18,426 million CFA francs, of which 14,926 million francs CFA were obtained from external sources, were allocated to the development of the Douala riverport. The seaports of Kribi and Campo had 536 million CFA francs and 168 million CFA francs respectively for their development.[36]

The abandoned Tiko and Victoria seaports and the Mamfe riverport on the Cross River prior to this period had played a vital role in the evacuation of produce from the hinterlands of the English sector to overseas countries. Export crops, e.g., cocoa, palm oil, palm kernel, timber, robusta and arabica coffee, were exported through these ports by the Produce Marketing Boards (PMB) to overseas markets. The Tiko and Victoria ports were of vital importance to the Cameroon Development Corporation (CDC) for the export of her produce such as tea, banana, rubber, palm oil and palm kernel.[37] The CDC's narrow gauge railway system linking the factories with the ports of Tiko and Victoria was rendered useless. A bulk of CDC produce had to pass through the congested Douala riverport. Owing to government pressure, CDC cash crops had to be exported through Douala, which is over a hundred kilometers from the ports of Tiko and Victoria, where the CDC factories and plantations were located. All of these additional costs were incurred merely for the political strategy of never having anything that Cameroon produces strictly from the English-speaking regions. Instead of developing the Victoria Cape (Limbe) deep seaport, the government preferred to spend millions annually to dredge the Douala riverport. The riverport is located 50 kilometers away from the Atlantic Ocean, has spots along its waterway that must be dredged frequently to enable big merchant ships to reach Douala, in addition to daily removal of sand from the ship terminus.[38] It had always been the wish of the Anglophones that the deep water seaport be constructed in Victoria to boost the economy of the zone and save the government from spending millions of francs dredging sand annually from the Douala riverport on the Wouri. Dr. E.M.L. Endeley in his address at the installation of a Limbe Senior Divisional officer (SDO) lamented that "we have the Atlantic Ocean here, right behind us, behind your backs and we lack a wharf. . . . Instead of using the wharf nature has given us, we are trying to use artificial means to live. Instead of using the wharf at our disposal, we want to change the Wouri river into a sea. Those incongruencies are before us; the ordinary people see them and they talk and I hear them."[39]

In line with the policy of Francophonizing the Anglophone institutions, the National Produce Marketing Board (NPMB) headquarters was moved from Victoria to Douala. The motive was not only to give it a national outlook but also to apply the Anglophone system of organizing the farmers under one authority to improve the earnings from their labor. But instead of keeping the top management in the hands of the Anglophones who knew the system, it was a Francophone who was put at the helm of affairs. This clearly justifies the views expressed by many Anglophones that an Anglophone is never put in a position where he can make binding decisions. The transfer of the Board's headquarters from Victoria to Douala and not Yaoundé, the nation's capital, raised the question as to why Victoria could not be the headquarters of NPMB. Some concluded that Francophones do not want any important establishment to be located in Anglophone Cameroon. The general decline in the economy of Anglophone Cameroon, particularly in the industrial towns of Tiko and Victoria, led many businesses in these localities to move to Douala. As the large enterprises moved to Douala, the survival of petty traders was hampered by the crushing effects of *patentes* (a business tax levied by the government). Limbe (formerly Victoria) became a ghost town, as its one time buoyant economy in the days of West Cameroon with ships calling on its ports, were now diverted to Douala riverport.

The following companies moved out of Limbe either to Douala or Yaoundé:

1. CAMBANK: Its headquarters was simply moved to Yaoundé
2. R & W King
3. Printania
4. Glamour

5. Emens Textiles

6. Cameroon Commercial Corporation

7. UTC

8. Socopsa

9. PMO nationalized and its headquarters moved to Douala

The following companies and banks closed down in Limbe altogether:

1. Power Cam

2. SONAC

3. Standard Bank of West Africa Limited

4. Alliance Company

5. Renault Motors

In Tiko, prominent among the companies that folded up were the Peugeot, Volkswagen and Opel motor companies. In the Bamenda region the coffee company Santa was closed down. The after-effect of the collapse of the West Cameroon economy was the exodus to French Cameroon of young Anglophones in search of economic opportunities. Many of these would-be workers had been schooled in the English system and did not have a strong command of French. Consequently, they were at a disadvantage in the labor market, which became very tight in the 1980s as the economy contracted and the central government was compelled to implement structural adjustment measures, which, among other things, meant freezing government hiring.

THE CASE OF OIL EXPLOITATION IN LIMBE (FORMERLY VICTORIA)

When the announcement of oil discovery along the Victoria coast was made public after the 1961 referendum, the people of Anglophone Cameroon were happy that the oil industry would bring life back particularly to Victoria, which had become dead economically. The French Company ELF Serepca located deposits of off-shore oil in Rio del Rey and Ndian Division, near the border with Cross River State of Nigeria. ELF Serepca spotted 21 areas and the company's preliminary estimates suggested that the largest oil fields contained as much as 1.5 million tons of oil a year, which was sufficient for Cameroon's internal consumption then.[40] When the main companies concerned at the time, ELF Serepca and Tepcam, started extracting oil, the atmosphere became saturated with rumors that the refinery would be built in Douala and crude oil would be channeled by pipeline from the Victoria coast to Douala. Cameroon at this time was a united republic with a single party, the CNU, and it was only Ahmadou Ahidjo who had the trump cards. He could do and undo. Those who spoke against the regime disappeared and were never seen again. These inhuman acts were carried out by the secret police organization *Service de Documentation* (SEDOC) and the *Brigade Mixte Mobile* (BMM).[41]

The rumors did not end with the building of the refinery at Douala. It was also rumored that the United Republic of Cameroon, with seven provinces, would be compressed into five provinces. The compression was to see the merger of the littoral and southwest provinces with headquarters in Buea and the western and northwest provinces with headquarters in Bafoussam. The speculation behind this merger was that if the refinery were built in Douala and crude oil from Victoria (now Limbe) pipelined to that city, there would be no indignation because the two towns would be in one province. Following these rumors the people of northwest province, at a provincial meeting with the CNU central committee delegation in Mankon, asked then-Minister of Territorial Administration, Mr. Ayissi Mvodo, to make a statement on the matter. Mr. Ayissi Mvodo expressed surprise and refuted the allegations. To buttress his point he rehearsed the usual political rhetoric that the aim of the government was to bring the government nearer the people and that it was even government wish to create more provinces in the future.

What equally promoted the building of the refinery in Victoria was the serious protest Dr. E.M.L. Endeley launched calling for the building of the refinery and the commencement of the tapping of the oil immediately. Dr. E.M.L. Endeley had just survived the hotly contested CNU section president elections in Fako against Mr. Luma Martin. As CNU section president he was in a better position to criticize from within.[42] Had he been beaten in the CNU reorganization exercise, which was aimed at eradicating radicals from the party, the story might be different today. Given vocal reaction from the northwest and the public appeal of Fako Section President Dr. Endeley, it became clear to Yaoundé authorities that the construction of the refinery in Douala would meet with resistance. Faced with these circumstances Ahidjo had to act in 1975 in his preparation for the presidential elections. He, like his able lieutenant Ayissi Mvodo, had to come to the public to refute all allegations pertaining to the building of the refinery in Douala and maintain instead that work would soon start in Limbe (then Victoria).

The construction of the refinery moved closer to reality in May of 1977 when the president, on tour of the provinces, revealed that the National Refinery Corporation would "have an initial investment of 25,000 million francs CFA and its headquarters will be in Victoria and in effect will generate subsidiary industries."[43] On December 7, 1976, the National Refinery Corporation, known by its acronym SONARA, was incorporated and on January 11, 1978, an established convention was signed between the government and SONARA. Feasibility studies stood at 4000 million francs CFA by November 1977. The construction of the refinery began in October 1978 and continued until the symbolic handing over in 1981. The refinery had a production capacity of 2,000,000 tons of crude oil annually and covered a total land surface of 54 hectares.[44] The state had 60 percent of the shares while related financial institutions that financed the project had 40 percent.

It has been impossible for most Cameroonians to know exactly the amount of crude oil exported in any particular year. For any official of the tutelage ministry—Mines and Power—or refinery official who talks to any researcher or anyone about oil production data in Cameroon must have authorization from the presidency. It is commonplace to see the SONARA manager feigning complete ignorance of crude oil production figures, and giving the impression that he is not even interested in knowing how much his plant is producing. Government rationale is that oil production should be kept secret so as not to distract Cameroonians from other pursuits, especially in the key agricultural sector. But this does not sound convincing to the average Cameroonian, who believes that government secrecy is simply for those who matter to swell their foreign bank accounts with petrol money. Worse still, oil income is not managed by the tutelage minister but by the president, which raises the question of who checks the other? If the tutelage minister were in charge of oil receipts the president could at anytime check him (or her), but if the president is in charge the minister cannot have a word, for he (she) serves at his discretion. The legislature cannot oversee the president either, emasculated as it is after more than forty years of executive dominance of the other branches of government. However, from foreign sources conservative estimates in 1984 put yearly oil production at 10,000,000 tons and that, when converted into barrels at a price of $28.00 per barrel, amounted to $700,000,000 in income per year.[45] Public speculation about oil income made president Ahidjo to admit in 1981 that there was a special account where the money is kept and is injected into the budget when it runs into difficulties.[46] The question asked always is, since oil income does not constitute part of Gross National Income (GNI) what amount is injected into the budget when it is in crisis and what happens to the rest of the money?

With the commencement of the exploitation of crude oil, and later the refining of crude oil in SONARA, Limbe became known as OPEC City. The people thought their dream of prosperity had come true. It was hoped that the one-time weekend jamboree town would be rejuvenated. With the tapping of oil, it was also believed that to a large extent unemployment would be reduced and the exodus of job seekers to the industrial and agro-industrial towns of Francophone Cameroon would end. Unfortunately, the location of SONARA in Victoria neither solved the unemployment problem of the area nor has it generated the subsidiary industries that Ahidjo had promised. The refinery is staffed mostly by Francophones; the Anglophones are relatively very few. When a General Manager (i.e., Bernard Eding) was once asked why the refinery had few Anglophone employees, even though it was located in an Anglophone province, he replied that Anglophones had not acquired the technological skills required to work in SONARA.[47] Lamenting the absence of locals in the ranks of oil refinery workers, a reporter of the government-owned national daily, *Cameroon Tribune*, commented that "I was admiring the beauty of the SONARA Satellite Village which I saw on the television last Saturday evening. It is within the periphery of Limbe, but it looks like a world of its own. The inhabitants of the shanties of Church Street, Mbende, Mile One, name the rest, admire it from a distance. What impresses me most is the homogeneity of the workers." He ended with the consolation that "It's national integration and work."[48] The Fako leader, Dr. Endeley, in his address to the Governor of southwest province, Nguimba Magloire, on the occasion of the installation of the Fako Senior Divisional Officer (SDO) in Limbe, told the administrators that SONARA had no impact on the people of Limbe; the so-called OPEC City and its structures were a decoration of a foreign organization among the people. He ended his speech by saying that:

> I gave the inaugural speech on behalf of the people when we were installing SONARA, a few years ago. And those of you who were here will remember that I quoted everything that the Head of State had promised SONARA would bring to us—hotels, night clubs, small industries— where are they now? And SONARA still lives, standing silent from the

southwest and this is a great conflict. The country will say these people are really fortunate and they will not know how unfortunate we are until they get here.[49]

Further, the royalties the oil companies were supposed to pay to the Limbe local government were instead being paid to the Douala local government under the pretext that the companies had their headquarters in Douala. Limbe had to fight for years until 1989, when SONARA began paying the city some revenue accruing from oil exploitation. Limbe and nearby Ndian equally do not benefit from income taxes levied on SONARA workers because their salaries are computerized in Douala.

In contrast to the debilitating effects that the unitary system has had on Anglophones, it has been a boon to Francophones. As mentioned earlier, the industries, financial institutions and organs of government moved east in the name of a united Cameroon in 1972. Since oil started flowing in viable quantity in the 1970s, the government can genuinely point to the completion of many important projects, most, if not all, probably paid for by oil from southwest province. One can cite:

- the magnificent presidential palace at Etoudi. The construction of the first phase stood at 450 billion francs CFA in 1980, more than the national budget a few years before then;

- the impressive extension of Douala decks;

- the equally impressive, though perhaps less justifiable, international airport at Garoua;

- Cameroon's only synthetic stadium at Garoua;

- the imposing hydro-electricity dams of the Noun (Songlolo) and the Benoue;

- the magnificent Ngoundéré-University centers and those of Dschang and Douala and the extension of Yaoundé University;

- the shooting skyscrapers on the 20 May Boulevard, Yaoundé, to give the town a new look;

- the multi-billion CFA francs television complex at Bala II, Yaoundé, and its nationwide relay stations;

- the Kousseri-Mora-Maroua-Garoua-Ngoundéré road in north Cameroon, the Douala-Yaoundé-Bafoussam-Bamenda road in littoral, center-south west and northwest provinces, the Bertoua-Belabo road in the east and the interroad network in the west.

Virtually all of the projects listed above are located in Francophone Cameroon, and therein lies the paradox of Ahidjo's May 20, 1972, "revolution" rhetorically based on national unity, balanced development and social justice.[50] Anglophone Cameroon, whence oil, the country's primary foreign exchange earner, is produced is neglected for the benefit of East (i.e., Francophone) Cameroon across the Mungo. Anglophone Cameroon remains the only zone where the provincial headquarters (Buea and Bamenda) are not linked by tarred roads.[51] In sum, Anglophone Cameroon has been left to wither on the vine, even though at least 40 percent of Cameroon's foreign exchange earning comes from one province: the Anglophone southwest.

CONCLUSION

Scholarly discourse on the state in the West has tended to imbue it with universal, i.e., non-exclusive, qualities. Similarly, western scholars tend to have a benign view of constitutions, treating them as the embodiment of political enlightenment. Both the state, as an organization, and constitutions, as their institutional underbelly, should be viewed critically in sub-Saharan Africa. In its contemporary form, the African state is a new and alien entity. It has yet to be universally accepted throughout the continent. In many ways the state in Africa is a source of conflicts, rather than an instrument in their resolution. Likewise, constitutions in Africa, far from reflecting elite, much less societal, consensus, are actually instruments of domination periodically manipulated by state elites to preserve their hold on power. It is naïve in the extreme to see constitutions in Africa as attempts to restrain the state. African politics cannot be understood without an appreciation of the tension between state and society and the arbitrary use of constitutions and of laws in general. In Cameroon, structural changes to the state, from federalism to unitarism, coupled with constitutional manipulations, often by decree, have led to a rise in tension between two important communities: Anglophones and Francophones. Further, the carting away of resources from one part of the country to another has made matters worse. If Cameroon unity is to be preserved, a fundamental restructuring of the state, which implied a return to the status quo of pre 1972, and a more equitable distribution of resources are necessary. Otherwise, the vortex of state disintegration that started in the Great Lakes region in the 1990s may well engulf Cameroon.

NOTES

1. Douglass North, *Structure and Change in Economic History*, New York, London: W.W. Norton and Company, 1981, p. 201.

2. Feder, G. and D. Feeny, 1991, "Land Tenure and Property Rights: Theory and Implications for Development Policy," *The World Bank Economic Review*, vol. 5, no. 1, pp. 135–153.

3. *Editor's note*: The imposition of the one-party state in Cameroon was de facto rather than de jure. This is important, for at the right moment (1989–1990) Cameroonians would use their dormant, but constitutionally guaranteed, right to free association to challenge the ruling party. No constitutional change was really necessary.

4. *Editor's note*: The author exaggerates somewhat the merits of the constitution that undergirded the Cameroon federation. In comparison to other federal constitutions, the Foumban constitution left much to be desired, although it was "better" than its successor. For an excellent study of the Cameroon federation, see Willard Johnson, *The Cameroon Federation: Political Integration in a Fragmentary Society*, Princeton: Princeton University Press, 1970.

5. Albert Mukong, *Prisoner Without a Crime*, Alfresco Books, 1975, pp. 72–75.

6. *Editor's note*: In fairness to Ahidjo, this view was widely shared among donors in the 1970s. Even now few donors work with local governments in Africa. Aid continues to be granted centralized authority even when it has become evanescent in many places.

7. Fongum Gorji-Dinka, "The New Social Order," Bamenda, 1985, p. 1.

8. Ibid., p. 2.

9. Author interview with Awudu Cybrien, Douala, June 7, 1988.

10. *Constitution octroyée* is that which is imposed on the people from above while *constitution évoluée* comes about through some sort of political arrangement or development.

11. The reference is to UN Resolution 1688 (XV) 994 of the Plenary Session of April 21, 1961.

12. Article 1 (IV) of the Unitary Constitution of June 2, 1972.

13. Victor Le Vine, "Political Integration and the United Republic of Cameroon" in David R. Smock et al. (eds.), *The Search for National Integration in Africa*, London: Macmillan Publishers, 1976, p. 276.

14. Article 4 of the Unitary Constitution of June 2, 1972.

15. Article 8 of the Unitary Constitution of June 2, 1972.

16. Article 2 of the Unitary Constitution of June 2, 1972.

17. One example is Ahidjo's dismissal of Moussa Yaya, who was the second vice president of the national assembly and a member of the CNU central committee in charge of women affairs, for opposing his handing over power to Paul Biya. *Editor's note*: The example is revealing, for it shows that there may have been opposition to Ahidjo from within his inner circle. Ahidjo may have been Cameroon's strongman but his power may not have been absolute and unchallenged. He had to balance the interests of divergent constituencies, which re-

quired political acumen, in addition to brute force. Further, Moussa Yaya was a Peul (i.e., Fulani) northerner. That Ahidjo was willing to dismiss a close ethnic kindred and a coreligionist in favor of Biya, a southerner and a Christian, undermines any argument that his regime was strictly "tribalistic."

18. Bill No. 153-PJI-ANF of May 23, 1967 promulgated by Law No. 67/LF/19 of June 6, 1967 (relevant sections: 1, 3,5 and 7).

19. Article 3 of the Unitary Constitution of June 2, 1972.

20. Law No. 75-1 of May 9, 1975, modifying Article 5 of the Unitary Constitution of June 2, 1972.

21. Article 9 (I) of the federal constitution of 1961.

22. *Editor's note*: As of the time of editing, there had been two Anglophone prime ministers in Cameroon.

23. Article 7 of the Unitary Constitution of June 2, 1972, modified on February 2, 1984.

24. Memorandum Presented to the Head of State and Chairman of the Cameroon People's Democratic Movement, Douala July 5, 1985.

25. President Ahidjo's speech to the special session of the fereral assembly, May 6,1972.

26. Pierre Flambeau Ngaya, *Cameroun, Qui Gouverne? De Ahidjo à Biya*, Paris, 1973, p. 71. *Editor's note*: The composition of the first post-federal government in fact shows a remarkable degree of regional representation. Of the 28 members of government, 6 came from Ahidjo's "home" region. Anglophone Cameroon and central south province, with 7 cabinet members each, had the most members. Based on numbers alone Ahidjo cannot be accused of stacking the government with either Francophones or fellow northerners. Superficially at least, he did take the notion of ethnic balance (*équilibre*) seriously. I emphasize superficially, because the numbers hide the fact that certain key posts seemed to have been reserved for key northern allies. Sadou Daoudou, for example, served as defense minister virtually for the entire time Ahidjo was in office.

27. *Editor's note*: This statement may be hyperbolic. The administrative- hegemonic character of the Ahidjo regime makes hiring practices more complex than the author is suggesting. This is not to say that the regime was oblivious to the needs of northerners, only that it had to be careful how it satisfied them since it had other goals.

28. *Africa*, no. 89, August–September 1984, p. 29.

29. Quoted in *Africa*, no. 51, September 1975, p. 70.

30. Author interview with N. Nfor, political scientist, Yaoundé, Cameroon, December 12, 1990.

31. Samuel Huntington, *Political Order in Changing Societies*, New Haven: Yale University Press, 1968.

32. Walter Rodney, *How Europe Underdeveloped Africa*, London: Bogle-L'Ouverture Publication, 1972, p. 244.

33. In all likelihood one of the hidden causes of the creation of the United Republic was the discovery of oil off the coast of west Cameroon. It is no accident that Cameroon went into the tapping of its crude oil soon after the "peaceful revolution." A unitary state allowed greater control of this essential product by the

central government. *Editor's note*: The people of the Delta region of Nigeria, whence oil is produced, have not seen a greater share of oil revenue gone to them simply because Nigeria is a federation. The structure of the state does not necessarily predict how equitably national resources will be distributed. Of greater importance is commitment to a vision of national development and social solidarity. In Cameroon the issue may not be so much federalism versus unitarism, but rather the unwillingness of the ruling elite even to divulge how much it earns from oil production, much less share it with the people.

34. *Editor's note*: Here the author is suggesting that the Ahidjo (and later Biya) regime was based on patron-client ties.

35. Cameroon News Agency, Yaoundé, May 23, 1972, p. 3.

36. *The Fourth Five-Year Development Plan—1976–1981*, Yaoundé, 1976, p. 140.

37. Tata Simon Ngenge, *The Socio-Economic History of the Ndu Tea Estate: 1966–1982* (unpublished master's thesis), Yaoundé: Department of History, University of Yaoundé, 1983, p. 72.

38. Author interview with Monsieur Priso, Director of General Administration (DAG) of the National Ports Authority Douala CTV, November 1, 1990.

39. *Day Dawn*, Limbe, June 11, 1985.

40. *Africa-Europe Publication*, 1975–1976, pp. 444–445.

41. Abel Eyinga, "Government by State of Emergency," in Richard Joseph (ed.), *Gaullist Africa: Cameroon under Ahmadou Ahidjo*, Enugu: Fourth Dimension Publishing Co., Ltd, 1987, p. 107.

42. *Editor's note*: Once again, the author acknowledges dissent within the Cameroon National Union (CNU). The reality was that even though the one-party state in Africa suppressed interparty competition, it did not end politics (and politicking) altogether. African politics, before the latest wave of "democratization," was less monotonous than has generally been assumed. To the extent that one of the functions fulfilled by political parties is interest articulation, they significantly enhance the vibrancy of politics. However, the absence of opposition parties does not signify the end of politics. Ahidjo apparently had to change the location of the oil refinery from Douala to Limbe, under pressure from CNU members from the southwest as well as ordinary citizens in northwest province. This would not have happened if he had complete control over the CNU and the institutions of state.

43. *Cameroon Information*, Yaoundé, March 1977, p. 17.

44. *SONARA Magazine*, France: Imprimerie SIRA/ASNIERES, October 10, 1984, p. 6.

45. *West Africa*, July 23, 1984, p. 1485.

46. *Cameroon Tribune*, Yaoundé, May 10, 1981, p. 6.

47. CRTV Interview, Limbe, April 10, 1989.

48. *Cameroon Tribune*, Yaoundé, June 23, 1989, p. 11.

49. Quoted in *Day Dawn*, November 6, 1985, p. 8.

50. *Editor's note*: The projects listed by the author have to be put in perspective. Yaoundé is the political capital of Cameroon. It is only natural that it hosts major government buildings, including the presidential palace, which is modern and allegedly well-fortified but hardly magnificent (which is of course in the eyes

of the beholder). Is Yaoundé the beneficiary of government spending because it is located in Francophone Cameroon or because it is simply the country's capital city? One cannot justify the growth of Yaoundé on ethnic ground either, for even though it is located in center-south province where Biya hails, virtually all of the projects benefiting Yaoundé listed by the author (projects 1, 7, 8 and the latter part of 6) were begun under Ahidjo. A stronger argument can be made that Ahidjo spent a disproportionate share of Cameroon's resources on his home province of the north. There is almost no justification for the ultramodern international airport at Garoua, which in 1991 played host to a grand total of one international flight per week. But, once again, was state spending on the north due to its location in Francophone Cameroon or its having been the birthplace of the country's first president, who spent money outside of his home base as well? Few would quarrel with the proposition that given its contribution to Cameroon's economy, the southwest has not received its fair share of government spending. However, whether this is the product of some conspiracy to marginalize Anglophones, I very much doubt. The projects mentioned by the author not withstanding, stagnation in contemporary Cameroon seems to be of a general nature. The mismanagement of the Biya regime appears to have equal opportunity effects. Since former West Cameroon, in comparison to former East Cameroon, was always the least developed part of the country, one would expect stagnation to be of greater intensity there. This no way justifies the conditions that prevail in the region nor does it absolve the government of responsibility for them, but it helps put things into context. (For the record, the construction of Ngaoundéré University Centre was financed by the French government.)

51. *Editor's note*: Some major cities within Francophone Cameroon are not connected by tarred roads either. Cases in point: Yaoundé and Ngaoundéré, Bertoua and Yaoundé. Even the road linking Yaoundé to Douala, Cameroon's two largest cities, is a single-lane "highway" in both directions. It is one of the paradoxes of Cameroon that a country so well-endowed in resources has such an underdeveloped infrastructure.

Chapter 4

Anglophone Political Struggles and State Responses

Nantang Jua

In Europe, presented in Western epistemologies as the sovereign theoretical subject of all histories, nation and state are coterminous. Although the validity of this assertion has been questioned by recent developments on that continent (especially in the former Yugoslavia), its purchase value has not been debased in the eyes of African leaders in their desire to foster a national imagining (Anderson, 1983). Countervailing historical evidence, however, confirm Appiah's claim that independence left Africa with states looking for nations (Appiah, 1992).

Cameroon has, arguably, remained an island of peace, despite the fact that a cultural divide born of its dual colonial heritage, English and French, has been suffused on ethnic differences. Official rhetoric would readily attribute this to the Cameroonian exception whose French rendition, *le Cameroun, c'est le Cameroun,* has become a common refrain in everyday life. That is, whereas relations imply similarities as well as differences, this official view has sought to ignore the differences between two important communities inside the Cameroon polity: the Anglophones and Francophones. It overlooks historical evidence of the spatial dialectic of integration and fracture that states tend to undergo. Paradoxically, the more the official line has tried to run roughshod over reality, the more it has brought it into sharper relief, that is, each action (or inaction) on the part of the Cameroon state elite toward Anglophones has provided energy for future struggles. These take many forms and cut across many realms including culture, politics and international relations. This chapter examines the "Anglophone problem" in all of its complexities, among them the fact that Anglophones and Francophones (or at least their elite) hold radically different views of the past, which they use to explain the present, and, in the case of Anglpohones, justify political struggles aimed at shaping the future.

RE-IMAGINING THE PAST

Addressing the National Assembly in 1990, the Minister of Defense, Ahmadou Ali, claimed that "Cameroon has always been one, not more" (*The Herald*, No. 8927 April 2000:3). This was a controversial claim, as just before the plebiscite in February 1961 that led to the reunification of the Republic of Cameroon and Southern Cameroons, it was affirmed in the British House of Commons that in the face of the difficulties facing the "countries federation is the only practicable system, certainly in the interests of the inhabitants of Southern Cameroons."[1] Ali was not alone in his assertion, which was seemingly informed by earlier declarations by Francophone political leaders. Ahmadou Moustapha, a former Vice Prime Minister and Minister of State, as well as President of the National Alliance for Democracy and Progress, noted that Anglophones had been "francophonized" (*Jeune Afrique Economie*, 20 novembre 1995: 63). Similarly, Ndam Njoya of the Cameroon Democratic Union (CDU) and Dakole Daissala of the Movement for Democracy and Progress (MDP) denied the existence of an Anglophone problem. That this view was common among the Francophone political elite gave it an institutional aura. Stored in institutional memory, Francophone (intellectual) elites repeated it *ad nauseum* over a popular radio program, *Dimanche Midi.* The objective of this proclamation was evident insofar as one accepts that the more powerful an agent (Francophones in this case) is seen to be, the higher the probability that the subordinate (Anglophones) would submit himself to the discretionary powers of the former. Although designed to shape social reality, this institutional position contradicts popular knowledge. In everyday life, Anglophones are repeatedly referred to as *les Biafrais* (Biafrans), a name that emphasizes their "otherness." Thus Cameroon has always been one, not more; by the same token, Anglophone Cameroonians are derided as foreigners.

"Naming," "identity," it has been argued, already has a sedimented history of its own; therefore, it is crucial to ask how the present historical instance of "naming" repeats or recuperates the general economy of the "name" (Radhakrihnan, 1990: 58). Biafrans (i.e., mainly Igbos) had of course tried to secede from the Nigerian post-colonial state. The naming of Anglophones as Biafrans was an acknowledgement of the historical and cultural differences that existed between the two communities. The political class tried to recuperate this while giving it a different spin. As Biafrans, Anglophones were to be seen as secessionists. This led Emah Basil, former mayor of Yaoundé, to refer to them as *"les ennemis dans la maison"* (the enemies within the house). As such, they had to be chased away. Mbombou Njoya, the present Sultan of Foumban, as Minister of Territorial Administration implicitly suggested this when he called on Anglophones, in the wake of the launching of the Social Democratic Front (SDF) in Bamenda in May 1990, *"d'aller au-dela de* nos *frontieres."* His position rested on a postulate that the land occupied by the Anglophone provinces belonged to the Republic. After all, Cameroon was recognized as a state under international law within these spatial boundaries. Its legitimate owners could therefore embark on what is referred to in Cameroon as *la chasse aux allogènes.* Naming in this context is therefore a mobilization resource, its goal being the galvanization of Francophone public opinion against the other with whom he may even share common experiences such as exclusion from public space.

The official position is based on a reading of present-day Cameroon, which has been widely refuted by careful research (Welch, 1966; Benjamin, 1972; Bayart, 1979; Jua, 1997; Konings, 1999; Konings and Nyamnjoh, 2000). Although colonized initially by the Germans, the Dankler report shows that seven years before the outbreak of World War I, Cameroon had not been effectively occupied and "the majority of the inhabitants were only nominally subjected" (cited in Nkwi, 1989:13). With a view to hurting Germany's *amour propre,* the territory (people as well as land), was converted into a League of Nations mandate after the War and placed under the auspices of the British and the French. Anglophone Cameroon—people as well as territory—became a League mandate and subsequently a United Nations trust territory under the auspices of Britain. The official position can be seen as a form of historicism. Modes of contesting this historicism have been varied. Prominent among them is the Anglophones' claim that oil-rich Bakassi Peninsula, which is disputed by Cameroon and Nigeria, belongs to them.

Colonialism, as a rupture in African history, turned Africans into hybrids endowed with two cognitive closures, one African and the other European. The Cameroon case was complicated by the fact that this rupture endowed Cameroonians with British and French cognitive closures. Early attempts to deal with this colonial heritage had caused the adoption of the reciprocal exchange of elites as a mode of state construction. Intellectual backing could easily be marshaled in support of this approach (Smith, 1983; Hobsbawm, 1990:10), which also has a rich historical lineage from Europe. In its pursuit, réseaux (networks) were commonplace in this rhizome state (Bayart, 1993). This had worked in the First Republic (1961–1982) for two reasons. Firstly, it sutured all the elites who did not place a premium only on the accumulation of material benefits. Secondly, these elites set up patron-client ties, which served (re) distribution purposes and contributed to a leveling process.

Because of their access to resources, barons of the regime were thought to have monopoly control over the imaginary means of production and reproduction (Godelier, 1978:767). Although correct, this explanation of Ahidjo's capacity to control the elites is not complete. Fear was a mode of social consciousness. Foncha confirmed this when he admitted that fear that Ahidjo would eliminate him, as well as his family, caused him not react to his dismissal from the cabinet (Soh, 1999:210). Reacting to a question on his failure to confront Ahidjo on critical issues affecting Anglophones, Solomon Tandeng Muna, who succeeded Foncha as vice-president of the federation, asked the journalist if he wanted him to commit political suicide.

The state's capacity to absorb elites was not elastic. If anything, there was a negative correlation between the increase in the former and the rate of their absorption. Anglophones were adversely affected by this trend as Francophones were employed in predominantly Anglophone areas. This was not anomalous, for disadvantage and political marginalization are normally distributed along lines of group identity (Calloni, 1998:226). As a bane, it caused the disaffection of several Anglophone elites, energizing some of them to refuse to continue "living within the lie" (Havel, 1985:147). Initially, this rejection took several forms, among them the creation of democratic spaces, such as popular theater, that were only obliquely related to resistance. Since dependence is an ambiguous concept eliciting both submission and revolt among the subaltern, their actions helped to usher in the revolt phase among this class, denying the institutional elite the monopoly claim over the laboring process in imagining a nation. Articulation of their grievances, using the frontal approach, came only on the heels of the creation of a political opportunity by Paul Biya, the president of the Second Republic. This opportunity translated the potential for movement into mobilization (Tarrow,

1994:18). Arguably, under duress from the public and as recognition of the shift in the balance of forces, President Biya signed the so-called liberty laws in 1990.

Liberty as a practice, Foucault notes, must be exercised not guaranteed by institutions (Rainbow, 1984:245). This need for exercise is reinforced in historical circumstances where actors are not normatively committed to this right. Anglophones had to seize the moment as official declarations denied the existence of their problem.

CREATING A DEMOCRATIC SPACE AND EXPLOITING A POLITICAL OPPORTUNITY

Anglophones, who, according to the Frost and Sullivan Political Risk Research Report on Cameroon (1987), have "nurtured a liberal and activist political tradition," have resorted to the use of their protest repertoire. As their life world has deteriorated, they have developed richer forms for its ideological defense. Proof of this is their ability to carve out new democratic spaces and their readiness to seize the chance to exploit political opportunities that have emerged in this system, where even a memorandum addressed to the president was considered a subversive document.

Obtrusive as well as unobtrusive modes of protest have been used for this purpose. Prominent among the latter has been the use of art. Art forms, it has been noted in another context, "do not merely reflect an already constituted consciousness, giving us a window to something already fully present. They are themselves important means through which consciousness is articulated and communicated. In times of rapid social change it seems likely that popular art forms, with their exceptional mobility (whether through technology such as radio, record and cassette tape, or through physical transportation from place to place by traveling performing groups) will play a crucial role in formulating new ways of looking at things" (Barber, 1987:4). Through the use of art Anglophone writers could re-center the Anglophone problem that had been bracketed out of public debate.

By the admission of a Francophone playwright, Anglophone drama re-centered international and national attention on the abuses (physical and cultural) against the Anglophone minority, contrary to the claims of official discourse (Doho, 1993:91). Victor Epie-Ngome in his *What God Has Put Asunder* points out Weca's (an acronym for West Cameroon) discomfiture during his marriage to Miche Garba (Francophone Cameroon) in 1961. Because of Garba's *machismo,* he inflicted a lot of suffering on Weca. Says Weca: "Once the festivities were over, he brought a fleet of trucks and bundled all my children and me out of our house. His drivers gathered our stuff trampling and damaging many things . . . and so he forced me to settle in with him. Since then, he has been forcing my children to learn his own mother tongue, and to forget mine with which they grew up; I must abide by the customs of his clan, not mine and , . . . in short he has simply been breathing down my neck since then (Epie Ngome,1992:53). What is this passage but a reference to the creation of the unitary state in 1972? It is not just a jeremiad.

Memory work is always embedded in "complex class, gender, and power relations that determine what is remembered (or forgotten), by whom and for what end"(Gills cited in Norval, 1998:254). Epie Ngome challenged national memory, which harped on the construction of unity and continuity. Nurturance of a transformational consciousness in this context augured well for the emancipatory potential of Weca. This is what happens in Bate Besong's *Requiem for the Last Kaiser,* when the docile student who had been apolitical undergoes a conversion after the woman had convinced him to "choose the side of the long suffering people of Agidigidi." As a sign of rupture, he says "We must break the chains that hold us in bondage" (Bate Besong, 1991:5). Only the recovery of this feeling (of possibility) makes emancipation a historical possibility.

Maximization of the intended effects of this drama can only be attained if it is accessible to the common man. Groups such as the Yaoundé University Theater Troupe and The Flame Players, who toured both Anglophone provinces staging the plays of Anglophone writers, carried out its propagation. The apparently postmodern turn in this art is designed to make the audience part of a collaborative process and involve it in the creation of meaning. Belief in this popular theater has caused Anglophones to extend the area of its coverage to Europe. Plays staged by the Mountain Mourners in Germany, for example, have brought the Anglophone plight to international visibility (*Cameroon Post*, No. 0251, March 2, 2001:3). Bringing this issue back to the consciousness of the international community is important, for even countries like Britain, which was the administering power of Southern Cameroons, seem to have forgotten about its existence. Thus, Baroness Scotland of Asthal, Britain's Under-Secretary of State in the Foreign and Commonwealth Office could note that "it is a compliment that a Francophone country such as Cameroon has chosen to join the Commonwealth" (*Cameroon Post*, No. 0200, August 1, 2000). Consciousness–raising efforts by troupes as well as other delegations have prevented the international community from sharing this narrow pattern of perception and valuation, if not reversed it. Proof of this was the condemnation of John Kenneth Galbraith, the former US Ambassador to India, of Biya's decision to include "his" Anglophones in his delegation to the UN Millennium Summit. He noted that "the SCNC leaders have always been termed misguided fellows by the regime. Why should the (SCNC) pose a threat to the extent that the President would want to address an issue posed by misguided Cameroonians to the UN?" (*Cameroon Post*, No. 0204, September 8, 2000:1). It is plausible that efforts such as these have also contributed to the examination of the Anglophone problem in academy. Post-graduate students in the Department of Peace Studies at the University of Bradford, for instance, examined this problem in a one-week seminar on "Early Warning and Conflict Prevention: The Anglophone Problem and Peace Prospects in Africa" (*Cameroon Post*, No. 0181, June 12, 2000: 1).

Theater in essence portrayed new fields of possibilities that were held out to the Anglophone during a period when political space was contracted. Biya's promise to liberalize the political arena as well as the impossibility to suture all the elites brought about a change in Cameroon's opportunity structure.[2] Acting as "tribunes of the people," some Anglophone elites who had been used to pluralistic politics seized the chance to create the Social Democratic Front (SDF) in May 1990. According to one of its founding fathers, Dr. Gemuh Akuchu, the SDF was created to fight the marginalization of the Anglophones (*Cameroon Post*, No. 0247, February 16, 2001:1). Despite the decision of the state banning the launch of this party, Anglophones turned out massively for it. Only their involvement in the same social networks could explain this defiance (Tarrow, 1994:22). And their collective definition of the Anglophone plight could allow for consensus mobilization. Despite the original intent of the founding fathers, the master frame that they adopted—struggle for voice through the practice of a pluralistic democracy—caused other Cameroonians to join the party. Growth in size as well a change in its sociological composition led it to refocus its attention on national politics. Given the Southern Cameroons National Council's embrace of the four-state option, with the Anglophone provinces constituting one of these, officials such as Albert Mukong, Ndoki Mukete, who was chairman of the party in the southwest province and chairman of the SCNC, and Nfor Nfor, a former chairman of the Political Affairs Committee and chairman of the northern zone of the SCNC, were compelled to resign from their posts in the SDF. Their position on the Anglophone issue contradicted that of the

The widening of the gap between these two was demonstrated w.. the SDF boycotted the SCNC's call for a boycott of the May 20 National Day celebrations which it dubbed a "Day of Mourning" (*Cameroon Post*, No. 0175, May 22, 2000:1).

In an attempt to contain the spiral of political contestation that had been unleashed following the launching of the SDF, the government convened the Tripartite Conference in October 1991. This was another political opportunity for the Anglophones. Four Anglophones—Sam Ekontang Elad, Simon Munzu, Benjamin Itoe and Carlson Anyangwe (EMIA)—who were members of the Technical Committee (TC) set up by the Conference to write a draft constitution instead presented a draft federal constitution to this TC. Although this proposal was rejected outright, the government's decision to call a constitutional conference in March 1993 provided them with another opportunity to convene the All Anglophone Conference I (AAC) in Buea. The symbolism wrapped up in this name was evident to all because Buea had served as the capital of the former West Cameroon. More than 5000 people attended AAC I. This conference was important for two reasons. Firstly, it issued the Buea Declaration calling for a return to the federal state (Konings and Nyamnjoh, 1997: 218–219). Secondly, it showed that social networks could be a form of power that could be differently reproduced. Initially scheduled to hold at the University of Buea, the venue had to be changed at the last minute because the vice-chancellor rescinded the permit. Despite the ambient fear that prevailed in Buea, only the use of social networks prevented the delegates from dispersing. They invested more social capital in the organizers of AAC I than in ethnic political entrepreneurs who actively discouraged its holding. This was an indication that the latter had failed to recover their social prestige in society, in spite of their "style shift." What was needed was not a "style" but a "positional" shift.

Trends already visible at the AAC I were confirmed at the AAC II held at Bamenda in April 1994. The relegation of Anglophones to the bottom of the social ladder had caused some activists to declare the "zero option," that is, a call for the total independence of Southern Cameroons in December 1993. It is against this backdrop that AAC II was convened. For its part, the regime tried to stop the conference from taking place. It even recruited Foncha who "endorsed a government sponsored plan to block the holding of AAC II . . . (while hosting) a CPDM teleguided anti-AAC II meeting at his Foncha Street residence" (Soh, 1999: 226). Foncha's identification with the position of the government on this issue was seen as a re-engagement with the CPDM from which he had resigned because of its marginalization of the Anglophones.[3]

The hardening of positions gave rise to a competition for ritual dominance between the pro- and anti-AAC II camps. Realizing that the people had vested the proponents of AAC II with social capital, the government resorted to the use of misinformation. It announced over Radio Bamenda, as well as the national news, that the organizers—i.e., Anyangwe, Elad and Munzu—had called off the meeting. They issued a disclaimer. A mammoth crowd showed up for the conference. Not even the presence of armed troops could stop the crowd from following the members of the Standing Committee, the group that had been mandated by AAC I to negotiate with the government on the opening day of the conference.

The Standing Committee's mandate in the talks was "not to accept any arrangement which does not envisage the restoration of the Anglophone federated state within the Federal Republic of Cameroon in recognition of the bicultural nature of Cameroon." Failing this, it was to "proclaim the revival of the independence and sovereignty of the Anglophone territory of Southern Cameroons, and take all measures necessary to secure, defend and preserve the independence, sovereignty and integrity of the said territory." And with a view to endowing the entity with structures needed for its functioning, the proclamation further stipulated that the Anglophone Council should "without having to convene another session of the All Anglophone Conference, transform itself into the Southern Cameroons Constituent Assembly for the purpose of drafting, debating and adopting a constitution for the independent and sovereign state of Southern Cameroons." Also significant was the vote of a change of name by the delegates as AAC was replaced by the Southern Cameroons People's Conference. For consistency, the name of the Council was also changed to the Southern Cameroons National Council (SCNC) in August 1993.[4] Similarly, the Advisory Council was renamed the Southern Cameroons Advisory Council (SCAC).

Although private newspapers questioned what constituted a "reasonable time" within which negotiations would have to start, the government persisted in its refusal to deal with the SCNC. Seemingly, it hoped that the group would become irrelevant. In furtherance of this goal, when Biya finally summoned the Consultative Committee to discuss the new constitution, the fourteen Anglophones invited were not members of the SCNC. The SCNC warned that these "chosen Anglophones" were participating in these talks in their private/individual capacities and the decisions to which they consented would not be binding on Southern

Cameroonians (*The Herald*, No. 170, 3 January 1995:1). Notable also is the fact that this committee was presided over by an Anglophone, Simon Achidi Achu, who was then prime minister. Operating in their private capacities deprived these Anglophones of cultural membership in their community. Membership, it has been observed, is an essential attribute of the individual's moral agency, "their ability to identify and pursue a way of life that they can affirm as good" (Williams,1995:75). This was reflected in a flurry of letters to various Anglophone newspapers, divesting these "chosen Anglophones" the prerogative of defining that way of life.[5] Rather, power was vested in the SCNC, which continued to wax strong. Several other factors contributed to SCNC's increasing fortunes. Notable among them were the creation of the North American SCNC, the embrace of the cause by a vibrant Anglophone press and diplomatic offensives (discussed below).

To proponents of the use of force, the continuous popularity of the SCNC may be enigmatic, especially as its motto was the "the force of argument not the argument of force." It is possible that this was largely due to its international presence. At the Commonwealth Head of States meeting in Nicosia, Cyprus, SCNC's two-man delegation successfully lobbied against Cameroon's admission. Ostensibly this was because Cameroon had failed to conform to the conditionalities of the 1991 Harare Declaration, which included the establishment of a democratic system, good governance and respect for human rights. Despite Cameroon's failure to make progress in these realms, it was admitted into this "gentleman's club" at the 1995 meeting in Auckland, New Zealand. This anomaly has been ascribed to a "deal" between Biya and the late Sani Abacha of Nigeria to defend each other against international criticism of their regimes as well as the acquiescence of the other members in the face of Nigeria's support (Konings and Nyamnjoh, 1997: 221–222). Not even the presence of the SCNC and its plea for the organization of a Quebec-style independence referendum for Southern Cameroons and its decision to file a separate application for membership elicited enough sympathy.

INTERNATIONALIZING ANGLOPHONE POLITICAL STRUGGLES

Its overtures to the Commonwealth having failed, SCNC now turned to the United Nations to protest against "the annexation of its ex-Trust Territory, the Southern Cameroons." This, as Konings and Nyamnjoh (1997) have pointed out, was not the first time Anglophones were petitioning the

UN. SCNC was preceded by Fon Gorji Dinka of the Ambazonia Movement as well as CAM. To the common man, this was the logical step to take
for resolution of the problem. This was based on the mistaken belief that
the plebiscite options contained an escape clause that allowed Anglophones to opt out of the union if it failed. Confidence was bolstered as the
delegation included Foncha and Solomon Tandeng Muna, both important
architects of reunification.[6]

Foncha, by his admission to a 2000-person crowd gathered in front of
his residence on 13 January 1995, was the leader of this delegation (Soh,
1999:234). History repeated itself; as reminiscent of the inability of the
leaders of Southern Cameroons to agree on the options for the plebiscite
in 1961, this delegation did not have a common position. Whereas some
of its members were for the "zero option," some like Foncha remained
disciples of federalism (Soh, 1999: 235). This, however, was not crucial
because the delegation simply sought to capture the attention of the UN.
This explains why the London Communiqué that the delegation issued en
route to the UN claimed, *inter alia*, that "the people of Southern
Cameroons are now with no defined citizenship or nationality. This situation has all the ingredients which could make Southern Cameroons a
flashpoint of a potentially destructive regional conflict in the Gulf of
Guinea, which could spillover into ethnic cleansing" (*Cameroon Post*,
No. 0257, June 26, 1995: 4–5). The UN trip also provided the delegation
an opportunity to lobby the US government to support its cause. A Washington lobbyist was even recruited for this purpose. However, the inability to pay his fees caused the contract to lapse.[7]

The delegation's return, and especially the crossing of the Mungo
Bridge that links the southwest and littoral provinces, was seen as the
penultimate step to the independence of Anglophone Cameroon. Significant are not only the rites that were performed at this bridge but the fact
that the delegation carried a huge UN flag. As a condensation symbol
(Edelman, 1964: 6), the flag had an expressive function, which is also one
of symbolic communication (Tarrow, 1994: 119). Members of the delegation exploited these, using re-interpretation as a mobilization sustain-
ing resource. It claimed that the flag had been given it to show that
Anglophone Cameroon was still a UN trust territory. Remarkably, this
claim was not challenged even by those opposed to the independence of
Southern Cameroons. Uncontested, this message reverberated across
Anglophone Cameroon and arguably contributed to the huge turnout of
crowds at rallies held in the Anglophone provinces. At Mbanga Bakundu,
I personally watched the security forces that had sealed off all entry roads

into Kumba withdraw because of pressure from the crowd that had come in vehicles and on foot. Escorted back to town by this crowd, the delegation met a throng of about 50, 000 people that had awaited its arrival all day. It was so energized that it stayed on late into the night, using torches and candles just to hear the "message of salvation." Talking analogically, Muna said that a proverbial traveler crossing a stream with the aid rod or staff inevitably makes a U-turn when his rod can no longer touch its bottom. The message was clear to all and its approval unanimous.

The failure of the UN to make any pronouncement following the return of the delegation to Cameroon can be seen as a disavowal of the foregoing claims, especially the symbolism of the flag. Undeterred by this, the SCNC saw the declaration adopted by the member states of the UN at its 50th anniversary as another window of opportunity. It reaffirmed the right of all peoples to self-determination, taking into account the particular situation of people under colonial or other forms of alien domination or foreign occupation, and recognizing the right of people to take legitimate action rule, in accordance with the Charter of the UN (Doc.A/AC.240/ 1995/CPR. I I/Rev. I). It is against this backdrop that one can begin to understand the decision of the SCNC to set October 1, 1996, as the date for the declaration of the independence of Southern Cameroons. Retrospectively, this declaration was a problematic bluff as on the day that it was supposed to take effect, the new Chairman of the SCNC, Henry Fossung, simply issued an "Independence Day" address in which he called upon all Southern Cameroonians to use their "national day" as a "day of prayers, imploring God to save us from political bondage" while reiterating that independence was "irreversible and non-negotiable" (in Koning and Nyamnjoh, 1997: 223).

HIKING THE STAKES

Anglophone political struggles took another turn on December 30, 1999, when Justice Ebong Frederick Alobwede, chairman of the High Council of the SCNC, proclaimed the independence of the Federal Republic of Southern Cameroons. Evoking the Enfant Relief Act of 1874, which states that "contracts between minors and adults are absolutely void upon attaining maturity, and that minors are not allowed by law to ratify that which is void *ab initio*," the declaration portrays Southern Cameroons as a minor before arguing that the results of the discussions that led to the birth of Cameroon unification were null and void *ab initio* (*Cameroon Post*, January 24, 2000:7). To give it effect, an attempt was made to seize the Mungo Bridge, considered the umbilical cord between Francophone Cameroon and Southern Cameroon, as well as hoist a UN flag over it. Unlike the Fossung declaration of 1996, Ebong tried to celebrate this independence in Victoria (Limbe), although he was foiled by state violence. Gendarmes arrested him as he drove to the site of the celebrations flying a UN flag on his car. He was transferred to Yaoundé along with Pa Sabuma and Chief Ayamba (*Cameroon Post,* January 17, 2000, 5). This was designed to preempt a snowball effect. Charges were not levied against them until their release in March 2001.

Following the declaration, Ebong, in quest for state recognition, immediately applied for membership in the UN, the Organization of African Unity, the Commonwealth, the Non-Aligned Movement, and, significantly, the Economic Community of West African States (*Today*, April 18, 2000, 3–4). With a view to endowing the new state with all the attributes of statehood, as well as guaranteeing state continuity, the Constituent Assembly, meeting somewhere in Bamenda in May 2000, adopted resolutions on the coat of arms, the flag and the national anthem while empowering Nfor Ngala Nfor, the Chairman of the Coordinating Committee for the Northern Region, to serve as Acting President (*Postwatch*, No. 006, January 2001, 8). A flag was designed and hoisted across several points in Bamenda (*Cameroon Post*, No. 0223, November 13, 2000:3). Similarly, the national anthem, *Freedom Land,* was released (*Today*, April 18, 2000:2). Revealingly, its lyrics make reference to "when our fight of honor is over, let our song of triumph fill the sky." I see this as suggesting that freedom has not been won as yet. Farce was sedimented into practice with the publication of the cabinet by Epie Johnson, chairman of the State Restoration Council. Ironically, Nfor saw this as a ploy by the Biya regime "to undermine the restoration of the independence of Southern Cameroons (*Cameroon Post*, November 17, 2000:3). The only significance of the publication of this purported government is that it brought back unto center stage differences between the northwest and southwest provinces. Several people from the latter saw the inclusion of the names of southwest ministers in Biya's cabinet as blackmail and a sign of contempt (*Cameroon Post*, No.0229, December 4, 2000:4).

Several factors prompted Ebong to issue his declaration. As a puritan, he must believe, like Albert Camus, that "it is better to die on one's feet than on one's knees." Given the similarities between the Anglophone problem and that of the French-Canadian Quebecers, he noted, as Claude Ryan did in the case of the latter, that "while French Canadians have always been united in their will to survive, they have been divided as to the methods whereby that objective could be realized" (Johnson, 1995:81). Arguably, there was an emerging consensus on the collective definition of the Anglophone plight. One activist argued that even the system's gatekeepers who are Anglophones "support the SCNC with their hearts in private, but pretend to speak against it in public in order to protect their positions" (*Cameroon Post*, February 7, 2000: 3). Focus should therefore be not on the public but private scripts. Empirical evidence exists to back up this assertion. An operation *coup de coeur* was launched among southern Cameroonians to help defray the costs of the trip by the Foncha-led delegation to the UN in 1999. In a SCNC meeting in Bamenda, Foncha, who had been assigned to contact Anglophone government ministers, informed the Council that they had agreed in principle to contributing but their only quarrel was with the levies that had been fixed for them. Similarly, when Biya decided to send ministers to the southwest province to convince people of the need to privatize the Cameroon Development Corporation, Anglophone ministers informed the Council, which was meeting at Tiko, about this mission, urging it to put up fierce resistance. Thus, like Fuh Stanley, the president of the Bafut Section of the CPDM, they could say "I am CPDM blood and bones, but we must admit that Anglophones have a problem" (*Cameroon Post*, February 14, 2000: 3).

The Cameroonian government's rebuff of all overtures by some Anglophones for a peaceful solution of the Anglophone problem may have led others to adopt "more extreme forms of collective action, violence and symbolism to draw attention to themselves and radicalize their confrontations with the authorities (Tarrow, 1994: 20). This logic explains the formation of the Southern Cameroons Youth League (SCYL) in the mid-1990s and its embrace of *the argument* of *force* as its operational principle. Comprising mostly young people who suffered from a double exclusion, that is, as minors in a system that privileged gerontocracy and as Anglophones, they preferred to die fighting rather than continue to submit to the fate imposed on Southern Cameroons by *la République du Cameroun*.[8] Not surprisingly, a strain occurred in SCYL's relationship with the SCNC in November 1996, a month after the Fossung's declaration of independence. Given the motto of the SCYL, it is plausible that this was due to its disapproval of Fossung's armchair approach. This may also explain why it placed itself under the umbrella of CAM that had metamorphosed into the Southern Cameroons Restoration Movement (SCARM) as posited by Konings and Nyamnjoh.[9] That a strain in a relationship does not necessarily signal a rupture renders this claim problematic. Buttressing this is the admission by the president of the SCYL, Ebenezer Akwanga, that his arrest came in the wake of his participation in a joint SCNC/SCYL meeting in Bui Division on March 24, 1997 (*Cameroon Post*, July 19, 1999:7).

Akwanga and the SCYL, which believes in the argument of force, were indicted for attempted theft of explosives from the Razel Company at Jakiri and the attacks on the installations of the forces of law and order in Bui and Mezam Divisions between March 27 and 31, 1997. According to official reports, three gendarmes and seven unidentified assailants were killed. *Le Patriote*, deemed to be an establishment newspaper, claimed that 2000 gangsters had been trained to effect the liberation of Southern Cameroons, while according to *Cameroon Tribune*, the government daily paper, "nearly 500 people had been trained to enable that part of the territory to secede" (cited in *l'Expression*, No. 107, 8 avril 1997: 8). Not even the passage of time has enabled the ascertaining of the truth of this charge. One thing that is evident is that the tenacity and fervor of the SCYL members have not been dampened. This explains Akwanga's submission before the military tribunal in Yaoundé that "I am the National President of the Southern Cameroons Youth League. Our fathers who took us into reunification have told us that (its) terms are being grossly and flagrantly disrespected. I believe in the SCNC which is fighting a just cause to see how the violation of the terms of reunification can be corrected" (*Cameroon Post*, July19, 1999:7). Largely because of this submission, I would posit, Akwanga was sentenced to jail.

Punishment is meant not only to normalize but also serves as spectacle that would deter conforming citizens from engaging in similar crimes (Foucault in Rainbow, 1984: 194). Akwanga's imprisonment failed to produce this impact in the SCYL. Clear evidence of this was their publication of a document entitled *The Southern Cameroons Independence is Here and Now*. This document advocates for "a peoples war" which "has to be aggressive, not cool and cautious; it has to be bold and audacious; violent and an expression of icy, disdainful hatred. (. . .) violence alone, violence committed by the people, organized and educated by leaders makes it possible for the masses to understand the froths and gives the key to them." In furtherance of this goal, it rearms that commitment of the SCYL to "make the revolution. Nothing can stop us. We are not intimidated by the specter of repression. Today it is me, tomorrow it would be you" (*Cameroon Post*, No. 0173, May 15, 2000:3; for a reiteration of this position see *Cameroon Post*, No. 0248, February 2001: 3).

REGIME RESPONSE: *IMMOBILISME* OR POLICY REVIEW?

Initial denial of the existence of an Anglophone problem in Cameroon by a Francophone dominated regime can be attributed to the phenomenon where those who wield power do not see why it should be contested. Anglophones, using a protest repertoire specific to them and exploiting a political opportunity, have reversed this impression. Acknowledgement in this instance, however, is not tantamount to justice. Rather, only policy reversals or innovations can reverse Anglophone marginality. The regime, on the other hand, is not committed to major policy shifts in the way the Cameroon *city* is governed. In its stead, it has conceived a series of measures, which might be described as the politics of muddling through (to borrow from Charles Lindbloom). In some instances, some of the measures have exacerbated the problem.

The government's preferred policy option has been to discourage collective action among Anglophones. Essentially, differential invitations to participate in this (patrimonial) regime (Konings and Nyamnjoh, 1997) have been used to sow discord in relations between the northwest and southwest provinces. Premium is placed on appointing elites from these provinces to "strategic posts." Claims that Biya's strategy has been efficacious (Konings and Nyamnjoh, 1997), I believe, are exaggerated as they fail to take into cognizance changes that have occurred in the nature of patron-client relations. Unlike the first generation of leaders, present ethnic barons preoccupied by Sisyphean tendencies tend to privilege private accumulation over redistribution (Kofele-Kale, 1986:58). Claims by clients that they maintain this network, else it falls into disrepair, are shrugged off. Members of the reigning elite in Cameroon are political entrepreneurs rather than barons, the difference being that the former are free agents, not heads of clientelistic networks. Occasionally, they even admit it. This was the case of Francis Nkwain, who claimed that he owed his appointment as minister to his friend Biya. This change in the nature of the relationship between the head of state and his subalterns has contributed to increasing the psychic distance between them and the population that they supposedly represent. Their trust in these barons has been depleted as a result of the perception that the barons are not working to bring home any benefit. Albert Hirschman notes that patronage is a moral resource whose supply can only be increased through usage. In some instances, feelings of *ressentiment* (resentment) have been developed by the common man vis-a-vis "their" elite.

Another strategy is the outright purchase of loyalty and its concomitant: "desalarization" of the outwardly disloyal. "Desalarization," or the threat thereof, has been used to dissuade Anglophone civil servants from identifying with the stance of the SCNC, as evidenced in the case of activists in Ndop who called for the boycott of the May 20 celebrations (*Cameroon Post*, No. 0246, February 2001: 6). The efficacy of this strategy is reinforced by monetarization of the economy and the breakdown of traditional safety networks. Confirming this, one of the victims of the policy states: "I cannot fight a cause on an empty stomach, since my salary has been suspended. By suspending my salary, the government has barred me from participating in any other activities. Take notice that I do not attend SCNC meetings any longer" (*Cameroon Post*, February 10, 2001: 4).

Failure of the use of symbolic violence to prevent collective action toward the Anglophone problem has caused the government to resort to the use of outright violence. In turn, the banalization of violence has led to libertinage, allowing Francophone frontline officials to frame Anglophones as secessionists. A love saga can easily be given political overtones. In Ndop, a quarrel between an Anglophone and a Francophone gendarme officer led to a raid in which several Anglophones were arrested and indicted for being SCNC activists. Instead of being held in Anglophone territory, the prisoners were transferred to Bafoussam in western province. Significantly, the arresting officer, in unilaterally deciding on the jurisdiction in which they would judged, told them that "You will be judged in Bafoussam. You say that you hate France and anything French, but you have no choice" (cited in *Cameroon Post*, No. 0225, November 2000:9). Their otherness was confirmed in prison where Francophone authorities "constantly and provocatively reminded" them that they are members of the SCNC "and that Anglophone can never receive the same treatment as Francophones, even in hell" (*Cameroon Post*, No. 0207, September 8, 2000:3).

Seen through another prism, this shows how the government's policy of integrating the two groups through administrative fiat has instead had the reverse effect. Reduction of the physical distance between them does not necessarily mean a reduction in psychic distance. On the contrary, the maltreatment of Anglophones, which sometimes results in death, creates among them a sense of persecution and martyrdom. Such is the case of Matthew Titiahonjoh, whose wife gave birth to twins while he was detained in Bafoussam Prison. In a letter from prison to his wife he lamented that she had to give birth in such difficult circumstances, attributing this to the fact that Togolo Jonas, the *gendarmerie* chief in Ndop, stole 300, 000 CFA francs while searching their house. Seemingly, it was his determination to recover this money that caused him to be killed in prison. In the wife's words, "when the coffin was brought for burial, I insisted that it should be opened so that I could see my husband for the last time, but the gendarmes refused" (*Cameroon Post*, No. 0226, November 24, 2000:5). Closure cannot take place in this circumstance and, reminiscent of several historical antecedents, the individual's private tragedy is appropriated not only by his family but the group. It informs group consciousness and cannot be allowed to recede into memory.

Policy defects that have, arguably, led to the marginalization of the Anglophone and impaired his imagining as a citizen of *la République du Cameroun,* have not de-energized the regime in flagging the bilingual character of the country in the discursive terrain of foreign policy, described as "a terrain of competition among the kinds of statements, in which a major discursive actor, the official strategic discourse, struggles not only to vindicate policy but the representation of that policy" (Shapiro, 1992:107). Evidence of this is Cameroon's membership in both the *Francophonie* and the Commonwealth. President Biya has used the duality to declare Cameroon's policy of bi-lingualism a success, while claiming that secessionist tendencies were manifested only by a small minority and that "he was even ready to call for a referendum, if it became necessary" (*Jeune Afrique*, No. 1990, 2 mars 1999). Biya's conditional argument can be held up as evidence of his ignorance, if not indifference, to the Anglophone problem. His (mis)reading is challenged by the results of the 1995 signature referendum in which the overwhelming majority of the Anglophones polled opted for secession from *la République du Cameroun.* Anglophones in North America have even pledged to bear the costs of the organization of this referendum, if it is organized by the UN (*Cameroon Post,* September 27, 1999:3). Given the experience of the Saharoui Republic (Western Sahara), would *la République du Cameroun* accept UN involvement in the organization of this referendum when and if it deems it necessary?

CONCLUSION

The Anglophone problem in Cameroon has been shaped by two competing, if not conflicting memories, the institutional and the social. Control over inscription into institutional memory is vested in the Francophone dominated regime and the social in the Anglophones.

Whereas the former has tried to erase, if not deny, this problem, the latter has mainstreamed it. The struggle for dominance between these two memories has for a long time precluded the possibility of a convergence and has impacted inordinately on the elaboration of the Anglophone agenda. Different resources have been used to this end. In the absence of a negotiated resolution, and in an attempt to pre-empt a collective definition of the problem, the government of *la République du Cameroun* recruited Anglophones who in their public script have insisted on a different reading of the differences between the two communities. Essentially, they have downplayed these, in some instances using even historicism to foster consensus mobilization The solution to these problems, they insist, is not in secession but in the adoption of a ten-state federation. This view is at odds with the call of the SCNC for the restoration of the independence of Southern Cameroon that has ossified into a standpoint over time. Divergence of positions on this crucial issue cannot be seen as evidence of the success of the government's policy of divide and rule. These differences are ephemeral and do not touch on the essence of the Anglophone identity. Recent proof of this was the coalescing of this community and its emotive validation of the identity following the victory of the Cup of Cameroon by an Anglophone football team, Kumbo Strikers, for the first time.

On the whole, there have been several defining moments in the attempt by the regime of *la République du Cameroun* and Anglophones to resolve the Anglophone problem. Contradictory stances have given the impression that both parties are engaged in a game of chicken. This is a no-win game as neither party has backed down. Rather, there has been an escalation, which has failed to produce the desired effects for either side. Succumbing to diverse pressures, the protagonists recently have made concessions that have allowed for a thaw in their relations, as demonstrated by the recent decision to release Justice Ebong, Chief Ayamba and Pa Sabum, who were charged with treasonable offenses. Failed policies of the past, even if discarded, would not only continue to be part of the historic memory of both communities but inform their consciousness, if adequate measures are not taken to redress extant grievances. In other words, the past cannot be erased. Resolution of the Anglophone problem will have to take the past into consideration because "it (would) present(s) policy makers . . . with information—indeed, ideas in all their meanings—about what may or may not happen when policies are designed in certain ways" (Peterson, 1997: 1084).

NOTES

1. G.M. Thomson, a lawmaker for Dundee East, cited in *The Washington Times,* June 1, 1995, A17. I believe reunification with Southern Cameroons was low on Ahmadou Ahidjo's scale of preference. His options were: (1) to lose in both Southern and Northern Cameroons; (2) to win in the North but lose in the South; (3) to win both; and (4) to win in the South but lose in the North (United States Department of State, Intelligence Report, No. 8423, March 10, 196:3). Given his affinity with the people of Northern Cameroons, Ahidjo probably would have preferred the second outcome. It has also been noted, as proof of his lukewarm attitude, if not total indifference, toward reunification that Ahidjo did not allude to it in his independence day celebration speech in 1960 (see Pius Bejeng Soh, *Dr. John Ngu Foncha: The Cameroonian Statesman,* Bamenda: Unique Printers, 1999, p. 109). *Editor's note:* The notion that Ahidjo was not interested in reunification is speculation. In his 1961 speech celebrating reunification, or, depending on one's point of view, unification, Ahidjo boasted that this achievement had been one of his goals all along. I believe him. French East Cameroon contributed to the financing of the referendum in West Cameroon. Why would Ahidjo have done this if he were not in favor of a "yes" outcome? Surely, one cannot argue that Ahidjo financed the referendum to lose. Further, Anglophones do not seem to realize that the argument undermines their case, for if the former West Cameroon joined the former French East Cameroon "uninvited," as some Francophone chauvinists have asserted, then Anglophones can hardly complain. In this saga both sides have distorted history, often using illogic, to bolster their position.

2. Clear evidence of this is the fact that John Fru Ndi, the chairman of SDF, had unsuccessfully ran for political office as a CPDM candidate before becoming the most visible figure of opposition politics in Cameroon.

3. One of Foncha's outstanding grievances in his resignation letter is that "the Anglophones whom I brought into the union have been ridiculed and referred to as 'les Biafrais,' 'les ennemis dens la maison' 'les traitres,' etc. and the constitutional provisions which protected this Anglophone minority have been suppressed, their voice drowned while the rule of the gun has replaced dialogue which the Anglophones cherish very much" (cited in Soh, 1999, op. cit., 222).

4. Although proposed for adoption at AAC II, this name had been rejected by some of the dovish councilors on the Committee. They feared that its resemblance to the National Council of Nigeria and the Cameroons (NCNC) may send out the wrong message. Its adoption therefore was indicative of a hardening of positions, even among this group.

5. One of them, addressed to Achidi Achu, states that "You are and have knowingly taken upon yourself to be a betrayer of your Anglophone brothers and sisters and your own children, so many in their numbers. As Christ said to Judas, "The son of man goeth according to prophecy. But woe unto him by whom the son of man goeth. Better for that man if he were never born" (*The Herald,* No. 171, 16 January, 1995, p. 4).

6. Being *bona fide* members of the group as a result of their membership in the SCAC, and considering that the participation of this group in SCNC meetings was not a privilege but a right, it would be wrong to argue that Foncha and Muna were merely co-opted into the delegation as Konings and Nyamnjoh (1997) suggest in "The Anglophone Problem in Cameroon" *Journal of Modern African Studies, Vol.* 35, No. 2, 1997, p. 221.

7. I was a Rockefeller Humanities Fellow at the University of Michigan in Ann Arbor during this period. When the delegation arrived in Washington D.C., I served as moderator of a seminar its members had with the Anglophone community there. As a counselor to the SCNC, I participated in most of the discussions that took place in the American capital. Hence the information given here is first-hand.

8. See interview of Mr. Fidelis Chiabi, Chairman of the former Anglophone Youth Council, in *Cameroon Post,* February 1, 1994, p. 7.

9. Konings and Nyamnjoh (2000) refer to this as a newly formed organization, the Southern Cameroons Restoration Council (SCRC). They are mistaken as the name of this organization does not occur anywhere in the almanac of Anglophone movements. But a cursory examination of the CAM and SCARM executives shows that the names on both lists are identical.

BIBLIOGRAPHY

Anderson, B. (1993), *Imagined Communities,* Verso: London.

Appadurai, A. (1990), "Disjuncture and Difference in the Global Cultural Economy," *Theory, Culture and Society,* vol. 7.

Appiah, A. (1992), *In My Father's House, Oxford* University Press: Oxford.

Barber, K. (1987), "Popular Arts in Africa" in *African Studies Review,* 30, 3.

Bate B. (1991), *Requiem far the last Kaiser,* Centaur Publishers: Calabar.

Bayart, J-F. (1979), *L'etat au Cameroun, Presses* de la Fondation Nationale des Sciences Politiques: Paris.

Benjamin, J. (1972), *Les Camerounais Occidentaux: La Minorité dans un Etat Bicommunautaire,* Presses de L'Université de Montrèal: Montreal.

Bevir, M. (1999), "Foucault and Critique," *Political Theory,* vol. 27, no.1, February.

Bob, H. and O. Ntemfac (1991), *Prison Graduate,* APCON Ltd: Calabar.

Bourdieu, P. (1986), *Ihzstinction,* Harvard University Press: Cambridge.

Bourdieu, P. (1990), *Outline of Theory and Practice,* Cambridge University Press: Cambridge.

———. (1990), "Force of Law: The Mystical Foundation of Authority" in *Cardoza Law Review,* vol. 11, no. 56, July/August.

Callum, M. (1998), "Neopopulism and Corruption: Toward a New Critique of the Elite," *Constellations,* vol. 5, no. 1.

Cameroon Post, various issues.

Challenge Hebdo, no.087, 4 Juin, 1993.

Conrad, J. (1989), *Heart of Darkness*, Anchor Books: New York.

Dahl, R. (1989), *Democracy and Its Critiques*, Yale University Press: New Haven.

de Certeau, M. (1988), *The Practice of Everyday Politics*, University of California Press: California.

Doho, G. (1993), "Theatre et minorites: le cas du Cameroon" in Lyonga N., E. Breitinger and B. Butake (eds.), *Anglophone Cameroon Writing*, Bayreuth African Studies, 30.

Epie-Ngome, V. (1992), *What God has Put Asunder*, Pitcher Books Ltd.: Yaoundé.

Escobar, A. (1984), "Discourse and Power in Development: Michel Foucault and the Relevance of His Work to the Third World," *Alternatives*, 10, Winter.

Foucault, M. (1979), *Discipline and Punish: The Birth of the Prison*, Vintage Books: New York.

Frost and Sullivan/Political Risk Research (1987), *Cameroon*, Syracuse, New York.

Gordon, C. (ed.) (1980), *Power/Knowledge: Selected Interviews and Other Writings*, Pantheon Books: New York.

Gramsci, A. (1978), *Selections from Prison Notebooks*, International Publishers: New York. Havel, V, ((!985), Open Letters, Vintage Books: New York.

Hobsbawn, E. (1990), *Nations and Nationalism Since 1780*, Cambridge University Press: Cambridge.

Jackson, R H. and C. Rosberg (1986), "Sovereignty and Underdevelopment: Juridical Statehood in the African Crisis," *Journal of Modern African Studies*, vol. 24, no. 1.

Jeune Afrique Economie, 20 novembre 1995.

Jeune Afrique, no. 1990, 2 mars 1999.

Johnson, D. (1995), "The Case for a United Canada" in *Foreign Policy*, no. 99.

Jua, N. (1991), "Cameroon: Jump-Starting an Economic Crisis" *Africa Insight*, vol. 21, no. 3.

———. (1997), "Spatial Politics, Political Stability in Cameroon" Keynote Address presented at a *Workshop on Cameroon: Biography of a Nation*, at Amherst College, Amherst, MA.

———. (1997), "Contested Meanings: Rulers, Subjects and National Integration in Post-Colonial Cameroon" in P. N. Nkwi and F. Njamnjoh (eds.), *Regional Balance and National Integration in Cameroon*, Yaoundé and Leiden: ICASSART and the African Studies Center, 1997.

———. (forthcoming), "Spatialization and Valorization of Identities in contemporary Cameroon" in J. O. Ihonvbere, J. M. Mbaku, and J. Takougang (eds.), *The Leadership Challenge in Africa: Cameroon under Biya*.

Kofele-Kale, N. (1985), "Ethnicity, Regionalism and Political Power: A Postmortem of Abidjo's Cameroon" in M. Schatzberg and W. I. Zartman (eds.), *The Political Economy of Cameroon*, Praeger Publishers: New York.

Konings, P. and F. Nyamnjoh (1997), "The Anglophone Problem in Cameroon," *The Journal of Modern African Studies*, 35, 2.

Konings, P. and F. Nyamnjoh (2000), "Construction and Deconstruction: Anglophones or Autochtones?" in P. N. Nkwi (ed.), The *Anthropology of Africa: Challenges for the 21st Century*, ICASSRT: Yaoundé.

Le Messager, various issues.

Le Temoin, various issues.

L'effort Camerounais, October 1991.

Lonsdale J. (1986), "Political Accountability in African History" in P. Chabal (ed.), *Political Domination in Africa*, Cambridge University Press: Cambridge.

Lyonga N., E. Breitinger and B. Butake (eds.) (1993), *Anglophone Cameroon Writing*, Bayreuth African Studies, 30.

Marx, K. (1987), *The 18th Brumaire of Louis Bonaparte,* International Publishers: New York.

Mazrui, A. (1986), *The Africans*, Little, Brown and Company: Boston.

Muclimbe, V. (1988), *The Invention of Africa*, James Currey: London.

Nkwi, P.N. (1989), *The German Presence in the Western Grassfelds 1891–1913*, African Studies Center: Leiden, Holland.

Norval, A.J. (1998), "Memory, Identity and the (Im)possibility of Reconciliation: The Work of the Truth and Reconciliation Commission in South Africa" *Constellations*, vol. 5, no. 2.

Pelczynski, Z.A. (ed.) (1971), *Hegel's Political Philosophy: Problems and Perspectives*, The University Press: Cambridge.

Peterson M.A. (1997), "The limits of Social Learning: Translating Analysis into Action," *Journal of Health Politics, Policy and Law*, 22, 4.

Postwatch, no. 006, January 2001.

Radhakrishnan, R. (1990), "Ethnic Identity and Post-Structiualist Difference" in A.R. JanMohamed and D. Lloyd (eds.), *The Nature and Context of Minority Discourse,* Oxford University Press: Oxford.

Shapiro, M.J. (1992), *Reading the Postmodern Polity*, University of Minneapolis Press: Minneapolis.

Sidney, T. (1994), *Power in Movement,* Cambridge University Press: Cambridge.

Smith, A. (1983), *State and Nation in the Third World: The Western State and African Nationalism*, Wheatsheaf Books Ltd.: Sussex.

Soh, P.B. (1999), *Dr. John Ngu Foncha: The Cameroonian Statesman*, Unique Printers: Bamenda.

The Herald, various issues.

Today, various issues.

Washington Post, March 12, 1967.

Welch, C.E. (1966), *Dream of Unity: Pan Africanism and Political Integration in West Africa*, Connell University Press: Ithaca. NY.

Williams, M. (1995), "Justice Toward Groups," *Political Theory*, February, Vol. 23, No. 1.

Williams, R. (1990), *Marxism and Literature*, Oxford University Press: Oxford.

Zartman, W. I. and M. Schatzberg (eds.) (1986), *The Political Economy of Cameroon*, Praeger Publishers: New York.

Zizek, S. (1994), *For they know not what they do*, Verso: London.

Chapter 5

Cameroon:
The Political Economy of Poverty

Tatah Mentan

Cameroon is richly endowed with natural resources, a diversified production base and a well-developed, albeit neglected, infrastructure. This impressive development potential, combined with appropriate economic
growth policies and a favorable external environment, produced real
growth averaging 7 percent a year from independence in 1960 through
1985.[1] Agriculture was the main source of growth and foreign exchange
earnings until 1978, when oil production started and quickly became the
cornerstone of economic growth. As in many oil-producing countries,
however, the oil bonanza was not wisely invested. It led to higher expenditures on the civil service (the padding of civil service payrolls with
names of blood relatives, ethnic kinsfolk, political clients and girlfriends
was the order of the day), subsidies to inefficient public enterprises, and
low-return, capital-intensive investments. After 1986 three major shocks
exposed the weaknesses of Cameroon's economy. The external terms of
trade declined by 60 percent through 1993 as coffee, cocoa and oil prices
fell sharply.[2] Oil output began a long-term decline with the result that oil
exports, at $531 million in 1994, were about one-third the 1985 level.[3]
The real exchange rate appreciated by about 54 percent from 1986 to
1993, greatly reducing Cameroon's competitiveness. Overall, Cameroon's macroeconomic experience alternated between cycles of booms
and busts, adjustment and privatization, from 1970 to 2001. This chapter
traces the vicissitudes of the Cameroon economy in an attempt to identify

the sources of continued poverty and underdevelopment in an environment of relative abundance.

ECONOMIC BUST

Cameroon started heading for an economic crisis in 1979, which marked the end of the coffee and cocoa boom. In the same year, the national budget changed from a balance to a 3 percent deficit and domestic credit expansion was reduced, due to overdependence on cash crops whose prices were determined by international buyers. One example captures the essence of the problem: between 1985 and 1987 Cameroon's export price index in CFA francs plunged by 65% for rubber.[4] Several factors, in addition to the one mentioned above, accounted for the worsening terms of trade. Cameroon's membership in the CFA franc zone implies that real exchange rates on a trade-weighted basis tend to move with the French franc, and the stability provided by the CFA umbrella has been far outweighed by the instability of export prices for coffee, cocoa and oil.

The fixed exchange rate deprives Cameroon of an instrument of economic policy during hard times. The effects of the decline in the prices of primary commodities, such as coffee, cocoa and rubber, should have been offset by the rise in the price of oil in 1979 following the Iranian revolution, but the worldwide recession of 1981–1982 choked off this possibility. Thus, the "oil crisis" of 1979 and the ensuing recession, combined with monetary inflexibility, were some of the external factors responsible for the downturn in the performance of Cameroon's economy. Internally, the institutionalization of "kleptocracy" (government by thieves), as part of President Paul Biya's strategy for survival, especially after the failed 1984 coup, crippled the economy. During the first five years of Biya's rule, some 600 billion CFA francs were stashed away in foreign banks.[5] Local banks were ruined by the "Big Men" of the regime who had been granted loans, which they were "hopelessly incapable of repaying."[6]

By 1993 the economy and its external accounts had deteriorated significantly. Continuous public finance deficits were generated as falling revenues were not matched by expenditure cuts. The burden on public finances was exacerbated by a large and inefficient public enterprise sector, payments for military-cum-paramilitary weapons for repression and payments to political cronies. Public sector deficits, fueled by central government expenditures and public enterprise losses, were partially financed by borrowing. Long-term external debt increased to more than 40 percent of Gross Domestic Product (GDP) in 1989, while domestic debt accounted for 6 percent of GDP in fiscal year 1987. Table 5.1 summarizes Cameroon's debt and capital flow a decade later.

Economic decline was accompanied by increased poverty as poor farmers suffered the brunt of the fall in producer prices and government cut expenditures on health and education. The middle class, which used to be one of the most developed in Sub-Saharan Africa, shrank.[7] In 1988 the government launched an IMF and World Bank-backed economic recovery program to streamline public finances, restructure public enterprises and banks, liberalize export crops, and deregulate internal commerce. The government also sought to improve incentives in the petroleum sector, reorient policies in forestry, health, and education, and establish special programs to mitigate the cost of adjustment. Little progress was made in structural reforms. More importantly, the internal adjustment strategy failed. A collapse in the terms of trade and severe appreciation of the real exchange rate had adverse effects on incentives and income distribution and were not matched by policy adjustments. Economic policy and management deteriorated after 1989, reflecting a lack of commitment to economic reform and the corrosive effects of the political tremors fueled by the sharp decline in

Table 5.1
External Debt and Resource Flows, 1996 (in millions US $)

Total debt outstanding disbursed	9,323
IBRD	520
IDA	513
Officials grants	0
Officials creditors	100
Private creditors	-133
Foreign direct investment	0
Portfolio equity	0
World Bank Commitment	254
Disbursement	163
Principal repayments	93
Net flows	70
Interest payments	51

Source: U.S. Department of State, Bureau of Economic and Business Affairs, August, 1998.

incomes in the 1990s. This externally determined recovery program targeted the financially burdensome public enterprises for privatization, closure and (or) restructuring.

CRISIS MANAGEMENT I: PRIVATIZATION

Privatization has become an important instrument for streamlining the public sector and promoting economic development in countries around the world. Privatization refers to divestiture of public sector enterprises (PSE)—enterprises owned and operated by the state—to private owners and, more generally, the placing of a large share of the economy in the private sector. Privatization gained a major thrust in the 1980s when international donor organizations—like the World Bank—made it a major component of structural adjustment programs, established as a condition for economic assistance. Structural adjustment itself refers to "a series of economic policies designed to reduce the role of government in an economy [by] replacing government control with market incentives."[8] Structural adjustment programs were initiated by the International Monetary Fund and World Bank as a result of the explosive debt crisis of "developing" countries like Cameroon in the early 1980s. The acceptance of neo-liberal economic ideas during the political tenure of the Reagan and Thatcher governments in the United States and Great Britain, respectively, accelerated the ascendancy of structural adjustment on the economic development agenda of Third World countries during that period.

While stabilization programs of earlier post-war decades achieved successful monetary, fiscal, and trade policies without economic restructuring, structural adjustment programs in the developing world during the 1980s and early 1990s were associated with the adoption of free-market policies as a condition for international assistance. Cameroon, dying for such international economic assistance, staggered into structural adjustment and privatization. State-owned enterprises were first created in Cameroon at the time of independence. This was a result of the transfer of public utilities and services previously managed by France and Britain. This movement gained momentum during the 1970s, when nearly half of the public enterprises were created as a result of government policy of substituting for the private sector. The private sector at the time was considered inefficient and incapable of financing the investments needed for Ahidjo's "economic take off."

With the economic boom resulting from oil exports in the late 1970s, expansion of the public enterprise sector was given further impetus. The cash surplus recorded by a number of public enterprises, such as the National Petroleum Company (SNH), the National Social Security Fund (CNPS), the National Commodities Marketing Board (ONCPB), and the National Investment Company (SNI), the holding created by the government to manage its portfolio, led to a new increase in the role of the public sector.

In pursuit of this policy of import-substitution industrialization, more than 200 public enterprises, of which 80 were owned by SNI, were scattered in all sectors of the economy by the late 1980s. They were especially dominant in oil, agro-industry, tourism and transportation sectors, as well as in public utilities such as water, electricity and telecommunications. In the early 1990s, public enterprises contributed about 20 percent of overall GDP, nearly 60 percent of the industrial sector's GDP, and 21 percent of Gross Public Investment. In addition, direct and indirect government subsidies, including tax exemptions, were estimated at about four percent of GDP. This excluded non-budgetary financing by SNH. In 1986, Cameroon's macro-economic situation deteriorated and budgetary revenues declined sharply. This bleak economic situation was a consequence of the "beticization" of public enterprises, whose managers embarked on massive looting of state resources. However, under pressure from external donors and lenders, the government launched an economic reform program with special emphasis on public enterprise restructuring in 1986.

One of the main objectives was to alleviate the burden generated by public enterprises, the losses of which were estimated at CFAF 33 billion, on June 30, 1986, despite CFAF 69 billion in government direct subsidies. This rehabilitation program, based on an in-depth analysis of 75 public enterprises, resulted in a new classification of the public enterprises in two groups: those that would be liquidated—59 enterprises outside the financial sector—and those that would remain state-owned—120, including 25 priority enterprises, to be rehabilitated under performance contracts. This first step was to be accompanied by the adoption of a new institutional framework to bring public enterprises to operating procedures closer to those prevalent in the private sector. In 1990 the government issued a decree listing 15 enterprises to be privatized. This program was to be implemented by a new government agency, the Public Enterprise Rehabilitation Mission (MRESP), attached to the presidency. The various components of this rehabilitation and privatization program were part of the structural adjustment loan approved by the World Bank in 1989 and supported by a technical assistance project.

Implementation of this reform program proved to be a difficult task. Financial institutions and the petroleum company (SNH) excluded, these enterprises accounted for about 10 percent of Cameroon's GDP and total assets amounted to US $4 billion. Losses represented about 10 percent of total revenues when taking fully into account the consequences of the 1994 devaluation. Total employment in these enterprises accounted for about 30 percent of the civil service and 14 percent of the formal private sector. Between 1989 and 1993 all enterprises in which the state was the majority shareholder accumulated losses, with the exception of three monopolies: *Société Nationale d'Electricite* (SONEL), *Cimenteries du Cameroun* (CIMENCAM), and *Société Nationale des Hydrocarbures* (SNH). Finally, the parastatals built up a large domestic debt amounting to CFAF 517 billion (about US $1 billion) by the end of 1994.

Performance contracts signed with the 25 largest public enterprises in the transportation, agriculture, water, and electricity sectors, showed disappointing results. Total financing granted by the government to these enterprises for the 1989–92 period amounted to CFAF 460 billion (about US $2 billion) in the form of operating subsidies, capital increases, assumption of debt and claims dropped. Such financing was partly inevitable, given that it only reflected the past losses of these enterprises and their inability to face debt servicing due to poor efficiency of past investments and the theft of public funds. However, it did not lead to a significant, overall improvement in the performance of these enterprises. Presubsidy operating losses were marginally reduced from CFAF -67.8 billion in 1989 to CFAF -52.2 billion in 1992 while overall productivity remained more or less the same.

Furthermore, despite an average 18 percent staff cut, the wage bill remained at approximately the same level because of rewards to clients within Biya's patronage cartel. With the exception of the electricity company, the largest agro-industries (HEVECAM, CDC and SODECOTON) and the national railways company, the productivity of which increased substantially, overall PE performance did not improve. The performance contracts essentially transferred debt from public enterprises to the central government without benefiting creditors. This was a way of shielding the regime's corrupt cronies.

The central government was unable to meet its obligations, because of growing financial problems, and effectively implement financial supervision of public enterprises, because of the absence of an institutional framework. The General Statute for Public Enterprises that was scheduled to be approved under the 1989 adjustment operation was never finalized. Although considerable efforts were devoted to setting up a data base, the data collected on a regular basis only covered 17 enterprises, mainly those whose general managers were to be witch-hunted out of office for political or ethnic considerations.

Between 1990 and 1994, out of the 15 enterprises to be privatized—listed in Decree 90/1423, October 3, 1990—5 were sold (one of them only partially), 3 were liquidated, 5 divestitures were unsuccessful, and 2 enterprises were taken off the privatization list. While these transactions brought CFAF 3.8 billion to the treasury, the state was still left with liabilities of around CFAF 10 billion. In addition to the small number of enterprises sold and the questionable nature of the list, the process was notoriously slow, given the cumbersome privatization framework. Privatization procedures were subject to more than 6 laws and regulations drafted between 1988 and 1994. Privatization strategies formulated for each enterprise by the Technical Committee had to be submitted for approval to an inter-ministerial committee composed of seven ministers, the prime minister, the secretary general at the presidency and finally the president himself. The same process applied to the final selection of buyers.

As a result, the numerous authorizations required at different stages of divestiture, French corporate pressure and the large number of participants with sometimes contradictory objectives, all created obstacles and delayed the transactions.[9] This heavily bureaucratic process was a reflection of the absence of a clear strategy for divestiture and visible discrepancies among the actors. Finally, the evaluation process, based primarily on asset valuation, led to unrealistic estimates and the rejection of bids submitted by operators. Moreover, differences in the assessments made by the government and SNI, a shareholder in these enterprises (the potentials for conflicts of interests here should be obvious), blocked the effort.

Out of the 59 enterprises liquidated in 1989–1990, 33 were companies owned by SNI and 26 were owned by the state. At the end of 1994, 55 of these 59 liquidations were still operating. For the 26 enterprises whose liquidation was supervised by the Technical Committee, audits performed on nine of them showed that basic asset protection procedures were not being observed and that the liquidation process lacked transparency. Also, some of the largest liquidations, especially the liquidation of the National Marketing Board (ONCPB), escaped any control.

Following the very limited results achieved in the public enterprise sector and the devaluation of the CFA franc in January 1994 (examined below), the government revised its economic reform strategy and decided to focus on privatization, instead of rehabilitation, as part of a comprehensive effort to further liberalize the economy. The strategies of reform and privatization were to create redundancy in the labor market, exclude certain ethnic groups from capital accumulation, marginalize civil society and accelerate the exploitation of dispossessed peasants and workers. The government's Letter of Development Policy, adopted in June 1994, in the context of the Economic Recovery Credit financed by the World Bank, was aimed at progressively achieving partial or full privatization of all industrial and commercial public enterprises. Limitation with regard to the public utilities went alongside further liberalization of the economy (i.e., creating a free market, allowing the unhindered movement of labor and maintaining an adequate growth rate).

In addition to the measures contained in the policy statement issued by the government in June 1994, a list of 15 additional enterprises to be privatized was published on July 14, 1994.[10] As Table 5.2 shows, this list included the largest enterprises in Cameroon and cut across a wide swath of the economy. In the transportation sector: CAMSHIP/CAMTAINER (a shipping company), CAMAIR (Cameroon's national airline), REGIFERCAM (a railway company) and SOTUC (a bus company). In the agro-industrial sector: HEVECAM (a rubber company), SODECOTON (a cotton development company), SOCAPALM (a palm oil company) and Cameroon Development Corporation (a colonial-era agro-industrial octopus with tentacles in tea, palm oil, rubber and banana production). In June 1995 President Biya decided to expand the scope of the privatization program by adding the public utilities (e.g., SONEL—electricity, INTELCAM—telecommunications) to the list. The total assets of the companies to be privatized were 1,103.3 billion CFA francs. Their staff amounted to 32,761 workers, well over half of the number of people who worked in government proper (50,000).

Based on the government's action plan, at least 18 state-owned enterprises were to be privatized "soon." In the Stand-By Agreement signed with the International Monetary Fund, the government also committed to raise CFAF 30 billion from privatization by June 30, 1996. Finally, the development policy letter attached to the on-going SAC reaffirmed the key role privatization was to play in the country's medium-term development plan.

To achieve the goals listed above and restore the credibility of the privatization program, which had been undermined by implementation problems, the government came up with a new privatization institutional framework.[11] A first step was taken in January 1996 when it split the technical commission into two different units: the Privatization Technical Commission and the Rehabilitation Technical Commission. This first step was to allow restructuring and strengthening of the privatization unit and avoid the previous confusion between two different missions: portfolio management and privatization. However, additional changes were needed to streamline the privatization decision making process and reduce the numerous approvals needed. During the negotiations of the ongoing SAP, the government agreed to review the institutional framework and address the remaining issues. The new framework had to be approved and implemented, at the latest, by the end of 1996. Meanwhile, to ensure the transparency and equity of sales, the government decided that bids would be opened to the public and selection criteria would be published. Given the failure of previous privatization schemes, bidding guidelines were specified, but they were thwarted with impunity to satisfy tribal and personal rather than economic interests. The government was made to ac-

Table 5.2
Parastatals to Be Privatized in 1993–94 and Their Assets
(in millions CFA francs)

Company	Total Assets	Turnover	Value Added	Net Profit/ Loss	Staff
CAMAIR	22.3	34.3	10.1	-4.5	1560
CAMSHIP	25.4	25.1	2.9	0.02	276
SOTUC	13.7	1.7	0.9	-13.9	990
REGIFERCAM	167.3	24.1	15.0	0.9	3,200
CDC	69.7	29.7	16.1	-0.5	13,500
SODECOTON	59.5	55.3	13.2	8.1	2,301
HEVECAM	45.1	9	5.8	1.1	4,236
SOCAPALM	26.2	11.6	6.1	-16.1	4,072
SCT	0.8	0.3	0.05	-1.6	NA
SONEL	323.6	57.6	43.6	3.1	NA
SNEC	203.8	13.1	7.5	-5	2,176
INTELCAM	145.9	12.5	9.1	-13.7	450
Total	1,103.3	274.3	130.35	-41.9	32,761

Source: Présidence, République du Cameroun, Decret No. 94-125, July 14, 1994.

cept that to be successful when implementing this program, it had to change the poor image of the privatization process, attract foreign investors, ensure broad participation of the Cameroonian private sector and the public at large, develop a competitive environment by eliminating all direct and indirect subsidies to public enterprises prior to their privatization and prepare for the social costs of divestiture. However, only six enterprises were privatized in 1995, due to political patronage and lack of transparency.

The crisis in the financial sector had a major impact on savings and investment in Cameroon. The banking sector was no longer in a position to take full responsibility for financing the economy, as is evident from the 58 percent decline in lending between 1989 and 1993. Following the near-bankruptcy of many banks and financial institutions, an additional 100 billion CFA francs worth of deposits were frozen. This situation considerably reduced investment capacity, since the unavailability of domestic savings, which could be used for investment purposes, was not offset by a large in-flow of foreign capital. In addition, the government confirmed its intention to exclude from the privatization process all the defaulters who did not straighten out their situation vis-a-vis the SRC. To succeed, the government had to launch an information campaign in a number of well-targeted countries to describe its program, design market-driven privatization strategies with the support of investment banks with incentives built into their contracts, establish realistic targets in terms of financial evaluation of the companies put on the market, and, given the corrupt nature of Cameroon's legal and judicial system, use arbitration mechanisms to solve litigation with the objective of mitigating the high country risk that could adversely affect some transactions.

CRISIS MANAGEMENT II: DEVALUATION

In January 1994 Cameroon and the other CFA countries devalued the CFA Franc, from 50 CFA Francs to 1 French Franc to 100 CFA Francs to 1 French Franc, as part of a comprehensive reform program supported by the IMF and World Bank. This was intended to stimulate export while reducing import, produce a trade surplus, shift spending to productive activities, hold yearly inflation to no more than 5 percent and generate annual GDP growth of 5 percent.[12] Cameroon also began far-reaching reform of trade policies. The few remaining non-tariff barriers were abolished. Subsequent measures included civil service reform, revision of public procurement regulations, privatization and public enterprise restructuring (see earlier discussion), tax reform, liberalization of coffee and cocoa marketing, revising the forestry code, and reforming the petroleum regulatory framework.

Balance of payments, as evidenced by the volume and value of Cameroon's major exports, increased by 12 percent in Fiscal Year 1997, resulting in an overall trade surplus, as Table 5.3 shows.

Non-petroleum receipts, however, did not meet expectations and an overall budget deficit of .4 percent of GDP ensued. The budget proposed for Fiscal Year 1999 (July 1998 to June 1999) reflects the shortfall and was reduced by 26 billion CFA Francs (USD 43.3 million) to 1,230 billion CFA Francs (USD 2,050 million). This budget attempted to bring more of the informal economy into the government's revenue producing stream. Non-petroleum exports rose by 12 percent over Fiscal Year 1996. Wood, coffee, cotton, rubber and finished products were the most productive sectors. Petroleum receipts rose by 42.6 percent, because of rising oil prices. Total imports rose by 19 percent over the 708 billion CFA level of Fiscal Year 1996; nevertheless, Cameroon's trade deficit dropped by a point to 1.2% of GNP.[13] Private capital investment (non-petroleum) was estimated at one percent of GNP, positive for the first time in the 1990s.[14] Private foreign investment in the Cameroonian economy is limited, as it is in most of Africa, by the three scourges of an inadequate judicial environment, infrastructure and market limitations.

Cameroon has been able to meet minimal external payment obligations only since June 1997. As a result, Cameroon's official debt with the United States and other creditors was rescheduled in October 1997. Cameron's external debt, which averaged USD 7.86 billion between 1991–1995, was estimated at USD 9.5 billion in 1996 and represented 4.2 percent of Sub-Sahara Africa's debt and 17.4 percent of the CFA franc zone's debt. Debt service was estimated at USD 528 million (25 percent of exports and 46 percent of revenue) and interest at USD 265 million. The ratio of Cameroon's external debt to the GNP is 124 percent. Multi-

Table 5.3
Cameroon Trade (in millions of US $)

	1995	1996	1997
Total country exports (FY, June–July)	1,761	1,978	1,820
Total country imports (FY, June–July)	1,201	1,347	1,376

Source: US Department of State, Bureau of Economic and Business Affairs, August, 1998.

lateral debt arrears reached 16.5 billion CFA Francs at the end of June 1997 which, together with current maturing multilateral debt amounting to 4.5 billion CFA Francs, meant that Cameroon owed multinational institutions 21 billion CFA Francs, (USD 42 million). Paris Club arrears amounted to 15.7 billion CFA Francs which, with 1.2 billion CFA Francs in maturing debt due, added up to 16.9 billion CFA francs (USD 33.8 million). Cameroon has expended great efforts to regain international confidence by servicing its external debt, to the detriment of development projects and payment of its internal debt (about 1,100 billion CFA Francs). Cameroon paid off 12.4 percent of its external debt but only 1.5 percent of its internal debt in 2000. This reflects the power that external creditors have over the Cameroon government and the relative weakness of Cameroon investors.

The European Union is Cameroon's main trading partner but there has been a shift away from northern Europe, specifically France. Italy imports 25.5 percent of Cameroonian exports, and Spain imports 20.4 per-

Table 5.4
Cameroon's Macroeconomic Statistics, 1998

	1996	1997 (est.)	1998 (projected)
GDP (in millions of US $)	9,251.9	9,455.4	9,447.2
GDP growth rate	5%	5.1%	5.2%
GDP per capita	682	610	670
Gov't Spending (% of GDP)	15.9	13.8	13.9
Inflation rate (percent)	4.3	3.0	2.0
Unemployment (percent)	35	35	35
Foreign exchange reserves (in millions US $)	2.45	2.92	NA
Average exchange rate ($1/CFA franc)	507	577	600
Debt service ratio to GDP	N/A	124%	NA
Foreign debt (in millions US $)	9,323	9,048	9,152
Debt outstanding/Exports	416.5	365.7	364.6
Debt outstanding/GDP	N/A	95.7	96.9
Debt Paid/Exports	38.7	43.6	38.7

Source: US Department of State, Bureau of Economic and Business Affairs, August, 1998.

cent. France imported 16 percent of Cameroon's exports in 1997 for third place. However, France is still the major supplier of Cameroonian imports, satisfying 25% of the country's import needs. In other words, France enjoys a surplus in its trade with Cameroon. The U.S. and Nigeria have an 8.4 percent share of Cameroon's imports each; Germany follows with a 6.7 percent share while Japan has ceded fifth place to Belgium, which supplies 4.8 percent of Cameroon's imports.[15] While Cameroon produces and exports heavy crude, it imports light crude oil suitable for refining from Nigeria (55 percent, valued at 56.8 billion CFA Francs), Equatorial Guinea (25 percent), Ivory Coast (12 percent), Angola (5 percent) and Italy (3 per cent).[16] Cameroon has effectively completed the neo- liberal agenda, and in so doing, is ahead of the other Central Africa CFA franc zone countries. However, the price in human terms has been high (see ahead).

Triggered by the 50 percent nominal devaluation of the CFA Franc, economic recovery has been under way in the tradable sectors. The volume of non-oil exports increased by 12 percent in 1994. Following a sizable decline, imports started to pick up in late 1994. As in other Central African CFA zone countries, Gabon excepted, budgetary performance was poor, with serious shortfalls in revenue in the first half of 1994. Disruptions caused by the tariff reform and fraud led to an abnormally low level of customs revenues; the situation improved remarkably after a new minister of finance was appointed in July 1994. Total revenues increased by 55 percent in Fiscal Year 1995, and non-interest expenditure declined from 20 percent of GDP in the early 1990s to 9 percent of GDP. As a result, the primary balance went from a deficit of 2.3 percent of GDP in Fiscal Year 1994 to a surplus of 2.9 percent of GDP the following year. Cameroon's performance in private savings and investment was stronger than that of the rest of the zone, but revenue mobilization was weaker, resulting in abnormally low public investment. In Fiscal Year 1996, revenues increased by a further 22 percent to 12.8 percent of GDP, somewhat lower than the target of 14.7 percent. On the expenditure side, outlays have been globally in line with targets, but only because an overrun in current expenditure has been offset by an equivalent compression of capital expenditure which remains at less than 1 percent of GDP.

After an eight-year period of economic decline, real growth of 3 to 5 percent picked up following the January 1994 devaluation of the CFA franc and the accompanying upturn in world economic activity. Despite the adverse impact of the Asian crisis in 1998, performance has continued to be good. Contrasting with the weak record in the implementation of programs under the previous four IMF-supported arrangements, performance in 1997/98 was on track, and all quantitative and structural performance criteria and benchmarks under the program were met. The results for the primary budget surplus (5.9 percent of GDP) and the overall budget deficit were slightly better than programmed in 1997/98. This outcome reflected higher than expected oil revenue, with non-oil revenues on tract and primary expenditures in line with the budget targets.

The encouraging performance continued in the first half of 1998/99 as strong revenue mobilization efforts, as well as better corporate tax collection, largely compensated for the shortfall in oil and trade related revenues. The focus of fiscal policy has been to strengthen public finances and raise the low non-oil revenue to GDP ratio by widening the tax base and reducing exemptions through a comprehensive reform of the tax system. An important aspect has been a reduction in anti-trade bias in the tax system through a lowering of non-forestry export taxes (to 5 percent on July 1, 1998) and an increase in domestic taxes. As part of this reform, the turnover tax was successfully replaced by a value-added tax (VAT) in January 1999, with the elimination of the differential tax rates under the old sales tax, the widening of the tax base and reduction of exemptions. Cameroon has implemented the privatization schemes demanded by international donors. HEVECAM (rubber), CAMSUCO (sugar) and SOCAPALM (palm oil) have been privatized.

The World Bank and the International Monetary Fund (IMF) are supporting a comprehensive debt reduction package for Cameroon under the Enhanced Heavily Indebted Poor Countries Initiative. Total debt relief from all of Cameroon's creditors is worth USD 2 billion. Debt relief under the enhanced HIPC framework significantly reduces Cameroon's annual debt service obligations, and immediately frees about USD100 million per year for the next three years, which could potentially be spent on health care, education, HIV/AIDS prevention and other critical social services. Debt service as a percentage of government revenue should be reduced to under 10 percent by 2008 (at the time of writing it was 23 percent). Under the enhanced HIPC Initiative countries with a satisfactory track record of macroeconomic and structural policy implementation and a NPV (Net Present Value) of external debt exceeding 150 percent of exports are eligible for debt relief.

The implication of Cameroon's entry into the club of heavily indebted countries is that it has committed itself to being under the structural adjustment yoke for decades to come. Cameroon will be required to produce exactly the same kind of crops and raw materials as it had under colonialism and to use its earnings to buy from the former masters machines and processed goods. In fact, this was the institutionalization of the neo-classical economic strategy, which combines the following elements: (a) abolition of all intervening "distortions" in the pricing mechanisms to achieve maximization of growth for the new owners of the erstwhile state enterprises; (b) liberalization of foreign trade in order to remove incentives for inward-looking economic behavior and to replace them with incentives for outward-looking and export-oriented economic activity; and (c) reduction of the public sector in size through privatization of public enterprises and the surrender of as many economic tasks as possible to private foreign companies.

THE BITTER HARVEST: POVERTY

As the foregoing analysis shows, in the 1990s Cameroon substantially liberalized its economy through such measures as privatization of state-owned assets and currency devaluation, which are themselves parts of the structural adjustment programs (SAPs) imposed on Africa in the last decades of the 20th century. However, the social costs of liberalization have been high. In particular, privatization has created unemployment and incalculable poverty, which, in turn, have exacerbated crimes such as armed robbery. Efforts to regain competitiveness and financial sustainability resulted in an 18 percent staff reduction for the 25 enterprises under performance contract in the early 1990s. For these enterprises, staff cuts were estimated at around 3,300, of which 1,600 came from SOTUC, a transportation company liquidated in January 1995. In the telecommunications and water sectors, overstaffing was high. On the other hand, staff downsizing in the agro-industrial sector was limited, especially in the case of the four largest enterprises to be privatized in 1996, since social plans had already been implemented under performance contracts, and the involvement of foreign operators in the management of these enterprises had reduced the risks of overstaffing. Indeed, past experience with the privatization of the Banana Marketing Board showed that, in some cases, production gains were so great that major staff cuts were not needed. There have been massive layoffs in the government ministries as well, and the civil servants who have been retained have seen their salaries cut, in some cases by 50 percent. This is on top of the 50 percent devaluation of the CFA franc in 1994, which is a wage cut in disguise (more on that later).

Basic public services, such as health, education and road construction, that used to be provided by the state, have stopped. Structural adjustment since the late 1980s, while leading to a turnaround at the macroeconomic level (economic growth has returned to a level of over 4% per year, inflation is under 3%, and budget deficits are under control), has led to a deterioration in the general quality of life for most Cameroonians. The incidence of poverty can be broadly defined as material deprivation (as measured by income, consumption or spending) and specifically manifests itself in food security, access to essential services such as housing, transportation, health, education, drinking water and the like. Both government and donor studies in Cameroon have used consumption measures to define poverty and demonstrate that at the national level, average consumption of goods and services fell by 30 percent from 1983/84 to 1996. Measures of relative and absolute poverty thresholds show not only increasing poverty but increasing inequality over the same decade.

School participation fell from full attendance in 1990 to 81 percent in 1996. Towns which knew almost no poverty, such as Yaoundé, Douala, Bafoussam and Bamenda, saw the incidence rise to 20 percent and 30 percent. Rural areas are poorer, even after adjusting for lower costs of living; there is also more poverty in the north and east. Of Cameroon's 6.5 million poor, 5.6 million live in rural areas, with the most intense poverty found in the plateau and forest zones. It is estimated that 50.5 percent of the population in Cameroon live in poverty, a further 31.4 percent could be characterized as middle class (with consumption between CFA francs 148,000 and 296,000 per person) and 18.1 percent as rich. Women and children are somewhat overrepresented among the poor. Also, more likely to be poor are export crop farmers, livestock farmers in the forest zone and in the towns, salaried workers and informal-sector operators, as well as the unemployed.

The impact of poverty is visible in the area of food insecurity; among its consequences in Cameroon: 36 percent of poor children are seriously underweight. While 250,000 children were malnourished in 1978, 466,000 were so in 1991. Twenty-nine percent of children under 3 were chronically malnourished in 1998. Severe malnutrition has risen to 7 and 8 percent in the northwest, north and far-north provinces. Another indicator is the percentage of school-age children attending school. As mentioned earlier, Cameroon's school attendance index fell from 101 in 1990 to 81 in 1998, in the process creating disparities between rural (though not urban) boys and girls, as well as sharp disparities between the north and south.[17] Among adults, illiteracy is falling steadily to a national level of 39 percent (45 percent for women), with a sharper deficit in the north, where up to 68 percent of the population and 73 percent of women cannot read. Government spending on education rose from the 1970s through the mid-1980s but declined by the end of the 1990s. Falling faster was household spending on education, as families coped with reduced incomes. As a result, 18 percent of young men and 32 percent of young women have not graduated from high school, the proportions rising to 29 percent and 46 percent in rural areas.

Health indicators have followed the country's downward economic trajectory, although not as strongly as education indicators. While the same regional inequalities exist, some indicators have remained constant since the 1980s at the national level, such as the number of pregnant women receiving prenatal care (about 80 percent). Infant mortality per 1000 births fell from 119 in the 1970s to 57 in 1989 but rose, albeit slightly, to 63 in 1997. Maternal deaths are among the lowest in Central Africa, and life expectancy increased from 44 years in 1970 to 57 years in 1997. At the household level, the rich and urban dwellers spend more on health, corresponding partly to the availability of hospitals (one per 100,000 in the far north, one per 30,000 in the south). The poor are more likely to visit a traditional healer than the rich (57 percent versus 22 percent). The poor are more likely than the rich to own their houses, although the materials used and amenities are of lower quality. Less than half the population has access to drinking water (77 percent in urban areas, 27 percent in rural areas; 26 percent of the poor as opposed to 68 percent of the rich). Very few have a piped water supply; wells, public fountains and rivers are the principal water sources. Although Cameroon has enormous hydro-electric potential, only 40 percent of households have access to electricity (only 22 percent in rural areas). A striking 36 percent of households have no durable goods at all. The most common asset is a radio (52 percent of households). Rich and urban households are the most likely to own a stove or television set, and about 13 percent of rich or urban households have a car. Similar proportions of rural, poor and middle class households own a bicycle.

CONCLUSION

From the 1960s through the mid-1980s the Cameroon economy, led by the state, attempted to enter Ahidjo's "promised land." The use of the state to promote import substitution industrialization resulted in inefficient industries requiring permanent subsidization, with no prospects of achieving international competitiveness. Extensive government intervention tended to generate "rent seeking" on a significant scale, that is, to divert the energies of economic agents away from production and into lobbying for increasing allocations of government subsidies and patronage. In fact, four causes of state-sponsored underdevelopment can be identified: the existence of a self-interest-seeking network of political cronies and other actors, who controlled the allocation of public resources and used the latter to further their narrow interests, incompetent administrators who lacked essential understanding of economics and business operations, lack of transparency in the functioning of government and the concentration of power in the presidency, which left no room for the other two principal branches of government (the legislature and judiciary) to play their check-and-balance role. These failures transformed the Cameroon state into a predator or vampire, sucking the blood out of the economy and society, which then paved the way for IMF and World Bank–imposed structural adjustment.

Cameroon's embrace of a market economy under Paul Biya has casually denied the devastating social impacts of macroeconomic reforms. In the name of efficiency, industrial plants have been closed down, small and medium sized enterprises have gone bankrupt and scores of professional workers and civil servants have been laid off. To survive, some unemployed workers have been driven into armed robbery, prostitution, and illicit logging damaging to the environment. Accumulation of wealth is going hand-in-hand with the distortion of production. Global economic restructuring through privatization is promoting stagnation in the supply of essential goods and services while redirecting resources towards lucrative investments in the luxury goods economy. With the drying up of capital formation in productive activities, profit is sought in increasingly speculative and fraudulent transactions, such as TIERCE, QUINTE and FOOTPOLLS, or what may be called casino economics.[18] This process of accumulation of wealth is taking place outside the real economy, divorced from bona fide productive and commercial activities, thus reducing Cameroon to a gambling den.

The principle of "minimizing employment," while simultaneously compressing workers' wages, obviously reduces consumer demand for necessary goods and services. The global cheap labor economy therefore expands output while paradoxically compressing the capacity of society to consume. Contrary to Say's law of markets, supply doesn't create its own demand. With the exception of beer, few "goods" attract Cameroonian consumers because of declining purchasing power. Finally, global integration is being contradicted by local disintegration. Entire branches of industry producing for the internal market, like SICAM (clothing company), are being eliminated. The informal urban sector, which historically has played an important role as a source of employment, was seriously undermined by the devaluation of the CFA franc in 1994 and import liberalization. Thus, the garment industry is being edged out by the market for used clothes made in Europe and Asia.

The economic crisis contributed to destabilizing an already fragile social environment. Cameroon's population is one of the most ethnically diverse in Africa, with some 250 ethnic groups, each with distinct languages and customs. Cameroon is one of the few African countries to have suffered a protracted armed struggle at the time of independence in 1960. It is also the only African country which started its independence with two parts, the larger under French colonial rule and the smaller under the British. During the first two decades following independence, the ethnic and regional differences were contained by a strong one-party and personal presidential rule.

The outbreak of the economic crisis after 1986 was accompanied by calls for political liberalization leading to civil disobedience. The Anglophone west and Muslim north did not entirely accept the results of the highly flawed presidential election in 1992. Subsequently, the government became sensitive to accusations of the opposition, the private press and pressure from major donors. In response to the latter President Biya appointed a strong economic team in July 1994 under a powerful minister of finance. In the new dispensation painful cuts in public spending and privatization, among other economic "shock therapy" treatments, are presented as ways of rendering the economy more efficient, more rational and more competitive in the global marketplace. Liberalization will undoubtedly open Cameroon to the predation of multinational corporations and the good grace of the lending institutions, but it remains to be seen whether this will benefit Cameroonians by alleviating poverty. In fact, the evidence, so far, point to the opposite.

NOTES

1. Bruno Bekolo Ebe, "Retrospective d'une decennie de croissance de l'economie camerounaise," *Revue Camerounaise de Management*, no. 3–4, 1986.

2. G.C. Abbott, *African Review of Money, Finance and Banking*, no. 1–2, 1994, pp. 5–31.

3. Ibid.

4. Bank of Central African States, *Annual Report*, June 30, 1987.

5. Tansa Musa, "Development Bulletin," *InterPress Service*, Yaoundé, September 9, 2000.

6. Forbes Global Magazine, October 1, 2001.

7. US Department of State, Bureau of African Affairs, *Republic of Cameroon: Economy*, March 1996.

8. World Bank, *Cameroon: Structural Adjustment Credit*, Washington, D.C., 2001.

9. On the struggle for influence by companies like Total and Elf, see *Lettre du Continent*, February 2, 1993. On rival interests in the banana trade within government circles, see *Lettre du Continent*, April 3, 1994.

10. Republic of Cameroon, Decree No. 94-125, July 14, 1994.

11. On conflicts between Cameroon and German investors, see *La Sentinelle*, no. 51, July 21, 1993.

12. Abbot, op. cit.

13. World Bank, *World Development Report 2000–2001*, Washington, D.C., p. 304.

14. Ibid.

15. *Finance Info*, June 30, 1998.

16. Ibid.

17. *Fako Net*, "World Bank, IMF, Biya Create Powderkeg," October 16, 1999.

18. TIERCE, QUINTE and FOOTPOLLS are gambling organizations that take bets on horse races, football matches, crickets, etc.

Chapter 6

Elections and Democratization in Cameroon: Problems and Prospects

Jean-Germain Gros and Tatah Mentan

Elections constitute one of the hallmarks of democracy. More than that, they are democracy's lifeblood, for "modern political democracy is a system of government in which rulers are held accountable for their actions in the public realm by citizens, acting indirectly through the competition and cooperation of their *elected* representatives."[1] For practical reasons democracy as "government of the people, for the people and by the people" must be representative and indirect in most settings.[2] Therefore, elections, while not exactly synonymous with democracy, become the primary instruments by which the *demos* rule indirectly through their representatives.[3] However, for elections to play their central role in democracy making, they have to meet certain criteria, specifically: periodicity, fairness and freedom. The first limits rulers' mandate and allows for continued re(assessments) of the voters' policy preferences, the second offers each aspirant to office roughly equal chances of being selected (or rejected), and the third confirms the empowerment of the citizenry by offering its members the opportunity to choose among aspirants without intimidation or fear of being punished. In free elections the citizen is given the chance "(1) to have his franchise recognized through registration; (2) to use his right to vote without being segregated into categories dividing the electorate and revoking the idea of popular sovereignty; (3) to cast his ballot free from external hindrance; (4) to decide how to vote, even to spoil his ballot without external pressure and (5) to expect his ballot to be counted and reported accurately, even if it goes against the wishes of those in power."[4]

The African continent was engulfed by the worldwide tide of "Democracy's Third Wave" in the early 1990s.[5] Since then at least forty-five African countries, Cameroon inclusive, have held elections, many of the multiparty type.[6] Further, elections have been organized at the roots and branches levels; specifically, there have been local, provincial (state) and national elections, as well as legislative and presidential elections, throughout Africa. However, significant variations from standard Western norms have been observed in elections organized in Africa since 1990. Elections that do not conform to Western standards have been called "elections without choice," "non-competitive elections" and "non- classical elections."[7]

Guy Hermet et al. distinguish between classical and non-classical elections thus: "Classical elections combine in a fairly coherent manner these three variables: voters' freedom, multi-party competition and results which affect what happens in government. Non-classical elections combine these three elements in so many ways that they induce a sort of taxonomic confusion—ranging from elections where the results change nothing through semi-competitive or non-competitive (free) elections with some political consequences, to elections which are not free and have no consequence for the voters, but where candidates compete to manipulate the electorate."[8] In other words, fraud characterizes "non-classical elections," or "elections without choice," and comes in different shapes and sizes, depending on the phases of the electoral process.[9]

Our aim in this chapter is, first and foremost, to analyze elections in Cameroon from 1992 to 1997, in an attempt to determine whether they have been "classical" or "non-classical," free and fair or flawed. But we do more than engage in sterile categorizing. Given the centrality of elections to the process of democratization, the chapter is an indirect assessment of democratization in Cameroon.[10]

FREE AND FAIR VERSUS FLAWED ELECTIONS: OR THE MECHANISMS OF DEMOCRATIZATION DECEPTION

All elections have at least three phases. First, there is a pre-election phase, which spans from the time an election date is set to the day when voters line up to vote. In some countries the law may mandate that campaigning stops a day or so before voting day, in which case the pre-election phase ends on the day candidates leave the campaign trail. Second, there is the election phase proper, which is usually much shorter than the pre-election phase, although in some countries, because of the sheer size of the electorate and for security reasons (e.g., India), voting may be scattered over a period of days, even weeks, to give all voters a chance to vote. In other countries, electoral laws may mandate a run-off for candidates who fail to receive more than 50 percent of the vote in the first round, in which case the election phase will be scattered, usually over two dates, and interrupted by the pre-election phase as candidates gear up for the final push toward the run-off *rendez vous*. Thirdly, there is the post-election phase, which spans from the time the polls close to the time winners are officially announced. Depending on the state of technology, among other factors, this can be as little as a few fours (e.g., the United States) or as much as four weeks (e.g., Bangladesh). In "elections without choice" fraud may be perpetrated during all three phases of the election process, or may be selective or strategic. Its preponderance depends on a number of factors, not least the ability of contestants to perpetrate fraud and get away with it. In this connection, and as a matter of general rule, incumbents have a greater capacity to perpetrate fraud than challengers, although in the universe of election fraud no one reigns supreme and unblemished. Below we highlight some examples of fraud according to the phase at which they occur. Our focus is on incumbent-engineered fraud, which we believe to be more widespread in the African context than challenger-engineered fraud.

Pre-election Fraud

The main objective of pre-election fraud is to give government candidates maximum advantages on Election Day. The timing of elections is crucial as opposition parties, many of which are (were) new, inexperienced and shell-shocked by the lifting of their illegality status in sub-Saharan Africa, may not have the time and resources to field viable candidates, develop credible alternative programs and mobilize supporters. Knowing this, shrewd incumbents (e.g., the late Houphouet-Boigny in Ivory Coast, Omar Bongo of Gabon) may call "snap" elections, even when constitutional statutes do not officially sanction them. For their part, opposition parties, enamored by the prospect of taking over power so they too can "chop" with impunity, may not be willing to slow down the transition, or to be perceived to want to do so. In sum, in its most basic form pre-election fraud, or perhaps more accurately ruse, may consist of government "blindsiding" the opposition. This may mean quick legalization of opposition parties followed by early elections, regardless of the state of readiness of the electorate and election officials.[11]

Pre-election fraud may take place during the registration process. Ultimately, the aim here is two-fold: to inflate support for the government and deflate it for the opposition. The government may attempt to disenfranchise some voters, whose loyalty may be suspect, by asking them to submit identification papers (birth certificates of ancestors, "valid" identification cards, tax receipts, etc) that the government knows they are unlikely to have. Failure to provide these documents may then be ground for expunging "ineligible" voters from the rolls or, in the extreme, denationalizing them. On the other hand, registration lists may be mysteriously lengthened by the addition of so-called ghost voters in areas known to be sympathetic to the government. In Africa the zeal displayed by election officials in the application of election rules, especially as they relate to registration, always seems to correlate inversely to the president's "home" region(s).

To a significant extent democratic politics is about communication. Candidates might be thought of as sellers (of public policies) and voters as buyers.[12] Thus, the ability of candidates to tell voters about their "products" is extremely important, if a successful transaction (winning office) is to be made. In Africa, as elsewhere, this is done by candidates in person (i.e., pressing the flesh) or through the media, specifically, radio and television but not so much newspapers, because of high illiteracy rates and poverty. For historical reasons media institutions in postcolonial Africa were government-controlled; in the few countries where media pluralism was tolerated, censorship was often applied to choke off criticism of the status quo.[13] Indeed, in some countries (e.g., Malawi, the former Zaire and Togo) journalism was as dangerous a profession as the soldiery.[14] The advent of democratization in 1990, which saw the legalization of opposition of parties, did not lead to immediate media liberalization. In many African countries the democratization of speech, and hence communication, continues to lag behind other reforms.

Pre-election fraud in "non-classical elections," or "elections without choice," consists of denying opposition candidates adequate time on the state-owned media (i.e., radio and television). Even when such times are officially agreed, they are routinely ignored on ground that "news" events take precedence over those relating to politicking. By contrast, even the most blatantly political utterances by ruling party candidates are deemed to have news value, and therefore worthy of being aired. Worse, the media may be used to spread rumors and assassinate the character of opposition candidates.[15] The most common accusations are that they have regional and "tribalistic" tendencies and that they are members of secret societies of the occult (Free Masons are especially feared in Francophone Africa).

Under circumstances where the electronic media cannot be counted upon as a neutral party in the transmission of information, "pressing the flesh" may be the only means for opposition candidates to communicate with their supporters. However, roadblocks may be erected here as well. In much of Africa public rallies often need to be authorized by local authorities (préfets in Francophone Africa). Permits to that effect may be denied on public security ground or withdrawn at the last-minute, both of which may be used to justify police breakup of "illegal assembly" and mass arrests. Even when such permits are granted, the time at which rallies must be held may be deliberately intended to depress turnout, thereby impeding communication. On the other hand, pro-government candidates often have a free reign in communicating directly with supporters; indeed, state resources are often available to facilitate communication in various ways, among them: early release from work of government officials, free transport to and from meeting places for rally attendees, police protection, free drinks, food and even clothing, and of course extensive media coverage. Pre-election fraud of the communication type is designed to disrupt the flow of information, thereby depressing the popularity of some candidates while raising the profile of others.

The institutional arrangements governing election administration make a difference in who wins or loses. Thus, who is in charge of election logistics (e.g., ballot making, storage, transport, counting, validation and invalidation, security in and around voting booths, etc.) has a significant bearing on election outcome. Pre-election fraud may consist of putting a government minister, usually that of the interior or territorial administration or home affairs, in charge of election administration, instead of an independent electoral commission. Even when such a body is constituted, the government may pack it with supporters, which subverts independence and impartiality.

Election financing is nearly as important as election administration, for, as suggested earlier, communication, even if it is limited to "pressing the flesh" as opposed to the more expensive means of campaigning, is not cost-free. In Africa few opposition parties are experienced enough to be prodigious at fundraising; fewer still have candidates rich enough to finance their own campaign (except perhaps in Nigeria, Africa's home of the profit margin, as Mazrui put it). The only viable means of supporting elections under this circumstance is state financing, which is usually entrusted to the ministry of finance, or again the ministry of the interior, rather than an independent electoral commission (e.g., Federal Elections Commission, FEC, in the United States). The disadvantage of this approach is rather obvious: ruling parties hold the very financial strings that have permitted their officials to live high on the hog while ordinary Africans have suffered and that elections may force them to relinquish. The monopoly that the state enjoys in election financing in Africa turns elections into political strip teasing contests in which candidates vie to extract money from election officials. "Parties" are formed for no other reason than to collect their allotment, and disappear into thin air soon after elections are over. The atomization of the opposition is one of the mechanisms of pre-election fraud in Africa. In this African leaders have proven to be astute students of history, for divide-and-rule, in addition to brute force, was one of the governing strategies of colonialism. The asymmetry of resources gives state power holders a strategic advantage over their competitors by facilitating the implementation of the divide-and-rule strategy.

Finally, pre-election fraud may consist of government creating an atmosphere of fear throughout the country, or allowing one to prevail. Impunity is the common term used to describe unofficially state sanctioned disorder. Thugs welcome election seasons in Africa, for their "services" are at a premium during such times. Pre-election violence, up to and including assassination, is usually well-targeted, that is to say, directed toward alleged opponents of the government, be they individuals (e.g., Etienne Teshekedi in former Zaire), members of a particular ethnic group, or entire regions of a country (e.g., the Rift Valley in Kenya in 1992 and 1998 where Kalenjin "warriors" fought virtual mini-wars against Kikuyus, Luos, Luhyas and anybody against Daniel Arap Moi).

Pre-election violence need not implicate state institutions (i.e., police, army, gendarmerie, etc.) directly, as state power in Africa is often shared informally with shadowy groups, which at strategic times can be called upon to engage in the more nefarious activities that state leaders may find "necessary" to remain in power but risky from the standpoint of international public opinion (not a negligible factor, given the dependence of most African countries). In extreme cases of state decay, these groups may become, for all intent and purposes, a substitute for the army and other coercive institutions of the state (e.g., so-called Ninjas and Cobras in Congo-Brazzaville in the conflict opposing Pascal Lissouba to Denis Sassou Nguesso).

It has been one of the paradoxes of democratization and economic globalization in Africa that, rather than fostering the rule of law, both have contributed to the further criminalization of the state and with that a weakening of its capacity to maintain order.[16] In this connection, calls for "good governance" by the international financial institutions and bilateral aid agencies (IMF, World Bank, USAID) seem rather simplistic, for they relegate "governance" to the realm of technicality. The experts who dominate these international bodies often ignore the reality of democratic politics, which may lead leaders to sacrifice long-term economic benefits for short-term political gains, even if the latter threaten the very future of the state and their own.[17] We do not mean to cast a pall on the desirability of democratizing Africa, but the coincidence between rising ethnic tension and violence and democratization on the continent is more than a coincidence and must be acknowledged.

One of the goals of pre-election violence is to frighten voters to the point where they may decide to sue for peace, even if this means rewarding their tormentors. Thus, a common refrain heard among Liberians when they voted for Charles Taylor was that he started the war that amputated their limbs and only he could stop it. Pre-election violence may also be intended to intimidate some voters (i.e., those thought to be against the government) into staying home. Where this is the goal, violence will be of a "surgical" character, that is to say, high in opposition strongholds, so voter turnout there will be depressed, but comparatively low in government strongholds.

Election Day Fraud

The activities that take place during this phase imply fraud much more directly than those associated with the pre-election phase. In fact, pre-election fraud is often meant to create an enabling environment for election fraud proper. Guy Hermet et al summarize the election-rigging tendencies of the powers-that-be when they assert: "the government aim is to prevent the authentic manifestation of popular wishes and pressures, while retaining a liberal facade which favors only those who support the existing order. In these situations, those in power dare not rely on the influence of an inadequately assimilated political culture or technical strategies such as gerrymandering or adopting a favourable electoral system to obtain the right results."[18]

Subtlety is not a quality often displayed by fraudsters in African elections. The most glaring example of election fraud is falsification of election results. This is done by stuffing ballot boxes with fictitious ballots in favor of government candidates; removing valid ballots in favor of opposition candidates; spoiling ballots (by checking off the name of more than one candidate for the same office) so they can be invalidated; stealing ballot boxes from areas known to be opposed to the government and, on the other hand, fabricating polling stations in government strongholds where none officially exists. Where fraudsters are somewhat more sophisticated (or less bold), other chicaneries may be employed, such as the late delivery (or the delivery in sub-optimal quantity) of ballots and ballot boxes in "problem" areas; the late opening and early closing of voting bureaux in those same areas; the deliberate printing of opposition ballots and government ballots on nearly similar colored paper, such that votes for opposition candidates can be "transferred" to government candidates; the inexplicable omission of elligible voters' names, or their misspelling, on voting registries, which automatically disqualify them from voting; and the location of polling stations inside the homes and (or) compounds of people known to be sympathetic to the government (e.g., chiefs, high level bureaucrats, entrepreneurs, etc.), instead of more neutral and open ground (e.g., schools, churches, union halls, etc.).

The act of voting in truly democratic elections is supposed to be a secret affair, involving the voter and her conscience. This is not the case in non-classical elections. Fraud here may consist of posting armed guards in full view of the vote casting citizen, such that she lacks privacy in making her choice and may feel compelled to vote for a particular candidate (or go home) lest she be punished for her "insolence."[19] The impact of these armed guards—sometimes soldiers, often thugs—may be felt in other areas. In the first instance, they may deter local election observers from monitoring what is taking place in and around the voting bureaux; in the second, armed guards provide the necessary cover for election officials to falsify election results if (or when) the need should arise.

Post-Election Fraud

In classical elections the means for resolving electoral disputes elicit the confidence of the disputing parties and, more importantly, the voters. The latter must be reasonably confident that their choices will ultimately be respected. This means that the authority in charge of electoral dispute adjudication must be perceived to be independent and fair. Further, it must have the capacity to enforce its decisions, or, in the very least, the parties must be willing to submit to such decisions, favorable or not.

Ideally, this authority should be placed in the judiciary, whether in the forms of specialized courts (e.g., administrative and constitutional courts) or ultimately the highest court in the country, since modern democracy and the rule of law are inseparable, although not synonymous.

Post-election fraud may consist of not formally constituting any adjudicating body, so whatever decisions election officials make are final, even when such officials are accused of malfeasance. It may also consist of limiting the power of judges to specific issues (such as determining who is eligible to vote and run for office) but not others (such as determining winners and losers or overruling the decisions of election officials). In the extreme post-election fraud may become a coup d'état, wherein an incumbent who sees he (or a favorite candidate) is about to lose either cancels the election (Ibrahim Banbangida in Nigeria in 1993, Robert Guei in Ivory Coast in 2000) or encourages the military to take over in order to preempt regime change.

In sum, in non-classical elections, or "elections without choice," the ruling party has the knife and the yam and can shape the entire electoral process (pre-election, election and post-election) to suit its whims and to the intended benefit of its candidates. By contrast, classical, or free and fair, elections meet at least some, preferably all, of the following criteria: universal suffrage for all law-abiding citizens regardless of race, ethnicity, class and gender; one person-one vote through secret balloting; security and stability in the overall political environment to insure that voters are not in any way intimidated into voting for this or that candidate (or party) or staying home; free flow of information about candidates and parties so that voters are reasonably well-informed about who and what they are voting for; freedom by all candidates and parties to mobilize support through mass rallies, media campaigns, etc.; honesty in the election administration process in all of phases, including voter registration (pre-election), vote counting (election) and reporting of the results and their adjudication in case of dispute (post-election); respect for whatever verdict is rendered by the people, meaning that voters must be reasonably certain that losing candidates will not seek to seize (or stay in) power by force; and, finally, periodicity, which time-limits mandates and office holders, thereby allowing for their renewal or removal by the *demos.*

Obviously, no election will ever be perfect (only saints could accomplish such a feat). All elections, no matter where they take place, will be chacterized by a certain amount of graft, errors and occasional (and not-so-occasional) acts of self-interest-seeking with guile. For example, incumbents, by virtue of their incumbency, nearly always enjoy certain advantages over challengers, especially money, which access to state resources gives them. The proverbial playing field can never be entirely level. The question is: Are deviations from the ideal type systematic, deliberate and so substantial as to fundamentally subvert the main raison d'être of elections, which is to (re)affirm the power of the *demos* over their rulers? At the end of the day, that really is the heart of the matter.

Having belabored the concept of election in both of its major categories, as well as in terms of its importance to democracy, the next focus of this chapter is on elections organized in Cameroon in the 1990s. We are concerned about one question: Do elections in post-one-party Cameroon fall under the category of classical or free and fair elections or nonclassical or "elections without choice?" Given the centrality of elections to democracy, the question may be rephrased somewhat: Is Cameroon democratic, or at least democratizing? In an attempt to answer the question, we will examine all the elections organized in Cameroon in the 1990s, namely: the legislative elections of March 1, 1992, the presidential election of October 11, 1992, the municipal elections of January 21, 1996, the legislative elections of May 17, 1997 and, lastly, the presidential election of October 12, 1997. Taking these elections as litmus tests of the democratic experiment in Cameroon, we will evaluate them in terms of processes and outcome(s). With respect to the former, we will examine the registration of voters and candidates; (b) the conduct of the polling; (c) the counting of votes; (d) and dispute resolution. With respect to the latter, we will dissect, province by province, the results of the 1992 presidential elections—in our view the most important in post-one-party (CNU-CPDM) Cameroon—in order to assess whether the will of the people was indeed respected.

We shall be parsimonious in answering the question that engendered this chapter: We believe that elections organized in Cameroon in the 1990s fall under the category of non-classical or flawed elections. We shall be considerably more generous in presenting the evidence to buttress the assertion.

PROCESSES

Contrary to other countries, elections in Cameroon are managed not by an independent electoral commission but by the Ministry of Territorial Administration (MINAT), whose titular head is appointed by the president. In France, which the Cameroon political system purports to emulate, this way of managing elections might elicit little objection from voters, since civil servants there are seen as officials of the French state. In Cameroon, putting MINAT in charge of elections all but guarantees that opposition candidates and, more importantly voters, will be suspicious, for civil servants in Cameroon are not independent. They serve at the mercy of the president. And, as stated earlier, a major requirement of free and fair elections is that voters have to be reasonably certain that their choice will be respected. For that to happen, the impartiality and independence of whatever authority is in charge of elections cannot be in doubt. President Biya has repeatedly been asked to allow Cameroon elections to be managed entirely by an independent electoral commission but has each time refused to do so. Cameroon ministers of territorial administration, including Gilbert Andze Tsoungui, has been unabashedly partisan in their conduct, thereby raising widespread doubt about their independence.

The registration of voters and candidates in all the elections held in Cameroon in the 1990s has been deeply flawed. Electoral malpractices at the level of registration are centered on selective registration of voters, selective distribution of voters' cards, the rejection of candidates of the opposition parties, and failure to publish the electoral lists, polling stations and parties contesting in each constituency. For example, during the municipal elections of January 21, 1996, voters were selectively registered in some areas. Suspected militants and sympathizers of opposition political parties in Yaoundé were calculatedly denied registration. This technique of exclusion weighed heavily on Anglophones and Bamilékés suspected of being supporters of the Social Democratic Front (SDF). Voters' names were either misspelled or their order on the voting lists misplaced. *The Herald* newspaper supports this assertion when it says, "voters' registers were so haphazardly entered that duly registered voters with valid cards either did not find their names on the registers or had their names jumbled up."[20] Some names simply disappeared from the voting lists on polling day.

Another method of hindering voters from exercising their voting rights was the arbitrary transfer of voters' names to unknown polling stations. This situation was true of large cities like Yaoundé and Douala where people suspected to be opposition members had their names in remote and difficult-to-identify polling stations. MINAT also proceeded to systematic rejection of candidates of the opposition political parties. Candidates' lists were scrutinized by senior divisional officers, governors and Ministry of Territorial Administration officials, who could decide who should stand for any elections. The Social Democratic Front (SDF) provincial chairman for Center and South provinces, Sani Alhadji, lamented the rejection of his party's lists in many councils thus:

> The Government rejected about 143 SDF lists. If we were present where we wanted to be, we could have performed better and the results would have been more positive. . . . That is why our lists were rejected in Maroua, Gidigis, Koulfata, Garoua Urban, Tibati, Banyo, Yaoundé III, Yaoundé IV, Okola. . . . Our lists were also rejected in Bandjoun, Mbanga, Dibombari, Ebone . . . this is however not exhaustive.[21]

It is noteworthy that, while the SDF was certainly most virulent in its accusing the government of "election rigging," other opposition political parties, even those close to the government, leveled similar charges. Thus, Minister Augustin Frederic Kodock of the *Union des Populations du Cameroun* (UPC), a CPDM ally, wondered aloud about the rejection of candidates presented by his party. Talking to the CRTV (television) Kodock said, "The CPDM party rejected most of my lists and prevented me from participating in all the councils I initially registered for. They didn't know that by doing this they were instead helping the number one enemy of the CPDM party, the SDF, to progress."[22]

The legislative elections of May 17, 1997 also witnessed a drastic rejection of candidates from the lists presented by the opposition. The SDF was most hurt in Bui Division of Northwest Province. Fai Mbu Yang Daniel and Shey Peter Nying of the Oku SDF Electoral District were unjustifiably rejected by the Bui administration. With regard to the presidential election of October 12, 1997, the Ministry of Territorial Administration rejected many candidates. In "Recours: La Cour Supreme Tranche," it is reported, *"On se rappelle que le MINAT avait rejeté sept des dix-sept déclarations de candidature qui lui avait été soumise pour examen. Une décision qui a suscité la réaction de quelques candidats recalés."*[23]

Another step in the disenfranchisement of voters is the selective distribution of voters' cards. Most opposition party supporters are routinely refused cards. This method is aimed at reducing the number of votes in favor of the opposition. The January 21, 1996, council elections give ample illustration of this fraud strategy. A glaring example is the incident at the Tsinga divisional office in Yaoundé. While voters were looking for their cards in vain, the same cards were being burned. It was reported that over 1000 cards, belonging mostly to Anglophones and Bamilékés, typically strong supporters of SDF, went up in flames.

Standard democratic rules provide for the publication of voters' lists, the total number of constituencies, parties contesting in each constituency and finally the total number of voters prior to voting. All the elections held in Cameroon in the 1990s violated these conventions, which led Boniface Forbin of *The Herald* to editorialize: "How could anyone call the elections free and fair when the SDF—Government's main challenger—did not, even on the eve of the election, know where it was allowed to contest?"[24]

As we stated earlier, elections are essentially about communication, of which campaigning is a vital part. In mature democracies, election campaigns are equitably (although not equally) covered by the state-owned media. Ideally, the field is a level playground for the contesting parties to canvas for support. The elections held in Cameroon in the 1990s were fraught with violations during campaigns. The state-owned electronic media, Cameroon Radio Television (CRTV), had the duty to cover all election campaigns, as did the state-owned print medium *Cameroon Tribune*. In addition, democratic tradition requires that these state-owned and publicly funded media show editorial neutrality, balance, objectivity, fairness and general interest. Viban further expounds on the duties of the public media: "that broadcasting responds to the demand for political information without also having unfair exploitation of (public) medium by one political party or another. That the party in power ... be prevented from dominating the political uses of broadcasting to consolidate its position. At the same time, broadcasting must prevent a party not in power from demagogic exploitation of broadcasting to overthrow the incumbent party."[25]

Since the outset of the democratic transition in Cameroon, the ruling CPDM party has monopolized the state-owned electronic and print media to its ends. All the election campaigns have confirmed the significant influence of the authorities over the media. The government employs the media personnel and dictates which political campaigns they must cover. The ruling CPDM uses CRTV and *Cameroon Tribune* as its campaign tools.

During the municipal elections of January 21, 1996, the Ministerial Order of the Minister of Communication stated that "All political parties and their candidates to the municipal elections have a maximum of 330 hours on radio and 15 hours on television from January 6 to January 20, 1996."[26] But the CPDM regime systematically monopolized campaign airtime by rejecting lists presented by the opposition parties in many municipalities. For example, the government rejected about 143 SDF lists, thereby reducing the total airtime of the SDF to 95 hours, while the CPDM had a total airtime of 306 hours. This example is just the tip of the iceberg.

In all the elections that took place in Cameroon in the 1990 s, the candidates were not placed on the same media coverage platform. Joachim Tabi Owono, presidential candidate for the Association for Meritocracy and Equal Opportunity (AMEO) during the 1997 presidential elections, complained bitterly: "We acknowledge the choice of Cameroonians. So far, my quarrel has only been with the absence of logistics at the disposal of some candidates. After screening the application files, I think the officials should consider those who go through this point as capable of ruling the nation. Therefore, all candidates would have been placed at the same level of competition, so that the difference should only come in the quality of the platform each candidate is presenting. Now we can't say exactly if Biya's lead is because the other candidates were unable to reach out to all Cameroonians or that the CPDM program is the best."[27] A survey of the elections held in Cameroon exposes the fact that when pro-government candidates go out on campaign, CRTV and *Cameroon Tribune* give adequate coverage to their campaigns as if these were news events of general interest. By contrast, only sporadic reports of opposition party campaigns are broadcast. Eighty percent (80%) of the pages of *Cameroon Tribune* are devoted to CPDM campaigns.

The ruling CPDM has made the campaign terrain rough and slippery for opposition parties in supposed CPDM strongholds. Administrative authorities, traditional chiefs, mayors, gendarmes, policemen and pro-government thugs have, in respect of CPDM instructions, prevented opposition parties from holding rallies in some parts of the south, center and east. The confrontation between militants of the National Union for Democracy and Progress (NUDP) and the traditional authorities of the Mayo Rey division in the north during the campaigns for the May 17, 1997 legislative elections is worth noting. During the 1992 presidential election (examined in detail below), the population of most parts of the so-called Grand South (center, south and east) was hostile to SDF militants. Suspected supporters of SDF, especially Bamilékés and Anglophones, faced harassment in the major towns of the south like Ebolowa.

The forces of law and order, expected to be neutral with the sole function of protecting the citizens and their property, have been very partisan. Taking the various elections held in the 1990s as a point of focus, these forces of law and order constitute the repressive machinery of the ruling

CPDM. As one of the writers of this chapter observed: "On March 25, 1995, SDF militants presented their permit, N0./RD/JO60/:SP, signed by Mbow Zanga Marcel, District Officer for Yaoundé, on March 15, authorizing them to hold a memorial service in remembrance of two SDF militants. Party Chairman John Fru Ndi also had an "important message" for his followers. A combined squad of policemen and presidential guardsmen volleyed into the venue, Carrefour Warda, teargasing, flogging, kicking and arresting militants."[28]

Still with regard to campaigning in the field, the CPDM regime during the elections of the 1990s used intimidation, threats and state funds to buy the conscience of innocent Cameroonians. Traditional rulers were compelled to militate for the ruling party and force their subjects to follow suit under the threat that their village would stop receiving government support. Civil servants, who are supposed to be apolitical, were sent to their villages of origin to canvas for votes for the CPDM if they intended to be promoted and appointed into ministerial positions.

CPDM rallies are usually held in conference rooms, so that the scanty crowds can be swelled using TV camera manipulation while the gendarmes and policemen roam the corridors sharing in the beer, rice, salt, loin clothes, etc. The public treasury absorbs the cost of these goods, and civil servants on CPDM campaigns in their respective villages ensure favorable election outcomes through generous offers to villagers of beer and other distractions.

Voting, like other electoral processes in Cameroon, has been flawed by the regime's apparatus. While the laws prescribe procedures for voter registration, there is no enabling legislation on the publication of registers for verification and correction prior to polling. The consequence is a dramatic shuttling of voters from one polling station to another right through polling day, searching vainly through one register after another for their names. This stratagem prepares the groundwork for effective disenfranchisement of voters in suspected opposition bastions. But the CPDM government has a multi-facetted approach to election rigging on voting day. The most brutal of these is intimidation of opposition supporters through beating and arrest.

A glaring case was witnessed in Ndu during the January 1996 municipal elections. "In Ndu, the CPDM Central Committee member, Ncho Adu, intimidated SDF militants in a polling station. He locked up the SDF list leader and eight others under the pretext that they insulted him."[29] Reacting to intimidation of opposition militants, Albert Dzongang lashed out bitterly against President Biya's corrupt practices in the October 12, 1997 presidential election. When unofficial results came in with Biya emerging the victor, Dzongang cried out in an interview in *Cameroon Tribune*, "Où étaient nos scrutateurs? On les a chassés dans les bureaux, même dans le Bamboutous, mon département d'origine. . . . Par la fraude, l'entourage de Biya lui permettra de voler ma victoire."[30]

Another method of excluding opposition supporters from voting on the day of polling has been the constant shortage of ballot papers of some opposition parties in certain polling stations. This shortage of ballot papers is a calculated step to turn the vote in favor of the ruling CPDM that had them in abundance. In reaction to this vote rigging technique, SDF chairman John Fru Ndi said during the 1996 municipal elections: "I have instructed all my militants to stop all voting and force the administration to supply more ballots or they should count what had been cast by the time the SDF ballot papers got finished."[31] SDF's Fru Ndi was not alone in his complaint. In a similar vein, Antoine Padoue Ndemmanu of the Rassemblement Démocratique du Peuple sans Frontière, candidate for the October 12, 1997 presidential election, accused the administration of fraud even in his native Menoua Division.[32]

Another tactic is multiple voting. The "floating" or itinerant voter is a familiar figure in Cameroon elections. The CPDM regime has transported voters from one polling station to another and from one part of the country to another to inflate support for the party. The case of Yaoundé is worth noting. During the 1996 municipal elections government-sponsored voters were moved one polling station to another so they could vote each time. These voters had many voting cards, supposedly those denied suspected opposition supporters. The first vice president of the central committee of the NUDP, Célestin Bidzigui, denounced the fraud in Lekie Division. His comment concerned the conduct of voting in the May 17, 1997, legislative elections: "The CPDM has issued thousands of cards for ghost voters in fictitious polling stations. Voters were allowed to vote several times in different polling stations. Our polling officers identified many of such voters and reported them to the prosecutor."[33] Again, what is significant is that the comment is made by a representative of a party close to the government and a Francophone, not by SDF, widely perceived to be the government's most ardent critic and Anglophone-dominated. CPDM has spared no one in its "winning" strategies.

Following the Janaury 21, 1996, municipal elections the president of the UFDC party, Victorin Hameni Bieuleu, said: "Pendant les élections, nous avons rencontré beaucoup de problèmes. Prenons le cas de Banna. Le RDPC a fait venir des votants de Douala. Et dans certains bureaux de vote des responsables ont carrément refusé de donner les procès-verbaux."[34] Another opposition leader, Louis Tobie Mbida, president of the Parti des Démocrates Camerounais (PDC), concurred: "à Elig-Mfomo particulièrement, nous avons la preuve que des allogènes ont été transporter par cargaisons et ont été inscrit sur des listes électorales, alors qu'au même moment, on refusaient aux autochtones de s'inscrire de peur qu'ils ne votent pour le PDC."[35]

The elections held in Cameroon in the 1990s were not managed by an independent commission, but by the Ministry of Territorial Administration whose titular head was a government (Biya) appointee. Vote counting, from the sub-divisional level upward, has been the prerogative of the Minister of Territorial Administration and his faithful disciples. The Senior Divisional Officer appoints the Divisional Supervisory Commission with a seat at the divisional headquarters. As was the case during the May 17, 1997, legislative elections, the commission members consisted of the president, who is at the same time president of the Court of First Instance of the division, with three other representatives appointed by the prefect and finally a representative of each of the political parties participating in the elections in the constituency.

In the May 17, 1997, legislative elections, the National Vote Counting Commission (NVCC) was appointed by Order No. 0225 of May 16, 1997, of the Ministry of Territorial Administration. While CPDM had a total of ten members on the commission, each political party had only one representative. At the level of representation, the entire vote-counting commission from the divisional level up to the national level was completely dominated and monopolized by CPDM.

The October 11, 1992 presidential election (examined later) demonstrates in a startling manner the absence of plurality in the National Vote Counting Commission. Ethnic and regional domination on this commission ensured Biya's victory. When one of Biya's appointees, then Minister of Territorial Administration Gilbert Andze Tsoungui, appointed members of the vote counting commission in charge of validating returns from the polls, 11 of the 13 members were people from his power base, the center and south provinces, or 85 percent representation by a geo-political entity that was barely 19.3 percent of the national constituency. Things were no better five years later. The National Vote Counting Commission of the October 12, 1997 presidential election had 22 members, 2 magistrates, 10 administrative representatives (also members of the CPDM) and finally a representative of each political party. Garga Hamman Adji, one of these representatives, lamented on the fraud practiced by the commission and gave reasons for his refusing to sign the final vote-counting report of the commission: "Je n'ai pas signé le rapport final de la commission nationale de recensement général de votes. Je ne l'ai pas signé parce que c'est un attrape-nigauds. Vous ne pouvez pas en même temps contester les résultats, dire que l'on a chassé vos représentants à Mayo Kani, Mayo Danai, Mayo Rey, Koupé Manengouba etc et signer le rapport final."[36] Hamman's reaction underscores frequent deadlocks on the commission, which always quotes electoral codes loaded with square brackets with unending references to "to be determined by law." These laws remain unknown despite efforts to find them.

According to the January 1996 constitution, the Constitutional Council has the duty to manage and control elections in Cameroon. Up to now (late 2002), the Constitutional Council has not yet been created. Hence the Ministry of Territorial Administration continues to manage and control Cameroon elections. In the absence of the Constitutional Council, the Supreme Court gives the final results of all elections. However, the competence of the Supreme Court to proclaim election results has been questioned. With the absence of the separation of powers between the executive and the judicial branches of government, the latter functions under the dictates of the former. The judiciary in Cameroon lacks independence. Members of the judiciary are appointed by the President of the Republic and each of them remains subservient to him in order to maintain his or her position and be promoted. The Cameroon Supreme Court cannot be counted upon to be objective, neutral and fair in handling matters related to elections. It is a brave judge, indeed, who would dare making a decision deleterious to the government.

The Supreme Court has, throughout the elections of the 1990s, demonstrated its partisanship and impotence. Petitions brought before it by the opposition parties concerning electoral malpractices by the CPDM have been discarded and dismissed. The contested results of the 1992 presidential election showed the incompetence and the firm grip of the Executive over the Supreme Court. Despite its acknowledgement of the irregularities that marred the elections, the Supreme Court could not defy the avowed will of the executive; it went ahead and declared incumbent Paul Biya the winner.

Another election in which the Supreme Court demonstrated its partisan nature was the January 21, 1996, municipal elections. The case of Yaoundé 6th District council is worth nothing. Here the SDF list was cancelled by the Vote Counting Commission under the pretext that it was headed by a "militant" of the CPDM, who had not yet resigned from the

CPDM. The SDF won in this council but because its list was cancelled, victory went to the CPDM. This was a blatant act of manipulation aimed at benefiting CPDM, for the same list had been examined and validated by the administrative authorities before the elections. Complains filed before the Supreme Court by opposition parties following this episode were deemed "unfounded."

Of course, electoral fraud is a frequent charge that African politicians level at their opponents. Africans tend to authenticate elections by their results: if they win elections must have been free and fair, if they lose the same had to have been fraudulent. In Africa, accusations of electoral fraud should not be accepted at face value. In the Cameroon case, however, the following observations should be made.

Firstly, electoral malfeasance has been a recurring development in Cameroon elections at least since 1992. We chose to explore all the elections conducted in Cameroon in the 1990s precisely because we wanted to see whether some were cleaner than others, but each election seems to exceed the previous one in its irregularities and failings. What we are dealing with here is pattern, not incident. The recidivism of the violations, in spite of repeated protests by the opposition and numerous exhortations by the international community, suggests one of two things, both equally deleterious to democratization: either the government does not care about the rules of electoral etiquette, or it has concluded that the only way to remain in office is by violating them.

Secondly, the charges are made by a variety of political parties, some close to the government some not. On rare occasions, even state officials have admitted wrongdoing. Such was the case during the 1992 presidential election, when the Supreme Court admitted that there were irregularities but that it had no power to annul the elections. Surely, it cannot be that everyone in Cameroon is fabricating lies against the saintly CPDM party and its government.

Thirdly, the charges have been corroborated by international election observers with no specific interest in who wins elections in Cameroon. For example, foreign observers in the May 17, 1997, legislative elections noted with dismay the wide spectrum of electoral malpractices. Among these observers were people from two key organizations in which Cameroon has membership: the Commonwealth and the Francophonie. The Commonwealth had representatives in 350 polling stations in all ten provinces of Cameroon. The Francophonie had representatives in 250 polling stations in eight of the country's provinces.

The Francophonie observers were shocked by sudden changes in the location of polling stations, in polling materials, unidentified ballot boxes, etc.[37] These electoral malpractices orchestrated by the government led the Francophonie observers to propose six changes that could help redress the democratic process in Cameroon. In the Francophonie report, published on May 20, 1997, the observers' recommendations went as follows:

- Harmonize the voters' registers and number of voters in the country. A similar job should be done to voters' cards so to insure a more efficient distribution of cards.
- Clearly identify polling stations ahead of polling day.
- Assemble and summarize all laws related to elections in a single document andmake them available those in charge of the exercise.
- Complete the training of election supervisors and supply to each candidate a copy of ballot counting forms.
- State precisely the procedure of transmitting polling station reports so as to guarantee security and confidence in the results.[38]

Fourthly, an analysis of election results, such as we do in the next section, largely substantiates charges of electoral malfeasance in Cameroon. In sum, election fraud in Cameroon has been authenticated by Cameroonians, foreign election observers, including the National Democratic Institute, and data analyses. In the latter connection, our focus will be on the 1992 presidential election, arguably the most controversial in Cameroon's democratic transition.

THE 1992 PRESIDENTIAL ELECTION: A POSTMORTEM THROUGH DATA ANALYSIS

The 1992 presidential election was a watershed event in Cameroon history. It was the first election since the political system was liberalized in 1990. It took place in an atmosphere of rising political unrest and economic malaise. It pitted an incumbent who seemed to be on his last breath against supercharged insurgents, not least the SDF's John Fru Ndi, NUDP's Bello Bouba Maigari, UPC in all of its mutations and countless others. For those who were in Cameroon at the time, it truly was an exciting period. In the transition to democracy the first national election, we believe, is the most important, for, depending on the outcome, it sets the stage for democratic deepening, stalemate or even reversal.

Throughout this chapter we have critiqued democratization elections in Cameroon based on how they have been conducted, in other words, the processes that have undergirded them. In this section we continue in our critique but our method is different. We use data from one election: the 1992 presidential election. [39] As a general proposition, the more implausible electoral data look—i.e., the more they deviate from "normal" expected patterns—the more questions should be raised about election outcomes. In the Cameroon case, a careful examination of electoral data is all the more important given that data provided by the government, as well as the main opposition party, the Social Democratic Front (SDF), suggest that the election was decided by fewer than 180, 000 thousand votes amongst more than 2 million cast, meaning that acts of fraud, even if they took place in a few voting precincts, could have had a significant impact on the final outcome.

Two criteria are used to determine election results plausibility. First, in comparing the government's versus SDF's second "final" results, it shall be asked which set of results shows the least surprising deviations from the general pattern of voting turnout, in other words, how do the total turnout figures in one province compare with the general pattern of turnout in the other provinces? Second, which set of results shows the least surprising areas of strength and weakness for the party reporting the results to the disfavor of its opponents, in other words, are candidates winning where they are not supposed to be winning? All results shall be presented by provinces, although district results are also available.

In the main, the data show significant variations in voter turnout by province, as Table 6.1 indicates.

Table 6.1 shows that two areas of strong opposition sentiments (littoral and southwest) had markedly lower levels of voter turnout than the national average (18% and 16% respectively, against a general pattern of about 25%). These areas are highly politicized and moderately to highly urbanized. [40] One would have expected voter turnout rates that are much closer to the national average in the two provinces. On the other hand, in the incumbent's strongholds, and in those of the main opposition party that was playing a "spoiler" role (i.e., NUDP), extremely high to high turnout rates are reported (43% to 33% respectively).

The attentive reader might note that in all but one of the provinces with "significant" deviations (i.e., southwest), government and SDF turnout figures are virtually identical. This requires an explanation. It may be that SDF did not or could not send its observers throughout Cameroon; as a consequence, the party was in no position to seriously challenge the gov-

Table 6.1
Turnout by Province as Compared to National Turnout Rates

Province	Gov't Turnout	SDF Turnout	National Turnout
Adamawa	25	26	25
Center	26	26	25
Far North	25	23	25
Littoral*	18	18	25
North*	33	33	25
Northwest	25	24	25
South*	43	43	25
Southwest*	16	23	25
West	26	25	25

* denotes cases of "significant" deviations from the national turnout average. All figures
are expressed in percentages.

Source: National Democratic Institute for International affairs, *An Assessment of the October 11, 1992 Election in Cameroon*, Washington, D.C.: National Democratic Institute for International Affairs, 1993.

ernment's results except in those provinces in which it had representatives. That SDF and government figures are close, if not identical, in many areas in no way validates the authenticity of those figures; they may, in fact, be a reflection of resource asymmetries between the government and the opposition, which prevented the latter from generating its own tallies nationally.

Table 6.1 only shows turnout rates by provinces. It does not show where the votes are going. In order to assess the overall plausibility of the 1992 presidential election results, one would need to know whether the three main candidates—Paul Biya of the ruling CPDM, John Fru Ndi of SDF and Bello Bouba Maigari of NUDP—won where they were expected to win. Voting patterns revealing "surprising" deviations may thus be used as red flags. Table 6.2 provides a district-by-district breakdown of voting results according to candidates in selected provinces. The data were lifted from "final results" tables submitted by the government and SDF on October 23 and 28, 1992, respectively. Once again, the focus will be on the areas of greatest discrepancies between government and SDF figures, so we can ask which sets of figures are more plausible.

Table 6.2
Voting Patterns Revealing "Surprising" Deviations in Selected Provinces

Province Disparity	Gov't-SDF Disparity for SDF	Gov't-SDF Disparity for CPDM	Gov't-SDF for NUDP
Far North			
Diamare	-4,138	7,138	0
Logone			
Chary	-7,697	0	0
Mayo			
Kani	1,857	—	19,594
Mayo			
Sava	0	0	6,000
Southwest			
Fako	-2,826	-4,808	0
Manyu	-35,063	11,471	13,013
Meme	-47,685	1,112	3,125
Ndian	-8,194	3,106	42
Northwest			
Donga-Matung	-3,416	9,774	85
Mentchum	0	0	19
Ngohk			
Entunjia	0	972	0
Boyo	0	-972	0
West			
Bamboutos	-288	-5	- 9
Menoua	0	269	0
Mifi	-100	0	0
Noun	-164	26,080	345

Note: All figures are expressed in thousands.

Table 6.2 shows a clear trend, namely: the largest discrepancies between opposition—read: SDF—and government figures were in the west, a SDF stronghold, the southwest, another SDF stronghold, and in the far north, a NUDP, or "spoiler," stronghold. In the west, particularly in Noun, the government gave itself 30,605 votes while SDF figures show it getting only 4,525 votes (hence a discrepancy of 26,080 votes for Biya). SDF-provided figures for votes received by the SDF candidate (Fru Ndi) in Noun stood at 9,231 votes, a number that is virtually identical to what the government said SDF received in the district, which was 9,067 votes. Thus, there is a 25,000-vote discrepancy between government and SDF figures in the west. The far north, where, significantly, SDF provided its own tallies, was also an area of significant variation between the government's and SDF results; more specifically, the government gave SDF 12,000 fewer votes there than SDF said it got. Two districts, out of a total of 6 in the Far North, accounted for 100% of the discrepancy—Diamare and Logone-Chari.

Southwest province, unquestionably a SDF heartland, has the largest variation between government and SDF data, with the government conceding many fewer votes—93,000—to SDF than SDF said it got. The discrepancy is particularly wide in Manyu and Meme: in Manyu the government conceded a little over 23,500 to SDF, while SDF gave itself nearly 59,000 votes; in Meme, according to the government, SDF received only 7,826 votes, according to SDF, it received over 55,000 votes there. The low number of votes given the SDF by the government is consistent with the relatively low voter turnout rate that the government said was experienced in the southwest (see Table 6.1).

Table 6.2 permits us to draw at least one general conclusion about the Cameroon 1992 presidential poll. Using the figures provided by both SDF and the government—and it must be reemphasized that those figures leave a lot to be desired—it can be conjectured that cheating, to the extent that it did occur, was highly concentrated, and in fact limited to a few districts in three provinces. Over 50% of the margin of victory claimed by the government—officially, only 180,000 votes separated Biya from Fru Ndi—came from a single province, the Anglophone southwest, which was one of SDF's two strongholds (the other one being the northwest). The apparent parsimony of possible acts of fraud does not, however, reduce their seriousness. As a rule, in close elections acts of fraud need not have occurred on a widespread basis in order for them to have a significant impact on the final outcome.

It is, however, somewhat surprising that the government apparently chose to "cook" the figures in SDF's own backyard. There is one explanation, which seems very plausible in light of a very important event. Shortly before the 1992 presidential election, one former provincial governor resigned from the government and made his main reason publicly known:

that Biya-appointed governors were under pressure from the minister of territorial administration to secure at least a 60% margin of victory for President Biya. It may be that the most zealous election officials were in the southwest, and that many felt obligated to deliver the prescribed margin, lest they ran the risk of falling out of favor.

Table 6.3 provides a breakdown of the votes for CPDM and SDF by province. Once again, the interest is in assessing the plausibility of the outlier cases as provided by the ruling CPDM and the main opposition party—SDF.

Table 6.3 shows that in a majority of provinces (5) SDF and government figures are identical. There are, however, four provinces (the far

Table 6.3
Comparison of CPDM and SDF Results by Province

Province	CPDM Vote as % of Reported Turnout according to CPDM	CPDM Vote as % of Reported Turnout according to SDF	SDF Vote as % of Reported Turnout according to SDF
Adamawa	26	26	6
Center	71	71	19
East	68	68	7
Far North*	48	45	7
Littoral	14	14	68
North	43	43	3
South	95	95	4
Southwest*	18	7	83
Northwest*	10	7	89
West*	12	5	72

Note: All figures are in percentages. * denotes cases of variations between CPDM and SDF figures.
Source: National Democratic Institute for International Affairs *An Assessment of the October 11, 1992 Election in Cameroon*, 1993. Data for tables 6.2 and 6.3 culled from Appendices XI and XII.

north, southwest, northwest and west) where there are discrepancies, and in one, i.e., the southwest, the discrepancy is in the double digits. More specifically, in the southwest the ruling CPDM said it got 18% of the votes, while SDF figures show CPDM obtaining only 7% of the votes there. The issue of differences in government and SDF figures was discussed in Table 6.2. What the writers wish to focus on in Table 6.3 is result plausibility. Both SDF and CDPM figures show the ruling party (CPDM) winning 95% of all votes cast in the south, with SDF obtaining only 4%. This leaves exactly 1% to the other parties. It is difficult to accept that a party like the old and still then widely-respected Union des Populations du Cameroon (UPC), even with all of its factional infighting, only got a fraction of 1% in the south, part of which covers the UPC's home turf: Bassaland.

In the center the table shows the government winning 71% of all votes cast. The center province was surely Biya's backyard since he is from there, but the center, especially its largest city, Yaoundé, is also very cosmopolitan. Yaoundé has populous neighborhoods, which might be expected to vote heavily for one or the other opposition parties (e.g., the Briquiterie, which is heavily populated by Muslim northerners, and Biyem Assi, where there is a large Anglophone population). While it is not surprising that President Biya received more votes than the competition in the center, there are legitimate reasons to doubt his wide margin of victory.

In the north both SDF and government figures show the ruling CPDM getting 43% of all votes cast there, with the NUPD, whose tallies are not shown in the table, coming first at 50%. Again, it is somewhat surprising that the NUDP candidate, Bello Maigari, only obtained a plurality of the votes in his own province and not a majority. In fact, of the three main candidates, Maigari is the only one who failed to win even a bare majority in the province of his birth. Born in Benoue, Maigari was well known throughout the north and the adjacent provinces; unlike Fru Ndi, he had superb administrative credentials, having served as finance minister in Ahidjo's last cabinet and as Biya's first prime minister; he was also politically savvy, as evidenced in his decision to identify himself as the natural heir to Ahidjo, who remain popular among northerners and who, in 1991–92, was undergoing something of a postmortem rehabilitation throughout Cameroon. Even with its control of election-related institutions, the ruling party should have fared much worse in the north, and the native son much better. After all, this was the pattern in the rest of the country.

We close this section on election data analysis with a brief discussion of the 1997 presidential election. In that poll there were seven candidates, including Bello Bouba Maigari of NUDP. But whereas President Biya tiptoed into power in 1992 with 39 percent of the votes, in 1997 he leap-frogged with a whopping 92 percent of the votes in a field of 7 candidates. In 1997, there was no discernible upsurge in President Biya's popularity compared to 1992. What then explains the more than two-fold increase in his share of the popular vote? It is true that the popularity of Fru Ndi, who boycotted the election, and Maigari had declined in 1997, but it is folly to think that the opposition candidates could not garner at least 10 percent of the popular vote. In the end, surprising electoral data variations from what one would consider normal, statistical implausibility, and unfair electoral rules justify labeling Cameroon elections profoundly flawed and the country's democratization a farce.

CONCLUSION

We set out to demonstrate in this chapter that elections in Cameroon in the 1990s have been "elections without choice." Much pains were taken to clearly differentiate such elections from truly democratic, free, fair and competitive ones. With varying degrees of scrutiny and using different methods, we focused on the following elections: the legislative elections of March 1, 1992, the presidential election of October 11, 1992, the municipal elections of January 21, 1996, the legislative elections of May 17, 1997 and lastly the October 12, 1997 presidential election.

We conclude that, through the aforementioned elections and other ruses, "the barons of the Biya regime have sought to adapt the structures of an authoritarian state to a new 'democratic' environment."[41] The democratic process, which guarantees free and fair elections through a transparent electoral code, neutral electoral arbiters and the like, has not been respected. The absence of an electoral code, in particular, supposes that of rules and regulations on the conduct of elections. Further, instead of a neutral authority, such as an independent electoral commission, elections in Cameroon in the 1990s have been supervised by the government-controlled Ministry of Territorial Administration, which has flaunted the contested electoral laws with impunity.

Government manipulation has twisted and marred all phases of the election process including (a) the timing of elections, (b) the registration of voters and candidates, (c) the conduct of the campaigns, (d) the conduct of the polling, (e) the counting of votes, (f) the proclamation of results and, finally, (g) the resolution of disputes. In the latter connection, the Supreme Court, usually endowed elsewhere with ultimate powers to settle all political disputes, has shown its impotence in adjudicating election disputes in Cameroon. The lack of independence of the judiciary compels the Supreme Court to act according to the whims and caprices of the government. The acting Chief Judge of the Administrative Bench of the Supreme Court confessed during the January 21, 1996, municipal elections that: "We declared our incompetence mainly over the failure of the Electoral Commission to carry out their task fully and because of the non-respect for procedures."[42]

If elections in Cameroon have not been the instruments by which the *demos* rule through their representatives, what then has been their political raison d'être? In our view, the politics of transition elections in Cameroon is two-fold. Firstly, elections are designed to give the regime a veneer of international legitimacy so it can remain in the good grace of "donor" countries and international lending institutions. Cameroon is now on the list of heavily indebted poor countries and is slated to have some of its debt canceled. Elections are an integral part of the regime's strategy to demonstrate adherence to so-called good governance, which has been made a sine qua non for debt relief. On the domestic front, transition elections are broadly designed to allow the regime to gauge popular support for the opposition parties so it can redistribute prebends to them on that basis. Herein, however, lies the rub: Paul Biya cannot allow for a true assessment of the ruling party and the opposition parties' electoral strength, for were elections to play this role, he might well have lost in 1992. Elections in contemporary Cameron play a more limited (and we daresay farcical) role: they are occasions for the regime to assign popularity (or unpopularity) to various parties and candidates, which it then uses to share with them the spoils of power on its terms. In this atmosphere, in which the ruling party is player and referee, complete control of the mechanisms of elections is an indispensable requirement to the regime's capacity to manufacture electoral victories or defeats.

In other words, elections in Cameroon are used to reconfigure the political map, to shrink and enlarge, depending on the need of the moment, the size and composition of the governing coalition at the center of which lies the ruling CDPM with its chairman of the board, President Paul Biya. The reshuffling of members of the governing coalition within whatever jigsaw puzzle is concocted by CPDM/UNC used to be the prerogative, *the domaine réservé*, of the head of state, be it Paul Biya or Ahmadou Ahidjo, but in the era of "democratization" such blatant misuse of presidential powers has become gauche, almost passé. After all, "democrati-zation" is supposed to usher in the "demonopolization" of political space by the executive branch and its sharing with other branches.

In the context of Cameroon's flawed democratization, however, the steely hands of monarchical African presidentialism are maintained in-side the velvet gloves of "elections," which are deliberately corrupted not only to sustain the myth of regime change for international consump-tion but also promote a deformed circulation of elites based, still, on the sole direction of the Prince. The recidivism and preponderance of fraud in elections after elections conform to this logic; similarly, continued mys-tery surrounding how much money Cameroon earns from oil production, the country's number one foreign exchange earner, gives the president complete control over prebendal allocation. Simply put, whereas before "democratization" who ate at the trough and for how long was a matter for the president to decide—the goat, after all, goes the Cameroon adage, feeds where it is attached—during "democratization" who does the same is still decided by the president but with the minor requirement, *circonstances obligent*, that beneficiaries go through the motion of "elec-tions."

As a result of the corruption of elections, some parties (although not their leaders), including NUDP, have been virtually eclipsed from the political scene, while official results show Biya's electoral strength (92 percent in 1997) approaching the stratospheric level of the pre-democratization era. Victory for the ruling party must be so overwhelm-ing as to make it clear to co-governing partners that they are peons sus-ceptible to being sacrificed at a moment's notice.[43] Biya is not necessarily unwillingly to share power, even though the size of his (post-1992) electoral victories suggests he does not have to, but in a sys-tem that is based largely on patronage, he must do so on his terms.

By his skillful use of the state bureaucracy, "politicians in uniform" (i.e., the military) and thugs, President Biya has stifled all efforts toward free and fair elections and institutionalized their antithesis: non-classical elections or "elections without choice." Worse, the use of ethnic militias to flush out so-called *allogènes* (or foreigners) from his electoral fief has paved the way for anarchy at election times with the decentralized vio-lence that accompanies it. In this regard, Cameroon may well be said to be going backward, or, at best, in a state of suspended animation demo-cratically speaking, rather than moving forward. The chronic uncertainty surrounding the use of the ballot box to choose who should rule Camer-oon has rendered citizens politically apathetic, if not dowright cynical.

What is the point of voting, they muse, we know who will win! Seeking light at the end of the tunnel, they shrug in impotence: Where is Ahidjo? Biya must go one day, but Cameroon will stay. The desire to cling to power tenaciously furnishes the regime with a tough and durable cement. Nevertheless, determination, buttressed by the administrative and repressive capacity to orchestratre electoral fraud on a massive scale, does not make any ruler outlive history. President Biya shall be no exception. The critical question is: How much damage will he cause before he leaves, and under what cirumstances (i.e., natural death, coup d'état, popular uprising, foreign pressure, ennui, or, less plausibly, elections) will he leave? What happens in Cameroon after Biya hinges significantly on how he leaves oofice.

If Cameroon seriously wishes to become democratic, it must remove the barriers to democracy and set up institutions that favor democracy. Clearly, the most visible human barrier to democracy in contemporary Cameroon is President Paul Biya. He has ruled Cameroon like a monarch for 20 years and as long as he is power, democracy, even in its minimalist incarnation, is not likely; nor is economic rebirth. The evidence in support of this conclusion is overwhelming; we present some of it in this chapter, as have others elsewhere.[44] The departure of Biya would facilitate the formation of a new political compact, which, if it is to favor democracy, should have the following characteristics.

Firstly, there must be clear separation of powers and independence among the executive, the legislative and the judicial branches of government. Executive domination of the political landscape in Cameroon has been the most visible manifestation of non-democracy or authoritarianism.

Secondly, all elections, as is the case in mature democracies, must be controlled and supervised by an authority trusted by voters. Given Cameroon politics and society, any electoral authority almost has to stand apart from the state, such as an independent electoral commission, if it is to be trusted. Bureaucratic culture has not developed to the point where bureaucrats of any ilk are expected to act independently and professionally. The preeminent role of the executive in appointing and firing public servants means that the latter cannot be counted upon to act with neutrality in any domain, including elections.

Thirdly, as elections by themselves do not constitute democracy (although they are a key element of the same), it may well be that the Cameroon state needs to be restructured before Cameroon can become democratic.[45] Democratization is aimed only at effecting regime change from non-democracy to democracy, and, we concur with Adam

Przeworski, with the acquiescence of existing rulers.[46] But democracy's fate is uncertain in a context in which unreconstructed authoritarian leaders are still around and even nascent democrats may turn out to be closet autocrats,[47] the structures of the state, if not its existence, are challenged by key sectors of the polity (e.g., Anglophones) and the political economy, led by so-called free market ideology, tolerates obscene regional and class inequality.

In other words, even if democratization is likely to be facilitated in a post-Biya Cameroon it could all come to naught in the end (i.e., it could fail to consolidate), unless the state itself undergoes profound transformation, so as to gain the loyalty of all of the *demos*,[48] and economic redistribution is left, front and center of the democratizing agenda, rather than an afterthought, so as to facilitate the emergence of a viable and modernizing middle class. This is a tall order indeed for democratization, which faces a dilemma in Cameroon and elsewhere in Africa. On one hand, democratization is taking place against the backdrop of neoliberal economic reforms, which are devastating the very middle class that democratization needs to anchor its institutions and values. On the other, genuine democratization may well result in slowing down, if not stopping, the neoliberal economic reforms, which the powers-that-be in the world say Cameroon and other countries must implement to "develop" (or at least receive foreign aid). The way out of this conundrum is as clear as Cameroon elections have been free and fair.

NOTES

1. Philippe Schmitter and Terry Lynn Karl, "What Democracy Is . . . and Is Not?" *Journal of Democracy*, vol. 2, no. 3, 1991, pp. 75–88 (Gros and Mentan's emphasis).

2. This definition has been ascribed to U.S. President Abraham Lincoln. By people Lincoln ostensibly meant all the people. In the original definition, as expounded by Aristotle, the meaning of people or *demos* is more specific; it refers to the "poor majority," the "commoners" or "populace." Thus, for Aristotle democracy was another form of government led by faction, in the same way that aristocracy (government by the best) and plutocracy (government by the rich) were. Aristotle did not even advocate democracy as the best form of government, which he thought could be easily hijacked by demagogues and transformed into tyrannies. Instead, he embraced the polity, or mixed government, as the best form of government, because it combined aristocracy (competent government) with democracy (responsible or accountable government). Aristotle, *Politics*, London, Oxford: Oxford University Press, 1948.

3. G. Bingham Powell, *Elections as Instruments of Democracy*, New Haven and London: Yale University Press, 2000.

4. Guy Hermet, Richard Rose and Alain Rouquié (eds.), *Elections Without Choice* (London and Basingstoke: The Macmillan Press Ltd., 1978, p. 3.

5. Samuel Huntington, "Democracy's Third Wave," *Journal of Democracy*, vol. 2, no. 2, 1991, pp. 12–34.

6. We refer to elections held in Africa in the 1990s as transition or democratizing elections, meaning they are meant to lead the continent from the despair of authoritarianism to the ecstasy of democracy. Whether this happens is open to debate, as is the ability of democracy in its liberal or bourgeois form to make a significant difference in the material lives of Africans.

7. We must note here that even in the West elections have not been entirely flawless. The 2000 presidential election in the U.S. offers irrefutable proof of this. Africa can hardly be expected to have perfect elections, when other continents and countries, more experienced at the democratic game and prone to sermonizing, have yet to play fully by the rules.

8. Hermet et al., op. cit. p. 5.

9. In this chapter we define fraud broadly, that is to say, as any act of self-interest-seeking with guile, as Oliver Williamson put it in another context. Thus fraud here certainly does include the blatant act of stealing votes, but it also includes the myriad ruses concocted by politicians, generally incumbents, to remain in power. We identify some of these ruses in the chapter and their raison d'être. Where Cameroon is concerned, we do not draw a distinction between flawed elections and fraudulent ones, although we understand that there are circumstances in which elections can be flawed without being fraudulent (i.e., when the flaws are not calculated to benefit particular candidates). In Cameroon, electoral flaws are not events of happenstance, therefore, they are frauds. We use flawed, fraudulent, non-classical and "elections without choice" interchangeably. On the flip side, we use classical and free and fair elections interchangeably as well.

10. By democratization we mean the gradual, often elite-negotiated, extension of political rights to the citizenry. Elections are obviously a major component of democratization; others include multipartyism, freedoms of the press, association, speech, etc.

11. In Francophone Africa the opposition has responded to this strategy with one of its own: the Sovereign National Conference. It has generally been the case that where insurgents have succeeded in forcing the SNC, incumbents have lost power in transition elections (e.g., Congo-Brazzaville and Benin).

12. We are idealizing things somewhat here. Voters, even in mature democracies, often have little more than cursory knowledge of public policy issues, and cast their vote more on personality and other types of shrillness than substance. This, of course, opens the electoral process to manipulation by savvy candidates and their public relations handlers and undermines the spirit of democracy.

13. In the aftermath of colonialism Africans leaders thought that the electronic media could be an instrument for development and nation-building. Further, the significant startup costs for television broadcasting and the small size of televi-

sion-viewing markets in African countries meant that, for all intents and purposes, the medium, if it was to be developed at all, would be government-controlled. The fact that television and radio were also excellent for disseminating propaganda and building up strongmen could not have escaped African leaders. The one country in Africa that consistently managed to avoid stringent censorship was Nigeria, but even there the buoyancy of the press depended, at least in part, on the sadism of the military regime in power.

14. In fact, being a journalist in Africa in the postcolonial period was more dangerous than being a soldier, since most African armies were more intended to quell domestic dissent by unarmed citizens than fight interstate wars. For a partial exposé of the travails of journalists in Malawi under Kumuzu Banda, see Sam Mchombo, "Democratization in Malawi: Its Roots and Prospects," in Jean-Germain Gros (ed.), *Democratization in Late Twentieth-Century Africa*, Wesport, CT: Greenwood Publishing CO., 1998.

15. The opposition usually responds by spreading equally malicious rumors about ruling party candidates, typically in opposition newspapers or through *radio trottoir* (word of mouth). The efficacy of the newspaper riposte by the opposition is limited by the low circulation of the print media for reasons explored in the chapter and the fact that censorship laws are still in existence in many countries even in the era of "democratization." In Cameroon the government has sought to silence the opposition press by suing journalists for defamation of the character of President Paul Biya and other government officials. Since the judiciary is not independent, this has been a very effective tactic.

16. Jean-Germain Gros, "Trouble in Paradise: Crime and Collapsed States in the Age of Globalization," *British Journal of Criminology*, vol. 41, no.1, 2003.

17. The tendency of political leaders to choose stagnation, however defined, over progress, however defined, or vice versa, is the stuff of public choice theory. For an example of a literature of this genre, see Bruce Buena de Mesquita and Hilton Root, *Governing for Prosperity*, New Haven, CT: Yale University Press, 2002.

18. Guy Hermet et al., op. cit. p. 5.

19. To be fair, intimidating voters in the exercise of their most sacred democratic right, the right to choose, is a strategy used as much by the opposition as governments in Africa. African women are particularly vulnerable to this kind of psychological pressure, since voting in a way that contradicts the choice of their husbands (or boyfriends) may be seen not only as a political act but also as one of rebellion against their mates.

20. *The Herald*, no. 279, 1996.

21. *Cameroon Tribune*, no. 6624, Jeudi, 25 Janvier. 1996, p. 8.

22. Augustin Frederic Kodock, Secretary General of the UPC talking to CRTV television on February 23, 1996.

23. Authors' translation: "MINAT rejected seven of the seventeen candidates under scrutiny, a decision that raised the ire of the disqualified candidates," *Cameroon Tribune*, no. 2735, Thursday 02 (incomplete date), 1997, p. 7

24. *The Herald*, no. 275, Editorial, 1996.

25. Viban Napoleon Bongadzem, *State-Owned Media and Partisan Politics: Political Reporting on Cameroon Television 1995*, Yaoundé, November, 1996, p. 38.

26. *Cameroon Tribune*, no. 6013, Mercredi, 10 Janvier, 1996.

27. *Cameroon Tribune*, no. 2744, Wednesday October 15, 1997. p. 5.

28. Tatah Mentan, "Cameroon: A Flawed Transition to Democracy" in Jean-Germain Gros (ed.), *Democratization in Late Twentieth Century Africa*, Westport, CT: Greenwood Press, 1998, p. 51.

29. *The Herald*, no. 278, January 25–28, 1996. p. 3.

30. Author's translation: "Where were our poll watchers? They had been chased out of the voting precincts, even in Bamboutous, my department of origin. . . . Through fraud Biya's entourage will make it possible for him to steal my victory." *Cameroon Tribune*, no. 2746, Friday October 17, 1997, p. 3.

31. *Cameroon Tribune*, no. 2746, op. cit. p. 3.

32. Ibid.

33. *Cameroon Tribune*, no. 6353, vendredi, 23 mai, 1997, p. 4.

34. Authors' translation: "During the elections we faced many problems. Take the case of Banna. CPDM brought in voters from Douala. And in some polling stations officials simply refused to surrender the results" *Cameroon Tribune*, no. 2314, January 26, 1996, p. 5.

35. Authors' translation: "In Elig-Mfomo especially, we have proof that non-natives were shipped in and had their names put on electoral lists, while at the same time natives were refused registration for fear that they would vote for PDC." *Cameroon Tribune*, no. 6627, March 30, 1996, p. 6.

36. Authors' translation: "I did not sign the final report of the commission. I did not sign because doing so would have set a trap. One cannot contest the results on the ground that one's representatives were chased at Mayo Kani, Mayo Danai, Mayo Rey, Koupé Manengouba and at the same time sign the final report." *Cameroon Tribune*, no. 2748, Tuesday October 21, 1997, p. 6.

37. The Francophonie's critique is especially revealing. Given the key role played by France in the organization, and the ambiguous positions France has taken toward democratization on the African continent, one might expect the Francophonie to be "soft" on African governments friendly to France. Apparently, the electoral delinquency of the Biya regime is too serious even for the Francophonie to ignore.

38. Reported in *Cameroon Tribune*, no. 6352, May 22, 1997, p. 4.

39. The data in this chapter and their analyses were also in Jean-Germain Gros, "Whither Authoritarianism in Cameroon? An Examination of the 1992 Presidential Election," in *The Democratic Challenge in Africa Working Paper Series*, The Carter Center of Emory University, May 13–14, 1994.

40. Douala, Cameroon's largest city, was the place in which the "ghost town" civil disobedience strategy was nearly 100 percent successful. If Cameroonians showed support for the opposition for weeks, even months, on end, it is difficult to imagine that on Election Day they would become reticent.

41. Tatah Mentan, op. cit., p. 54

42. Quoted in *Cameroon Tribune*, 22/7/96.

43. In the 2002 legislative elections, the ruling CDPM won 163 seats out of 180. NUDP won a grand total of 1 seat, with Bello Bouba Maigari failing to win in his constituency of Laindé in North Province. Nevertheless, President Biya retained him in his cabinet as minister, for which Maigari has publicly expressed gratitude.

44. Nicholas van der Walle, "The Politics of Non-Reform in Cameroon," *African Governance in the 1990s: Objectives, Resources and Constraints.* Working papers of the Second Annual Seminar of the African Governance Program. The Carter Center of Emory University, Atlanta, Georgia, March 23–25, 1990.

45. We are using the concept of state here in the Weberian sense—i.e., as a territory ruled by a centralized authority that has a monopoly over the means of repression and that is (a) recognized by the international community and (b) at least tolerated, if not entirely supported, by the citizenry. Regime simply refers to the rules, formal and informal, and norms of the political game. Thus, democracy is a regime. When there is dissonance between state and regime the outcome is usually the overthrow of the latter by the former. During the period of democratization the state must be postured so it is not in a position to overthrow the nascent, and therefore fragile, regime being put in place.

46. According to Przeworski, "A transition to democracy [in other words, democratization] can be made only at the cost of leaving economic relations intact... Freedom from physical violence is as essential a value as freedom from hunger, but unfortunately authoritarian regimes often produce as a counter-reaction the romanticization of a limited model of democracy." Adam Przeworski, "Some Problems in the Study of the Transition to Democracy," in Guillermo O'Donnell, Philippe Schmitter and Laurence Whitehead (eds.), *Transitions from Authoritarian Rule: Comparative Perspectives*, Baltimore: Johns Hopkins University Press, 1986, p. 63. In Cameroon, the removal of Paul Biya would presumably reduce the amount of concession that would have to be made to pro-status quo forces, and with that the possibility that democracy might be diluted, if not entirely subverted, at some future date.

47. It has been one of the distressing pictures in Africa that democratically elected leaders, even when they come from the opposition and may have even been personally victimized by authoritarianism, have not behaved differently (i.e., better) in office than their predecessors. Frederick Chiluba of Zambia and Launrent Gbagbo of Ivory Coast confirm this observation, although Abdoulaye Wade of Senegal and John Kuofor of Ghana have not—to date.

48. A return to federalism, more genuine this time around, may be a way to tie Cameroonians, especially Anglophones, to the state, while making the latter more democratic (i.e., closer to the people and, therefore, more likely to be subject to popular control). Thus, federalism may be a minimal precondition for not only democratizing Cameroon but also preserving it as a nation-state at peace with its citizens.

Chapter 7

Football and Identity in Cameroon

Bea Vidacs

We are at the Ahmadou Ahidjo Stadium of Yaoundé, Cameroon on 22 June 1997 immediately following Cameroon's disappointing tie against Gabon as part of the qualifying rounds for the African Nations' Cup Finals. Cameroon has done rather badly in the match. After trailing by 2–0 and then 2–1, at the last minute Gabon managed to score an equalizing goal, leaving Cameroon's qualification for Ouagadougou in doubt. As a dispirited Cameroonian team and a jubilant Gabonese team are leaving the stadium, a corpulent older man comes up to me and my companion, a Cameroonian coach, in great agitation. He starts by saying that he is very angry. He then pointedly remarks that he is angry at the Second Vice President of the FECAFOOT, the football federation, because the latter had prohibited a man, wearing a bishop's hat, a bishop's staff and a white robe sporting the green-red-yellow of the Cameroonian flag, from encircling the stadium during half-time. In fact the 'bishop' is a familiar figure at all international matches at the Yaoundé stadium. In excited tones our friend exclaims, "It's the Bamileke, always the Bamileke!" ("Ce sont les Bamilekes, toujours les Bamilekes"). He goes on to explain that, had he been allowed to proceed, the bishop would have protected the national team, and that he (our speaker) had been told that the result was going to be 2–0, and would stay that way. "It's impossible that every time there is an international match the Bamileke betray us. Because the bishop would have protected us, but Colonel Tchatchou didn't let him."

CAMEROON'S ETHNIC MAKE-UP: THE BAMILEKE-BETI QUARREL

In order to understand the deeper meaning of these accusations, I should explain first of all that Cameroon is a multiethnic nation where there are upwards of 200 ethnic groups and the Bamileke are one of the largest of these. The FECAFOOT official in question is a Bamileke whereas the speaker himself is a Beti, which is a collective name for people of the south, and from whose ranks Paul Biya, the president of Cameroon, hails. Cameroon's triple colonial heritage is unique. The country was first colonized by the Germans (1884–1916). Following the First World War, the former German colony became a League of Nations trusteeship administered by the British and the French, dividing the territory into British and French Cameroon. The west province referred to in the present essay as the "homeland" of the Bamileke belonged to the French administered territory. The people of the southern half of former British Cameroon voted to rejoin French Cameroon (East) just before independence, whereas the northern half voted to join Nigeria. As a result of the British colonial legacy, an English-speaking minority (about 20–25 per cent of Cameroon's population) came into being which has developed a separate "ethnic" identity as "Anglophones." They mostly live in the present northwest and southwest provinces. This identification as "Anglophone" overrides other ethnic divisions among them and, in many instances, sets them apart from the French-speaking majority of the country. Other major divisions within Cameroon are between the Muslim north and the Christian south.

The Bamileke originate in west province, but have also migrated and settled widely all over Cameroon. They are seen by many as controlling the economy of the country. Indeed, because of their economic dynamism, they are resented by many people in Cameroon, and the phrase "the Jews of Cameroon" has been used about them in debates. Although the phrase obviously compounds stereotypes, it does indicate the nature of the structural position of the Bamileke in Cameroon, and the kinds of prejudices they face. In addition, the Bamileke are in political opposition to the current political regime. They are not the only ones. Cameroon's Anglophone minority was in the forefront of initiating multipartyism. In fact, Cameroon's most important opposition leader, Ni John Fru Ndi, is an Anglophone. There are prominent opposition figures among the Beti as well, but certainly the Bamileke are perceived by Cameroonians as being among the most staunch critics of the current regime.

Like many other ethnic groups in Africa, the Bamileke have been constructed as a group as a result of colonization.[1] The term Bamileke unites a number of groups from Cameroon's Grassfields who live in highly hierarchical societies. However, these are fairly independent units which do not really constitute a centralized whole. The Beti as a group are of even more recent origin, consisting of ethnic groups which, until recently, were seen as separate entities (Ewondo, Boulou, Eton, and so on) and the word Beti was originally a linguistic term describing the interrelated languages of these various groups. Their emergence under the collective name Beti dates to the 1982 rise to power of Paul Biya, who is a Boulou. Traditionally, these societies of the southern forest region of Cameroon were small, autonomous acephalous societies, with very little sense of commonality.

In recent years, Biya's regime has increasingly tried to put more and more administrative power into Beti hands, and in the ethnic charges and countercharges that are now rife in Cameroon both groups accuse each other of ruining the country. The Bamileke see the Beti as being lazy and using their closeness to power to enrich themselves at the expense of the country, while the Beti accuse the Bamileke of likewise enriching themselves and disregarding the needs of the country. The relationship of the two groups has become increasingly bitterly antagonistic over the past couple of years since the beginning of multipartyism in Cameroon in the early 1990s, and P. Geschiere,[2] following J. Lonsdale,[3] has characterized it as an example of "political tribalism."

THE PLACE OF FOOTBALL IN CAMEROONIAN SPORT

Football is the most important sport in Cameroon. People refer to it as "sport roi" (literally the "king sport," meaning the most important sport) and it animates their feelings in many ways. As most men have played it in childhood, and often in their teens and early manhood, it is a game everybody claims to understand, and thus have an interest in. Also, given the proliferation of teams of various levels, a very large number of people have taken an active part in football, both as players and as managers or officials of some sort. Everywhere in Yaoundé, where there is a team playing there will be spectators as well, no matter how impromptu the team is. People even stop to watch children play, and often comment that they like to see children play because they play a more original and interesting kind of football.

Thus, it is not surprising that sport news is dominated by football. For example, the popular *Sport Matin* program on the radio, which broadcasts every morning, is almost entirely composed of football-related news and announcements, and other sports will be mentioned only rarely; usually on account of a good home performance in an international competition. The same can be said about the sports pages of newspapers appearing in Cameroon. They too are dominated by football news. For example, a quick overview of the first 21 issues of the weekly paper *Génération*[4] shows the following coverage during an approximately five-month period: in the sports section there were 36 longer features dealing with sport, of which 28 dealt with football; there were also 27 shorter articles, usually less than ten lines long, and of these 15 covered football; while 12 dealt with other sports. In addition, there were 11 further articles about football outside the sports section, six of these in one issue of the paper,[5] where the investigative central theme was the much debated collection for the Indomitable Lions for the 1994 World Cup.[6] No other sport merits mention outside the sports section. *Génération* is a paper of the Cameroonian intelligentsia opposed to the current political regime, and is the most intellectual of all the Cameroonian newspapers. It combines investigative journalism and serious social analysis with bourgeois general interest articles. *Challenge Sport*, a weekly paper devoted entirely to sport, also shows an overwhelming interest in football. The issue of March 28, 1995, for example, devotes approximately 9 pages out of 12 to the sport.[7]

We can see that the coverage of football in Cameroon is extensive, becoming almost exclusive during an event such as the World Cup. The national radio (CRTV) devoted five and a half hours daily to the 1994 World Cup, besides covering the matches and providing football-related news coverage under the regular news. This is without counting the special football-related programming of provincial stations. During the 1994 World Cup, as part of this coverage, CRTV ran a call-in radio program, *Bonjour l'Amérique*, and its English-language counterpart, *Hi America,* which was supposed to rally Cameroonians to support their team. In the event of Cameroon's early elimination from the World Cup, it also served as a safety valve to allow Cameroonians to express their bitterness and frustration at their poor performance.[8]

BRIEF HISTORY, AND THE OFFICIAL AND UNOFFICIAL ORGANIZATION OF FOOTBALL IN CAMEROON

Football, according to S. Tsanga,[9] was introduced in Douala in the 1920s by African migrants, and quickly spread to Cameroonians. As elsewhere in Africa, and in the colonial world in general, the colonizers attempted to exclude the *natives* from playing against them, and thus several early clubs had a European and an *indigenous* team.[10]

The first Cameroonian teams evolved in Douala and Yaoundé, respectively, the economic and political capitals of the country, and until recently these two towns remained the centers of the sport. This, however, seems to be changing, as some Western Cameroonian and other provincial teams gain more and more prominence. At first these teams were recruited on a strictly ethnic basis, and as Clignet and Stark[11] demonstrate, this went to the point that transfers of players to ethnically different teams were regarded as betrayal. These days this is less important, as players and coaches are fairly mobile, but the supporter base and the managers and officials of most teams remain ethnically determined, although, especially in the case of the more prestigious teams such as Tonnerre, Canon and Union de Douala, they draw on a wider set of supporters than the merely ethnic.

In the English-speaking western part of the country (Northwest and Southwest Provinces) which was under British colonial rule until 1961, football had a somewhat different history, because there the most important teams became those sponsored by various "corporations and governmental agencies."[12] Even today, PWD Bamenda (Public Works Department Bamenda) is the foremost team of the Anglophone Northwest Province.

The formation of the Cameroonian football federation (FECAFOOT) followed in 1959, just before independence, and it joined FIFA in 1962. Cameroon has been participating in international football ever since, won the African Nations Cup twice (1984, 1988), and has participated in four World Cups (1982, 1990, 1994, 1998). In 1990, the Indomitable Lions, the national team, created a sensation in the World Cup by reaching the quarterfinals, and defeating Argentina, the holders of the title, on the way.[13]

The structure of official Cameroonian football is as follows. There is a first division where 16 teams compete from all over the national territory. Each of Cameroon's ten provinces organizes second division championships, the champions of which vie for the three places that become vacant in the first division through the "Interpoules" competition, which traditionally has been held in Yaoundé and Douala, although in recent years there have been some attempts to move Interpoules to other parts of the country. For example, in 1994 they were held in the regional towns of Bamenda and Bafoussam; and although in 1995 they were back in Douala and Yaoundé, they have been alternating among various provincial towns, so that in 1998 they were held in Ebolowa and Buea. In addition, there is also the third division or "la ligue," where teams compete at the departmental or district level. In theory there is also a "championnat de corpos et veterans" (championship of corporations and veterans) organized by the FECAFOOT, but these tend not to function very well, even though both corporations and veterans do play all over Yaoundé, and presumably elsewhere too.

There is also the Cup of Cameroon for which all teams of all three divisions compete. The final of the Cup of Cameroon is a much awaited festive event where the President of Cameroon always appears to provide further pomp to the proceedings by his presence. The fact that he never fails to attend the Cup final is a reminder that the state in general, and the President in particular, take football very seriously. The President is the one who hands over the Cup and he personally congratulates the players. There is also a championship in women's football, as well as the women's version of the Cup of Cameroon, but most female teams are located in Yaoundé and Douala, and the female version of the sport is not yet practised very widely.[14]

In addition to these official forms of football, there are many other ways in which football structures Cameroonians' spare time and interests. There are the "championnats de vacances," organized in school holidays, sometimes referred to as "les interquartiers," where various neighborhoods of Yaoundé hold mini-championships. In addition, there are the "2–0," the "old boys" teams, and village championships, which will be discussed later.

ETHNICITY AND FOOTBALL

As mentioned above, the ethnic component has not disappeared in Cameroonian football, and in fact on lower levels of the competition and especially outside the official system of national championships, there are many instances of ethnicity being *the* driving principle of football. Village championships, organized by migrants bringing together members of the village in town, are an important addition or alternative to traditional village meetings. The expressed goals are to "animate" and allow the town-born young members of the village to get acquainted with each other. I observed the village championship of the Bamendjoun, a Bamileke chiefdom, over a six-month period in 1995. The Bamendjoun grouping (groupement) consists of six villages and are united under the leadership of a chief. The six villages organized a football championship and a cup competition in Yaoundé. The most important criterion for playing in one of the six teams was that the players had to be a descendant of the village, either paternally or maternally. Some of the players were also actively playing in "official" teams (sometimes in the second, but usually in the third division) and therefore teams that fielded more "professionals" had an intrinsic advantage. As a result, it became important to scrutinize the origins of the players. I have witnessed debates about the legality of a certain player on a team, including calling for elderly witnesses. Because the witnesses then explain how the player can be considered a member of the village, such disputes also lead to revisions and relearning of traditional ways of reckoning kinship.

The organization of the championship was along official lines, so much so that the various forms and administrative details followed closely those of official football. The referees, too, were active referees of the second and third division. The organizers of the championship volunteered their time and, apart from the president and treasurer, consisted mostly of the players themselves. The matches I observed were a community event, 100–300 people attended them and, unlike at the official championships, the number of women present almost equalled the number of men. This is a clear indication of the community nature of these events. Unfortunately, this village championship has stopped functioning because of controversies over the handling of money that came in at the post-cup gala. One of the organizers remarked to me that it was a pity because the championship had become like a post office for the village: everyone knew where to go to find everybody.

Village championships also take place locally, when youngsters who regularly arrive "home" for the summer holidays are organized to participate in impromptu championships all over Cameroon. This is so widespread that many "official" teams have difficulty holding on to their players during the summer holidays as youngsters disappear into the villages.

Despite the continued importance of ethnicity in football, thus its role in maintaining ethnic distinctions and boundaries, it is also undoubtedly leading to a crossing of boundaries on the level of the everyday practice of the sport. Not only does football create non-traditional standards of behavior, such as a new notion of time, or a turning upside down of patterns of respect (e.g., age v youth), but also, and most importantly, it creates linkages among people who would not otherwise be linked.[15] In the course of a sporting career, football players come into contact with a great many people from all walks of life. As players, they often play on multi-ethnic teams and, even when they play on a team that is ethnic, that is to say its supporters and leadership are identified with a single ethnic group, the players themselves will come from a variety of ethnic groups. This is because, despite ethnicity, teams and especially coaches, who do much of the recruiting, are often willing to find the best players regardless of ethnic origin. The average football player will have played in at least three or four teams and the ethnic mix he will have been exposed to is far larger than would be the case were he not playing football. In addition, teams, especially in the first division, but even at lower levels of competition, often play official and unofficial matches outside their regular milieu and inevitably will make contact with coaches and players from other teams and other ethnic groups. In Yaoundé, players often recruit each other and, interestingly, in many cases they will not be of the same ethnic group.

RELATIONSHIPS BEYOND FOOTBALL

Football creates relationships which endure beyond an active career. Much of the human structure of Cameroonian football is made up of former players, so much so that the innumerable more or less volunteer coaches, the officials of the federation and the referees for the most part have played football in their youth, and all seem to know each other as former team mates, coaches and players. This leads to a complicated set of alliances, which do not necessarily conform to the rules of ethnic exclusivity.

Then there is the "2–0," which is an institution in itself, uniting former players in recreational football. These matches consist of the "old boys" teams, which play on weekends. The name "2–0" originates in the practice (dictated by having too many would-be players) of having two teams play until one of them leads by two goals, at which point the losing team will yield its place to those still waiting to play.

The "2–0" team, of which I was an honorary member, contained the representatives of at least six ethnic groups and the friendships that developed were very far from being ethnically determined. The team, AMIAF constituted what could be seen as a voluntary association, but instead of the ethnic homogeneity characteristic of many urban African voluntary associations it consisted of a variety of ethnic groups. Among the noticeable interethnic friendships was that between a Bamileke and a Bassa; the two were practically inseparable. If you saw one of them you could be sure that the other was not far away. The former had been the coach of the latter. Another, for some time inseparable, pair was a Bamileke and a Douala. The former had his own young team and the latter for a while was its only supporter. Supporter here means turning up for training sessions, providing advice and financial support.

Another man on the team, a former second division player who is Bamileke, started his career in a team in Douala and played not in a Bamileke team in Yaoundé but in a Beti team of Sangmelima, a nearby town. He describes his experience with football as something that helped him establish himself in his career as a carpenter because, instead of money, he asked the leadership of his Sangmelima team to provide him with contacts for job orders. At present he does most of his work for a government company which sells goods to government employees on credit. This ensures that he has a steady source of income, which in the current economic climate of Cameroon is especially important. His access to the company's store is through a Bassa member of the "old boys" team, and he faced great difficulties getting paid for his delivery when his team member was on summer leave. Incidentally, this carpenter was also instrumental in organizing the village championship mentioned above. Thus, being ethnic and co-operating across ethnic lines are not necessarily contradictory.

THE NATIONAL TEAM

While football is an important vehicle for the maintenance and continuation of ethnic identities and differences, it is just as important in the creation of national identities and national distinctiveness. Cameroonians support the national team even when, fearing that the government is going to take advantage of victories, they resent football. The government in fact does try to do this whenever possible. For example, the victorious performance of the national team in Italy in 1990 went a long way to calm Cameroon's turbulent political climate in the wake of the country's transition to multiparty politics. Paul Biya has done everything to appropriate the image of the Lions in order to claim their victories for himself. Among other forms this appropriation has taken are election campaign posters, a postage stamp showing him with a football and the image of a lion, and having a popular football player endorse him in election advertisements. These attempts were only partly successful, however, because, even though Biya managed to maintain his hold on power, his attempts to usurp the success of the Lions has earned him the ridicule of a large part of the population and, after the national team's 1994 World Cup fiasco the government, despite all efforts to deflect the censure for the defeat, got blamed by most people.[16] Interestingly, the government handled the 1998 World Cup much better, and when Cameroon was eliminated, to a large extent as a result of questionable refereeing, the government managed to turn the event to its advantage, by making it look like a victory, "stolen" by the Hungarian referee. Even though in the latter case the Cameroonian people found themselves on the same side as their government, some opposition papers were quick to point out that this incident should show everyone (including and especially the government) how bad it felt to have a clear victory snatched away, in a clear reference to the 1992 presidential elections where, according to the opposition, John Fru Ndi's victory was "stolen" by Biya.[17] In any case, in the heat of the moment, when actually watching an international match where Cameroon is playing, people root for the national team, and derive great pride from the exploits of the Lions.

Cameroonians themselves recognize that the national team brings unity and holds them together. As one caller to *Bonjour l'Amérique* expressed it during the 1994 World Cup, "football is the only thing that unites practically all Cameroonians."[18] This sentiment was often echoed both in *Bonjour l'Amérique* and my interviews.

A *Bonjour l'Amérique* listener, who had gone to the studio in person, said the following just before Cameroon played Russia, its last remaining match in the first round of the 1994 World Cup:

> I myself would say that no matter who plays, that the people know, that the people who are in the United States know, that the Cameroonians have done all . . . have done all, didn't they . . . to show; that they love their national team. Well, no matter who plays, that he should play thinking . . . that he should play Wednesday thinking of the fact that we . . . that we count on this team, we count on it because it is a question of national pride, we count on it that the remainder of the competition should go very well and if later on we leave [the competition] that we leave it honorably.[19]

His comments were in part addressing the ever-present question of bonuses, and the effort Cameroonians made through the Coup de Coeur, the nationwide collection set up to help the Lions before the World Cup. In part he was reacting to the news of dissent among the team members regarding who would play. But what is really significant is his sentiment that the team should uphold the honor of the nation.

Another caller, this time an Anglophone man, was also keeping the honor of the nation in mind:

> Yes, I think I am a football fan and I have been trying to watch all the matches that are ... that are played and really football brings honor to a nation. If you look inside Africa you'll find that Cameroon is being honored by most African countries and why not Europe, European countries, because of the performance in 1990.[20]

In fact, what people lamented most about Cameroon's first round elimination was that Cameroon's prestigious image, gained in 1990, had been lost. When listening to these statements it is hard not to realize that the national team elicits nationalist sentiments in Cameroonians.

NATIONALISM AND SPORT: THE SIMULTANEOUS MOMENT AND THE IMAGINED COMMUNITY

Sport is the vehicle par excellence for national sentiments. Given the way international competitions are organized, it is nations, however defined, that are pitted against each other, and such structures have a way of imposing themselves on the popular imagination. With the advance of mass media into quite remote areas, the simultaneous moment, about which Benedict Anderson is so eloquent, regarding the relationship between the novel and the rise of nationalism in Europe and elsewhere, is particularly evident when the majority of the population of an entire country is able to watch a football match at the same time.[21] Add to this that in Cameroon, and in Africa in general, the majority of these spectators are literally watching the match together because in Cameroon, for example, most people watch international matches not in their living rooms with their immediate, nuclear families, but in public spaces: bars, for the most part, where for the price of a few beers people unrelated to each other gather to watch matches. In fact, even if they are watching at home, chances are that there will be neighbors, relatives, servants or friends availing themselves of the opportunity to watch the match, thus once again the event is more public than one would expect. There are also giant screens set up in large cities where hundreds of people can and do gather together to watch a match. There are simultaneous radio broadcasts of international matches as well, so even people in remote areas can follow the competition, again usually in public rather than in private, as not everyone owns a radio. So the imagined community is rejoicing and seething, literally all at once, and of course it is both real (in the immediate sense) and imagined in the Andersonian sense, because people in their immediate communities know that there are other immediate communities of the same kind experiencing what they are experiencing. They know this for no other reason than because, the day after the match, the radio will broadcast man-on-the-street reactions to the match from all ten provinces of Cameroon. D. Spitulnik,[22] analyzing radio in Zambia, also sees the broadcast of international football matches as one of the main instances where Zambian national identity is articulated, with football serving as an effective rallying cry for national unity.

To extend Anderson's thesis on the rise of nationalism, football is a major force in imagining the nation. This is not only so in the above outlined scenario of imagining the nation through the communal experience of watching and rooting for the national team; it is also evident in the very structure of the national championship and the Cup of Cameroon which helps make the abstraction of Cameroon as an idea, as a unit, real in the minds of the people. Although this structure is not so different from the rest of the world's, its significance in terms of the imagined community of the nation is not to be ignored.

THE INTERPLAY BETWEEN ETHNICITY AND NATIONALISM IN AFRICAN SPORT

What is really striking about our stadium friend's explanation of the Indomitable Lions' disappointing performance is that it highlights an often neglected aspect of the influence football plays on the relationship between ethnicity and nationalism in Cameroon, and I suspect elsewhere in Africa too. And that is that sport, and especially football, incites the loyalties of people on different levels so that they can act to promote national as well as ethnic sentiments.

Much of the rather sparse literature on sport in Africa seems to deny that it has national integrative functions, although such functions have been amply illustrated elsewhere, especially in Europe.[23] Rather, the emphasis has been on the divisive aspect of sport, which brings out the "ethnic" in Africans.[24]

Similarly, in the anthropological literature of the past 30 years, ethnicity is seen as the most important dividing line in Africa. There has been an almost rigid division, more often than not unacknowledged, where Africans are seen as ethnics, and Westerners as nationalists. Yet ethnicity and nationalism are not the mutually exclusive categories being presented. In analyzing ethnicity, anthropologists have come to describe it as situational and flexible.[25] Ronald Cohen defines ethnicity "as a series of nesting dichotomizations of inclusiveness and exclusiveness . . . where . . . the cultural identifiers used to assign persons to groupings . . . expand or contract in inverse relation to the scale of inclusiveness and exclusiveness of the membership."[26]

There is an argument for adding nationalism as one more of these flexible and situational identities, an alternative that can be chosen at certain times from among other identities. The various alternatives need not be consonant with each other. This makes sense also because of the segmentary nature of sports competition. When lower level teams are opposed to each other the identities that come to the fore are local identities, when higher level teams are opposed to each other the inclusiveness and scope of the identities evoked match the level of the competition, and this allows for, or even invites, these "nested" identities.

Thus, at issue is not so much whether sport is promoting unity or divisiveness. It clearly does both. In Africa it even goes beyond nationalism in promoting even more overarching, pan-African identifications. For example, after Cameroon's stellar showing in the 1990 World Cup, *Jeune Afrique*,[27] in a band headline cutting diagonally across the lower right corner on its title page, said "Africa among the great," referring to Cameroon's and Egypt's showing at the World Cup. A few weeks later, upon the conclusion of the competition, which of course had been won by Germany, the *Jeune Afrique*[28] headline declared "It is Cameroon that Won"—in handwritten block letters superimposed over the photograph of a stadium covering the entire front page.

Certainly in 1994, after Cameroon was eliminated from the competition, Cameroonians were quick to shift their allegiance to Nigeria, the only remaining African side in the competition. Many bought the Nigerian flags being sold in Yaoundé on the night of Nigeria's match against Italy. When Nigeria lost the match a Francophone Cameroonian friend told me the next morning that he had been so upset that he almost cried. This is despite the fact that Cameroon has had a continuing border dispute with Nigeria over the Bakassi peninsula. The dispute is closer to the hearts of the government than the people at large. Nevertheless, Cameroonians on the whole are convinced that they can beat Nigeria in football any time.

How easily this identification is made, and how one African country is made to stand for the whole of Africa, is shown by the following statement by a woman caller to the English version of the call-in radio program, the day of the Nigeria-Italy match: "Well, to start off the Nigerian side showed up a good game and I am sure they defended the . . . the *African nation* as a whole and all I can wish them that they should keep on and try to, at least fly the flag of Ni. . . . Africa. . . . I hope [they will attend may be even the semi-finals."[29] The ease with which she treats Nigeria and Africa as interchangeable terms shows that she sees the good performance of Nigeria as holding up the honor of Africa as a whole. Given that by this time Cameroon had already been eliminated, she, like many others, is now rooting for Nigeria as the African team, hoping that they will go far in the competition. One could object that Europeans do not automatically support the next European team when their own has lost, but shifting of loyalties in such a case is a question of power relationships, where such switches are facilitated by Africans' perception of a commonality of fate vis-à-vis Europe, which is of course the product of their colonial history, of being dominated and exploited by Europe and the continuing structurally weak position that African countries share in relation to Europe and the United States today.

This line of argument follows to some extent what J. Lever[30] has to say about the interplay of the unifying and divisive functions of football in Brazil. I agree with her that football is capable of both uniting and dividing people, however, while she sees this as paradoxical, I regard it as an outcome of the segmentary nature of the game's organization. At the same time, I include nationalist and pan-Africanist (as well as ethnic) sentiments in the framework of co-existing and available identity choices, where the scope of inclusiveness will be triggered, and to a great extent determined, in relation to situation. To what extent it will be "determined" seems to depend on the level at which we find ourselves. That is to say, Cameroonians followed this system of increasingly widening nesting identifications throughout the 1994 World Cup to the point where, in the final, the majority supported Brazil against Italy, on the grounds that Brazil is a Third World country like Cameroon and possibly also because there are blacks on the Brazilian team.[31] However, at this level of inclusiveness the identification was much less binding, and a minority felt perfectly at ease supporting Italy, whereas it is unlikely that it would have been possible to support Italy against Nigeria openly.

J. Athena[32] objects to Lever's analysis on the grounds that conceivably watching international football, a *global game*, could work to wash away not only ethnic, but also nationalist divisions, as he puts it, "in favor of a greater sense of transnational community, if only through a sense of shared experiences and the consequences of operating within similar institutions and regulations."[33] Athena's argument that football in and of it-self does not uphold governments, and that the gains in popularity of regimes and leaders is only momentary, is well taken, but my point here is on a different level. In this proposed framework of nested identities, pan-Africanism today does not make nationalist or ethnic sentiment impossible tomorrow or even the next minute, as can be seen from the contribution of the woman caller quoted above. Nor does nationalist sentiment exclude ethnic sentiment (and vice versa) as evidenced by our friend's statement at the stadium.

Put somewhat differently, in all the debates about ethnicity and nationalism, little attention has been paid to nationalism in areas, especially Africa, where we are not expecting to see it. In a 1996 volume on African ethnicity, Fardon,[34] for example, devotes only one paragraph to nationalism in his conclusion to a highly imaginative analysis of the constraints imposed on *ethnic narratives* by their respective interethnic contexts. As an aside (actually, in brackets) he mentions that nationalism should be evident in Africa, if at all, on the level of organized sports.[35]

NATIONALISM AND ETHNICITY: TWO SIDES OF THE SAME COIN

To return to our stadium interlocutor, he is being ethnic and nationalist at the same time. His very presence at the stadium is an indication that his interest in football goes beyond the purely ethnic. Presumably someone with an ethnic interest in football would go to the stadium only when his ethnic team plays. I happen to know this man and know that he is present at every match played at the stadium, but there are many other people who only turn out for the matches played by their own team, and that often happens to be an ethnic team. His fervent need to find an explanation for the result is also proof of his national sentiments. Yet the exegesis he chooses to present, apart from its magical undertones, is purely ethnic. He singles out an individual, who, even if the story of his constraining the bishop is true (about which I have no information), was only doing his duty, presiding over the peaceful unfolding of the match. And, in addition to blaming the Colonel for the result, he jumps from him (an individual) to his ethnic group and generalizes that the entire group is always trying to sabotage Cameroonian success in all international matches. The point is that in one breath our man is being both a nationalist and an ethnic chauvinist, questioning the patriotism of groups other than his own in a way that also involves questioning who exactly constitutes the nation.

Many of the contributions to the radio program, *Bonjour l'Amérique*, bear witness to the fact that indeed football on the international level elicits from Cameroonians the same kind of nationalist fervor as we are used to elsewhere. In many of my interviews, the majority of interviewees predictably supported their own ethnic teams, but at the same time they also supported the national team. Often what we find is that people go to matches only when their team plays and when the national team plays. This is no different from any European fan who will support his own team (chosen on whatever basis) and the national team, and no one sees any contradiction in this. Cameroonians act in exactly the same way and we are surprised because we supposed them to be ethnic to the exclusion of all else.

What they debate is the definition of the nation, who is a true patriot, who is betraying us. And this is where nationalism, the "unifying force," becomes divisive, in denying other people's intentions to uphold the honor of the nation.[36] This chapter has demonstrated that football is a two-edged sword and, while it can be both ethnic and nationalist, even when it is nationalist it can be devisive.

CONCLUSION

Football in Cameroon reinforces ethnic ties and cuts across them. Whether it does one or the other will vary contextually: people do support their local "ethnic" teams, but in the same breath also support the national team. What they contest is whether everyone supports the national team to the same extent and, by implication, whether everybody deserves to be part of the nation. At the same time, through the experience of football as a practice, people gain a wider social network which cuts across ethnic links and binds them together in novel ways.

NOTES

This chapter was originally published as "Football in Cameroon: A Vehicle for the Expansion and Contraction of Identity," *Culture, Sport, Society*, Vol. 2, special issue 2.3, 1997. Permission to reprint the material has been granted.

1. See P. Geschiere "Kinship, Witchcraft and the Moral Economy of Ethnicity: Contrasts from Southern and Western Cameroon," in L. de la Gorgendière, K. King and S. Vaughan (eds.), *Ethnicity in Africa: Roots, Meanings and Implications* (Edinburgh, 1996), for a discussion of the constructed nature of the two groups and the differences in the way in which they cope with new inequalities in their midst.

2. Ibid.

3. J. Lansdale, "The Moral Economy of Mau-Mau," in Bruce Berman and John Lonsdale (eds.), *Unhappy Valley, Conflict in Kenya and Africa* (London, 1992).

4. *Génération Yaoundé* (August 1994 to early January 1995), that is to say, at the tail end of the 1994 World Cup.

5. Ibid., 1, 17, 12 December 1994.

6. For more detail on the Coup de Coeur see P.N. Nkwi and B. Vidacs, "Football: Politics and Power in Cameroon" in G. Armstrong and R. Giulianotti (eds.), *Entering the Field: New Perspectives in World Football* (Oxford, 1997).

7. *Challenge Sport* (Yaoundé) II, 61.

8. For a more detailed analysis of the program and changes in its tenor see "Football."

9. S. Tanga, *Le Football camerounais des origines à l'indépendence* (Yaoundé, 1969) (hereafter *le football*).

10. See W. J. Baker and J.A. Mangan, *Sport in Africa, Essays in Social History* (London, 1987); Laura Fair, "Kickin it: Leisure, Politics and Football in Colonial Zanzibar, 1900s–1950s," *Africa*, 67 (1997); P. Martin, "Colonialism, Youth and Football in French Equatorial Africa," *International Journal of the History of Sport*, 8 (1991); B. Stoddart, "Sport, Cultural Imperialism, and Colonial Response in the British Empire," *Comparative Studies in Society and History* (30) (1998); *Le Football* (Yaoundé, 1969).

11. R. Clignet and M. Stark, "Modernisation and Football in Cameroun," *Journal of Modern African Studies*, 12 (1974).

12. H.M. Mokeba, *The Politics and Diplomacy of Cameroon Sports: A Study in the Quest for Nation-Building and International Prestige* (unpublished PhD thesis, University of South Carolina, 1989); see also "Modernisation and Football in Cameroun."

13. J.-C. Kudo-Ela and A. M. Masika, *Il était une fois . . . les Lions Indomptables du Cameroun* (Yaoundé, nd) Collections Hommes et Evénements.

14. S. Kuper, *Football against the Enemy* (London, 1994).

15. "Modernisation and Football in Cameroun."

16. See "Football" for further details of how the government is trying to take advantage of football victories.

17. *La Nouvelle Expression*, 381, 26 June 1998, 6.

18. *Bonjour l'Amérique*, 27 June 1994, 7.

19. *Bonjour l'Amèrique*, 28 June 1994, 1.

20. *Hi America*, 2 July 1994, 7.

21. B. Anderson, *Imagined Communities*, (London:1983).

22. D.A. Spitulnik, *Radio Culture in Zambia: Audiences, Public Words, and the Nation State (I and II)* (unpublished doctoral dissertation, University of Chicago, 1994).

23. J. Hargreaves, *Sport, Power and Culture: A Social and Historical Analysis of Popular Sports in Britain* (New York, 1986); J.A. Mangan (ed.), *Tribal Identities: Nationalism, Europe, Sport* (London, 1986) (hereafter *Tribal Identities*); J.A. Mangan, Richard Holt and Pierre Lanfranchi (eds.), *European Heroes: Myth, Identity, Sport* (London, 1996).

24. T. Munnington, "The Politics of Black African Sport," in Lincoln Allison (ed.), *The Politics of Sport* (Manchester, 1986); T. B. Stevenson, "Sports Clubs and Political Integration in theYemen Arab Republic," *International Review for the Sociology of Sport*, 24 (1989).

25. J. Vincent, "The Structuring of Ethnicity," *Human Organization*, 33 (1974); R. Cohen, "Ethnicity: Problem and Focus in Anthropology," *Annual Review of Anthropology*, 7 (1978).

26. Ibid., 387, emphasis in the original.

27. *Jeune Afrique*, 1538, 20–26 June 1990.

28. *Jeune Afrique*, 1541, 11–17 July 1990.

29. *Hi America*, 2 July 1994, 7, emphasis added.

30. J. Lever, *Soccer Madness* (Chicago, 1983). As she puts it, "Sport's paradoxical ability to reinforce social cleavages while transcending them makes soccer . . . the perfect means of achieving a more perfect union between multiple groups," p. 7. In the case of Cameroon it is impossible to share this optimism; the processes I am talking about are much more indeterminate.

31. I have not heard the latter explicitly stated in the case of the World Cup final, but judging by the commentary and keen interest with which Cameroonians scrutinized the racial composition of foreign teams, it is more than likely that this factor played a part in the ready identification of many Cameroonians with Brazil. To give an example of this kind of scrutiny, there were many jocular comments on why Saudi Arabia was considered an Asian team in the World Cup when clearly many of its players were black.

32. J. L. Arbena, "Nationalism and Sport in Latin America, 1850–1990: The Paradox of Promoting and Performing 'European' Sports," in J.A. Mangan (ed.), *Tribal Identities*, op. cit.

33. Ibid. p. 225.

34. R. Fardon, "Crossed Destinies: The Entangled Histories of West African Ethnic and National Identities," in L. de la Gorgendière et al. (eds.), op. cit.

35. Ibid. p. 142.

36. B.F. Williams, "A Class Act: Anthropology and the Race to Nation Across Ethnic Terrain," *Annual Review of Anthropology*, 18 (1989).

Chapter 8

Politics and Music in Cameroon

Francis Nyamnjoh and Jude Fokwang

In order to grasp the extensive breadth of political thought and forms of political expression in Cameroon, it is important to examine the myriad ways through which Cameroonians express their political views, overtly and covertly (cf. Mbembe 1997, 2000, 2001; Monga 1997, Nyamnjoh 1999a). One of these ways is found in the realm of music. This chapter examines music's pervasive role in the socio-political landscape of Cameroon. We attempt to put music in historical perspective with changing political regimes and rhetoric. Under President Paul Biya, Bikutsi (a genre of music from his Beti ethnic group) is shown to have rivalled Makossa, which flourished in the public media, official festivities, bars and dance floors under Ahmadou Ahidjo. Given the dominance of the Beti elite in the state bureaucracy and the state-owned electronic media, i.e., *Cameroon Radio Television* (CRTV), it became obvious why Bikutsi tended to praise Paul Biya and his entourage as representing the interests and aspirations of the entire Beti ethnic group. However, with dwindling economic and political fortunes in the late 1980s and early 1990s, criticism and protest began to emerge as evidenced in some of the Bikutsi songs produced by rural dwellers, whose benefits from the regime were always more imagined than real (cf. Onguene Essono 1996).

This was the period when civil society witnessed a remarkable resurgence through the "anger" and efforts of students, journalists, cartoonists, hawkers, taxi drivers, musicians and others searching for space to articulate their rights and against the might of the state (cf. Monga 1992, 1995, 1996, 1997; Takougang and Kriger 1998). During this period Lapiro, a Douala-based Makossa singer distinguished himself as the foremost critic of the Biya regime through his brand of Makossa (cf. Modo Asse 1995:127–130). It is against this background that Lapiro, among others, is examined at length as a case study of protest music in Cameroon. His involvement in civil society issues further determined the ambivalence of his relationship with the Biya government. Matters became worse when he fell out with his fans and colleagues over accusations of bribery and treachery. By putting Lapiro into focus, we demonstrate that as much as music plays the role of tranquilizer within situations of economic anxiety and violence, it is also a vehicle for the expression of felt injustices and related problems. Furthermore, Lapiro's music and socio-political experiences as an activist offer a window through which to appreciate the articulation of Cameroon's attempts at democratization.

A BRIEF HISTORY OF CAMEROONIAN MUSIC

The development of popular music in Cameroon dates back to colonial times and is closely associated with urbanization and the need for entertainment by the Cameroonian city dwellers in Douala and Yaoundé. Although lured by the city and its promises of modernity, Cameroonians in the cities did not feel that this should be achieved at the expense of the cultural forms of entertainment they were accustomed to. This included indigenous music from the diverse ethnic and cultural regions of colonial Cameroon that had fed migrants to the cities. Attractive though it was, European music was not often available or affordable or desirable in popular entertainment spaces such as bars in the African sections of the cities. Already harnessed or modernized familiar forms, such as Congolese rumba, Cuban salsa and highlife music from Nigeria and Ghana, proved ready and popular substitutes. But indigenous Cameroonian music was sorely missed, and bar owners began exploring ways of keeping their customers and attracting others by bringing music from their home villages into the bars. Makossa and Bikutsi, the respective music forms of the indigenous Douala and Yaoundé (Sawa and Beti) populations, became the first to be invited into the bars by Cameroonians thirsty for local cultural entertainment in the 1940s and 1950s.

Douala's strategic position as a seaport and Cameroon's largest commercial center gave Makossa an early lead. The fact that this brand of music was more easily electrifiable was an added advantage to its rapid development and modernization. Its gentle, bourgeois, cosmopolitan and adaptable rhythms and dance styles made Makossa the perfect music for urban Cameroon at a time when expectations of modernity were highest. That some of the pioneer Makossa musicians migrated to France gave Makossa an early opportunity to export itself, and to influence and be influenced by music from elsewhere. Among these was Manu Dibango. Born in 1933 in Douala, Manu Dibango was sent by his parents to study in France when he was only 15 years old. In France he met Francis Bebey with whom he formed a band and began to experiment with different modern instruments, such as the piano and the saxophone. Manu later migrated to Brussels where his music career began to blossom. In the early 1970s, Manu Dibango brought international recognition to Makossa with his album "Soul Makossa." This was followed by other releases celebrating Makossa, including his 1994 "Wakafrika" album done in collaboration with some of the leading superstars of African music.

Manu Dibango has remained an inspiration to younger musicians in Cameroon, and especially to the new and more innovative generation of Makossa musicians. That Makossa has blossomed can be seen from the sheer number of musicians identified with it. Nkotti Francois, Toto Guillaume, Eboa Lotin, Charlotte Mbango, Ekambi Brilliant, Johnny Tezano, Manulo, Guy Lobe, Guy Manu, Douleur, Ben Decca, Grace Decca, Moni Bile, Hoigen Ekwalla, Prince Ndedi Eyango, Dina Bell, Lapiro de Mbanga, Nguea Laroute, Tom Yom, Kotto Bass, Petit Pays and Longue Longue have all benefited from and enhanced the popularity of Makossa in Cameroon, Africa and the world. The strength of all these artists has been ties with the West, France in particular, that have yielded better production and technical quality and greater international exposure for their music. Such cosmopolitan connections have also exposed Makossa to influences by other music forms such as Zouk from the French Caribbean, Soukous, Kwasakwasa and Ndombolo from the Democratic Republic of Congo, disco from Europe and North America, and Salsa from Latin America. In Cameroon, Makossa has served in all capacities, proving to be an indispensable ingredient socially and even politically.

If Makossa started as the music of Douala and assumed a nationwide appeal, nowhere has it faced stiffer internal competition than in Yaoundé, especially after the coming to power in 1982 of President Paul Biya. Bikutsi, the music of the Beti, has risen to rival Makossa nationally and internationally. In colonial Yaoundé, where the bar had "come to serve as a weekend hangout, often catering to various ethnic groups and offering a taste of home for the ex-villagers," bar owners, "hoping to cash in on the profitable alcohol trade," encouraged Bikutsi musicians to form orchestras. One such orchestra that became quite popular was the Richard Band de Zoetele, but it soon faced difficulties electrifying the sound of the balafon to suit new technologies and the tastes of the times. This hurdle was later overcome by Messi Me Nkonda Martin, who shifted from balafons to electric guitars and keyboards, earning himself the status of "father of modern Bikutsi music." His band, Los Camaroes, became "a landmark in Bitkutsi evolution because the traditional role of the music remained while the instruments which expressed them were changed." Traditionally, Bikutsi, like other indigenous music in Cameroon, has distinguished itself by focusing on social issues such as commentary, frustrations, sex and relationships, and the private lives of prominent individuals (cf. Fuller H & C 1997).

Among the earliest and most resilient Bikutsi musicians is veteran singer Anne-Marie Nzie, whose first recording dates back to the 1940s. Her vocal excellence and popularization of Bikutsi earned her the title "Queen Mother" of Cameroonian music, and brought her to the attention of the post-colonial political leaders, including Presidents Ahidjo and Biya. Equally popular nationally and internationally, especially since the failed coup d'état against Paul Biya in1984, have been groups such as Les Veterans, Les Têtes Brulées, Mbarga Soukous, Mekongo President, Otheo, Titans de Sangmelima, Ange Ebogo Emerent, Seba George, Elanga Maurice, Nkondo Si Tony and Jimmy Mvondo Mvelé. With the artistic and technical assistance of Jean-Marie Ahanda, Les Têtes Brulées in particular, became a household name by 1987, with their "New Form" Bikutsi that was more creative, exciting, profound and innovative.

Since 1982, when Biya became president, the prominence of Bikutsi has improved remarkably. Not only have Biya's governments been dominated by ministers and collaborators from his Beti ethnic group (cf. Takougang and Krieger 1998), they have consistently paid special attention to the promotion of Bikutsi and other cultural products from his home area, notwithstanding official rhetoric on balanced regional development and national integration. The advent of national television in 1985 with a Beti as the general manager brought Bikutsi to the living rooms of viewers even in regions originally dominated by Makossa and other music forms, and inspired an unprecedented craving for stardom among budding Beti musicians of all generations. The fact that the management of CRTV has remained firmly in Beti hands since the advent of television in 1985 has meant more than 20 years of privileged attention for Bikutsi on national radio and television.

Bikutsi has defined itself principally in opposition to other music forms, Makossa in particular. Promoters of Bikutsi music started by criticizing the dominance enjoyed by Makossa since independence, arguing that the time had come for a Cameroonian music that was vigorous, cultural and modern. They were critical of the tendency to devalue or trivialize Bikutsi as a "primitive," "erotic," "sexually suggestive" music that galvanized the "forest savages" to pound the ground with their feet and shake their bodies in frenzy as if in a trance. Some Bikutsi advocates argued the contrary: far from celebrating savagery and promiscuity, Bikutsi, especially in its new "accelerated, savage, and brutal" form, was a very necessary therapy to the urban and rural poor trapped in misery and threatened by death. As demonstrated by the popularity of a new Bikutsi movement since 1993 known as *Pédale*, once a moving Bikutsi piece is played in popular bars around Yaoundé, "dancers crush together, shaking in frenzied trances on the square dance floor, expressions of physical and drunken pleasure plastering the face. It's the accelerated beat that does it, and as each song progresses, the realties and frustrations of the past week fade deeper and deeper into oblivion. *Pédale* offers a way in which to escape from *la crise economique* no other art form has previously offered Cameroonians. [It is] a revolutionary message by the people against the economic and social situations that they must face during the week." But as someone as shrewdly remarked, "one can pedal away the weekend and forget that during the week the children are needy." All the same, it is an investment in hope that the end to their sufferings is near. (Fuller H & C, 1997).

The result of the strategic effort to revalorize Bikutsi has been a noted insensitivity by the Beti in government towards cultural recognition and representation for the music of other ethnic areas in Cameroon. Bikutsi musicians and bands have dominated the airwaves and official cultural delegations to represent Cameroon abroad, or to cheer the Indomitable Lions of football in their various international exploits. The national and international popularity that Makossa had enjoyed under President Ahidjo was seriously and continues to be challenged by Bikutsi produced at home and in France with the financial and political blessings of President Biya and his Beti entourage in power. And the arrogance and sense of achievement that once characterized Makossa musicians have shifted to Bikutsi bands and singers. It is similar to the arrogance of being in power, which has been noted by various scholars on Biya's regime and the role of the Beti elite therein.

We are not arguing that only Bikutsi artists have benefited from the introduction of national television, but that there has been a deliberate political effort over the past 20 years to favor and privilege Bikutsi over music from other ethnic regions of Cameroon. Coming to power for Biya in 1982 meant power as well for the Beti as a cultural community, and for Bikutsi, as a symbol and medium of Beti culture, to be beamed to Cameroonians and the rest of the world by the Beti-controlled national television and radio. Thus, although the following assessment was true of all music in Cameroon, it was particularly true of Bikutsi: "Television introduced a new medium over which artists could express themselves and their music, and if they were creative enough, even forge an image and hence a nationwide identity for their group. Overnight, television shows such as Elvis Kemayo's Tele-Podium were to air, broadcasting to a virgin public music videos that enhanced the marketability of musicians as audiovisual performers and entertainers (cf. Fuller H & C 1997).

Thus, although Cameroon has a rich variety of folk music from the different ethnic groups and regions, some of this music—Makossa and Bikutsi in particular—has been popularized better than others. However, music from other ethnic groups has developed as well, although none has quite achieved the same prominence as Makossa and Bikutsi. Assiko and Ambasse Bey of the Bassa ethnic group has attained prominence, thanks to the efforts of musicians such as Salle John and Petit Papa. Various types of music from the Bamiléké area have been popularized over the years by different artists: Mangambeu by Tchana Pierre and Pierre Didy Tchacounté; Makassi by Sam Fan Thomas, especially through his 1984 album titled "African Typic collection;" Bendskin by Talla André Marie. The Arab, Foulbé and Kirdi provinces of northern Cameroon have produced a few stars, such as Ali Baba, but little to compare with the above. From the southwest has sprung Makossa type music by Sammy Macfany and others, and the East has been represented by Eko Rousvelt who did an album on the music of the pigmies—*gros nez.*

In general, although Cameroon has had an impressive list of stars with proven track records since independence, budding musicians find it difficult to make a breakthrough, because few of those who have succeeded have bothered to invest in the industry at home. Success seems to imply going to live in France, and coming home briefly for concerts or on the invitation of the ruling elite to celebrate this or that event. The Bamenda grassfields are arguably the region where there has been the least achievement in producing local pop stars. The reasons are not obvious, but it is clear that grassfielders love their indigenous music heritage.

Gatherings and occasions at home in Cameroon or in the Diaspora are always an excuse for singing, drumming and dancing to grassfield rhythms. Amateur audio and video recordings are easy to come by, and are reproduced infinitely and circulated among grassfielders at home and abroad. Dedicated performers of various dances are not difficult to find in cities were grassfield elites may want to show off or entertain their guests with a bit of "our culture." Not wanting to be totally eclipsed, some elites have attempted to sponsor the production of local grassfields talents, some of whom (Francis Ndom, Prince Afo-AKom, and "Bottle Dance" musicians like Richard Nguti, John Minang, Ni Ken and Depipson) have made it to the national scene with music from their home area. These and other budding talents in the region and elsewhere shop around for sponsors ranging from businesses to NGOs and publicity-seeking elites, through other artists and the national orchestra.[1]

The quest to make it does not exclude prostitution in various forms,[2] and the outcome is not always a forgone conclusion. But few give up too readily, even if this means a form of success limited to performing in bars, market places and private functions like itinerant musicians for very little pay. However limited the financial rewards, the local performers do more than ensure continuity for their home cultures. They often have more space to articulate social criticism than their better-known foreign-based counterparts, and their poverty is in a way a blessing since it compels them to stay within Cameroon instead of migrating to France to celebrate success. Critical music in tune with popular expectations is not limited to the most disfavored regions of the country. Even among the Beti, whose Bikutsi music has been given greater prominence on state television and radio by sheer fact of association with President Paul Biya, not all voices have heaped praise on the regime. Critical Bikutsi songs have arisen among local performers to challenge complacency and support for President Biya, "a son of the soil" who has repeatedly failed to deliver on promises even to his own ethnic kin (Onguene Essono 1996).

MUSIC AND POLITICS: A CLOSER LOOK

Music and politics have had a love-hate relationship in Cameroon even before independence (cf. Modo Asse 1995:127). While politicians have consistently relied on music and musicians to disseminate their ideas, dramatize their popularity and maintain a semblance of legitimate power, they are seldom tolerant of music and musicians indifferent to praise singing or critical of politicians. But how successful politicians have been in domesticating music or making good bedfellows of musicians has varied with governments and the nature of politics.

During the Ahidjo years (1960–1982), especially from 1966 when the politics of one-dimensionalism became the norm, music, like every other aspect of Cameroonian life, was harnessed for purposes of national unity and development. As the national anthem dictated, Cameroon expected all her children, "to give their heart," "serve their land" and "with constancy play their part" in defending her flag "as a symbol of . . . [her] faith and unity." Musicians generally reflected themes in consonance with these goals, with the hope that "one day at last we'll see all achieved" as a nation of liberty, peace and development. Songs were composed on the importance of independence, on Cameroon as a land of unity in diversity, and on Ahidjo as the architect, founding father and wise guide of the nation. Cameroonians were familiar with verses such as "Ahidjo, Ahidjo notre President, Père de la Nation, Ahidjo Toujours Chaud Gars," and on official feast days, schools practically competed among themselves to come up with a winning "patriotic" composition in honor of the President (Modo Asse 1995).

Room was created in the national orchestra and budget for promoting such music, in praise of Ahidjo as "chef d'état" and "chef de caisse."[3] Almost every musician of distinction had compositions in tune with Ahidjo's expectations as the leading politician of the day. Thus, for example, Tala André Marie celebrated "20 years of peace and progress" under Ahidjo, while Manu Dibango hailed his policy of "national unity," and Medzo Me Nsom invited Cameroonians to turn out en masse and vote for Ahidjo (Modo Asse 1995:126). Tchana Pierre, Francis Bebey, Eboa Lottin and Anne-Marie Nzie are other examples of leading musicians who have participated either by volution or as commissioned musicians in bringing their art to serve their country by singing the praises of President Ahidjo and or his achievements. Talla André Marie and Manu Dibango's music in praise of Ahidjo was used as signature tunes for news, current affairs, sports and other leading programs on national radio. The president's pervasive presence was not only evident in national politics, but also in music and the different uses to which it was put.

In other words, few could reflect, relax, dance to or enjoy music without reflecting, relaxing, dancing or enjoying with President Ahidjo. Music brought him home even to those who would have wanted him kept at bay, and showing even marginal appreciation for praise music in his honor was in a way accommodating Ahidjo. Any criticism had to be very subtle and deep in metaphor to avoid the risk of repression for the artist concerned, as few could dare to openly question established authority. In Bikutsi circles for example, Ahidjo was generally known as "le pasteur de la-bas" (Onguene Essono 1996:60). Even then, some still fell victim when the ambiguity of their compositions was interpreted by officialdom as a veiled attack on the President. A case in point was Messi Martin's song, "Amu Dze" (Why?), on suspicion that he was reproaching President Ahidjo of having snatched someone else's wife, even though the song had not mentioned Ahidjo in name (Modo Asse 1995:127).

Not only mass produced or popular music was expected to support the government's development initiatives though praise songs. Folk music in remote villages was just as liable to co-optation by politicians and civil servants seeking attention to their home regions through compositions in honor of the government and Ahidjo as "founding father of the nation." Ahidjo's politics of regional balance also applied to music, and this meant creating space, in no matter how marginal a form, for music and musicians from the different cultural regions in the national orchestra and/or on national radio. Politicians and civil servants made regular visits to their home villages armed with recording devices and instigating the local populations to acknowledge the development opportunities brought to their communities by the President through their elite. Back at the regional and national capitals, the folk music collected was fed into radio for wider dissemination, and how regularly it featured depended, among other things, on how appreciated it was by the men and women in power. In principle, radio was expected to feature mainly indigenous music in its programs and entertainment packages, and music has regularly dominated the airwaves since independence. In the days when radio was the only electronic medium, programs with a focus on Cameroonian music included "Le Club des Noctambules," "Magie du Chant Noir" by Jean-Paul Nanga, "Melodie et Symphonies du Cameroun" by Michel Essang, "Big Music" by Anne-Marthe Mvoto, "Dash Show" by Njomo Kevin, and various variety and light entertainment programs on national and provincial radio stations. When television was introduced in 1985, programs featuring budding and established musicians and bands became very popular. These included such programs as "Tele Podium" presented by Elvis Kemayo, a popular musician, and "Tam Tam Weekend," presented among others, by musicians such as Rose Epie and Folley Dilan (cf. Nyamnjoh 1989, chapter 8).

If poverty and fear of state repression made most musicians literally play along, riches and a certain degree of independence did not always come with a critical distance from the government and politicians. Migrating to France, where musicians hoped to strike it rich, did not necessarily imply a severing of links with the patron state. In certain cases more financial success and artistic prominence only led to greater recognition and co-optation by the state. It meant, for example, that one had graduated to the club of an elite few to be flown in for anniversary or national day celebrations to perform for the president and his guests, songs specially composed to suit the occasion. Such recognition and attention accorded established musicians by the state, it must be admitted, was too tempting to be resisted, especially in a society where a career in music was generally looked down upon, and musicians treated as people who had failed to be successful by more respectable means. Such recognition or co-optation was added evidence that elusive success and status had come at last, and usually served as an opportunity for musicians to challenge friends and relatives who had branded them "social failures" simply because they had opted to play music instead of going for more socially acceptable careers in medicine, law, politics, academe, etc.

It is therefore not surprising that under Ahidjo two types of lyrics dominated popular music in Cameroon: pro-establishment political songs and music on social virtues (love, honesty, etc.) and social ills (jealousy, corruption, prostitution, etc.). Politically critical music was rare, and when available, was usually very subtle in its criticism, using understatement, irony, double entendre, Pidgin English, or a mixture of broken French and Pidgin English to escape the administrative axe of the censor who targeted all critical voices in society. Repression was the order of the day, and one of the effects was for musicians and others to yield to a narrow idea of politics common at the time: "la politique aux politiciens," and to reproduce official propaganda either by conviction or as flattery. Others found comfort in defending foreign causes, such as the plight of Nelson Mandela in prison (cf. Sam Fan Thomas), anti-colonial struggles in Namibia and Mozambique, and the exploitation of Africa by France and the West.

Ahidjo resigned as president of Cameroon in November 1982, and was succeeded by Paul Biya, who promised a "New Deal" government of political "liberalization," "rigor" in the management of state affairs, and "moralization" of the civil service, politics and society. The rhetoric articulated a determined break with an autocratic past, and a *glasnost* that would bring about a democratic Cameroon. Most Cameroonian musicians bought into the rhetoric and euphoria of Biya's early years as president, and composed songs to celebrate his new deal government.

Anne-Marie Nzie composed and dedicated "Liberté" to Paul Biya, and his Cameroon People's Democratic Movement (CPDM), and when John Fru Ndi and his Social Democratic Front (SDF) attempted to use the song for his presidential campaign in October 1992, she was "vehemently opposed" to the idea (Modo Asse 1995:126). Archangelo de Moneko's "Renouveau National de Paul Biya" replaced Manu Dibango and Talla André Marie's compositions as signature tunes on national radio and television, and soon became just as popular as the tunes it had replaced. The song was worded as follows (cf. Modo Asse 1995:125):

> Paul BIYA nous te disons
> Nous fiers militants du RDPC,
> Tu es l'homme de la dynamique nouvelle
> Par la volonte de Dieu et la confiance de la nation,
> Jamais, Jamais, tu ne failliras.
> Va de l'avant, Paul BIYA, va de l'avant
> Le Peuple camerounais te dit Paul BIYA,
> Va de l'avant Paul BIYA, va de l'avant
> Nous soutenons ton action de foi et d'unité.

It seemed as though a new deal government needed a new deal music to celebrate the end of an era and mark the beginning of another. Bikutsi, a rigorous music with a rigorous dance style that had lived under the shadow of Makossa since independence, seemed the perfect match for a government that promised a clean sweep of the northern Cameroonian hegemonic alliance that had kept Ahidjo in power for over 22 years. Bikutsi musicians mushroomed to thrill people in bars and nightclubs with songs of welcome to the new political landscape that should mark as well the end of marginalization and unfair competition for Bikutsi and the Betis. George Seba sang "Renouveau National" that also made it the signature tune of radio news at one point. Like his predecessor, Paul Biya also became "Notre President, Père de la Nation, Paul Biya Toujours Chaud gars" (Modo Asse 1995:124–126). He was even "God's chosen messenger" who deserved "respect and veneration" ["Papa Paul, assume ta tâche, c'est Dieu lui-même qui te l'a confiée"]. The Beti people wished him well with his mission, assuring him their support ["Continue ta mission, nous sommes avec toi"] (cf. Onguene Essono 1996:54–55).

As noted earlier, the fact that Bikutsi has known its heydays under Biya's presidency is no accident. There has been connivance and complicity between the two, which does not imply that the state has directly funded the production of Bikutsi, nor does it imply that relations between government and Bikutsi musicians have always been harmonious. The general attitude of tolerance and heightened expectations by the Beti people toward Paul Biya as their kinsman in power meant a mobilization of cultural resources, talent and creativity in his support, so that state power and resources could stay under their control as an ethnic group for as long as possible. The government might or might not have funded the production of Bikutsi directly, but the fact that it created an environment for musicians and their promoters to think that investing in Bikutsi was economically and politically worthwhile was support enough. With Biya's coming to power in 1982, Bikutsi musicians also benefited from the ready availability of government jobs and business opportunities for the Beti elite.

Biya's excessively narrow focus on his ethnic community disillusioned most other Cameroonians shortly after the euphoria of his first few months in power. Soon critical songs began to filter through, especially in the Makossa music genre, questioning the repression and hardship that had come in place of the promises of freedom and prosperity made by Biya and his new deal government. Makossa artists joined critical sections of the increasingly disillusioned public to ridicule the official rhetoric of rigor and moralization. Rigor was corrupted by different musicians in different ways: to Uta Bella, it had became a slogan for mobilizing people towards political vengeance, and for Ngalle Jojo, Cameroonians had to condemn with rigor the thieves that masqueraded as leaders: "à bas les voleurs, vive la rigueur" (down with thieves, long live rigour). Everywhere, rigor took on a very negative and cynical connotation: the poor suffered and drank their beer with rigor, while the rich enjoyed their stolen wealth with rigor. Betis were said to play, dance Bikutsi, devastate the national economy and feast on the sweat of fellow Cameroonians with rigor (cf. Mono Ndjana 1997a:13–21). It was a sign that rigor as intended by Biya had failed to materialize. Even the tune for introducing radio and television news, was corrupted by cynical Cameroonians from: "Va de l'avant Paul Biya, va de l'avant. Nous soutenons ton action de foi et d'unité," to "Mange ta part Paul Biya, mange ta part, et laisse les Camerounais tranquille" (Eat your share Paul Biya, eat your share, and leave Cameroonians in peace).

Even for the Beti masses, the collective celebration of power and expectations of abundance lasted only until 1987 when, overnight, the new deal government announced that the country was under a severe economic crisis. To non-Betis, this did not come as a surprise, since Biya and the elite few of his ethnic kin had devastated Cameroon with the impunity of white ants. A structural adjustment program was adopted, the stiff conditionalities of which dictated a freeze in the mass employment policies that had favored the elite Beti to the detriment of Cameroonians from other ethnic groups. As the situation worsened, salaries of civil servants were slashed significantly, followed by a 50% devaluation of the CFA franc in 1994. As the flow of jobs, opportunities, largesse and resources that had made it possible for the Betis as a group to throw their weight behind the illusion of ethnic power dried up, so too did the rigor of Bikutsi and its celebratory songs and dances (cf. Onguene Essono 1996). Bikutsi artists started raising eye brows through an upsurge of questioning songs, with some like Sala Bekono, even going as far as to insinuate that President Biya had forced a bad death upon his own wife Jeanne-Irene, who had died with her "eyes open" ("Mis Meyo"), symbolizing a troubled conscience and unsettled debts to the living (Modo Asse 1995:127). The moral decadence and corruption in the regime became the center of attacks, as more vibrant versions of Bikutsi—*Pédale* type referred to above—sprung up as a coping strategy (or musical therapy) for victims of the regime, its false promises and the economic crises its lack of "rigor" and "moralization" in public management had precipitated.

The first sustained use of Bikutsi to criticize President Biya for failed promises came from traditional musicians in rural areas, who, despite years of repression, have largely maintained their freedom of expression. Bikutsi to them has maintained all its dimensions, and they have used it to sing praises and celebrate, admonish and attack, ridicule and humiliate, nurture and educate, challenge and disperse rancor, when each was called for (cf Onguene Essono 1996:52–53). In his study of democracy in song, Onguene Essono (1996) discusses 107 critical Bikutsi songs composed by popular and village musicians, men and women alike, disillusioned by a regime that has promised without fulfilling, and that has capitalized on Beti solidarity and community spirit for the selfish interests of the elite few in power. The tarred roads, electrification and other development initiatives Biya promised his Beti community upon assuming office in 1982, have not been delivered. In return for their support, the president has simply compounded their hardships with his callous indifference to their plight and the bleakness of the future of their children. The songs reject the god-like status President Biya has assumed based on false promises, and the torture that the insensitivities of his regime have imposed even on his own supporters from the same ethnic origin. The disappointment and frustrations are such that the Bikutsi messages addressed to the Head of State and government is no longer enveloped in metaphors, as was the case under President Ahidjo and during colonial times (Onguene Essono1996:60). They are direct and clear and without fear, in the spirit of the democracy that the regime has purportedly brought about. The songs are critical of the economic crisis, denounce surging social injustices and the slow pace of development, and condemn government inaction and complicity in the face of corruption and misappropriation. Biya is even compared unfavorably to his predecessor, President Ahidjo, during whose leadership, money was available, and peasants were at least sure to sell their cash crops, feed themselves and keep their children in school.

Onguene Essono cites a verse in which the women of Nkol-Afeme are asking Paul Biya where he has kept the money of the country for life to become so expensive. Their farm products sell poorly, but the price of meat, salt and other essential consumer items has skyrocketed. Yaoundé has become unbearably expensive, and President Biya must say what he has done with the country's money. Yet another group, *Espoir du Renouveau* (New Deal Hope), is not pleased with the president's indifference to the development of their village: "Papa Paul Biya, why have you abandoned New Deal Hope? It is important that we live a decent life Papa Paul, we need funds." They are suffering, and their crops sell poorly, but they work very hard, and are not happy with the way Papa Paul has abandoned them to themselves. A third group invites the people to meet Paul Biya with pertinent questions and demands; he should have foreseen the economic crises, and has the responsibility "to save them from death or to let them perish" (Onguene Essono 1996:56–57). Schools are without teachers, hospitals without drugs, and harvests have ceased to fetch money, yet the President is insensitive to all this. He must be reminded that it is his duty to bring things back to normal, for "your team is working without output," and some seem to have been born to watch a minute few enjoy the country's resources. It cannot be true, the women of Obala sing, that Paul Biya knows what is going on in his country and decides to sit quiet: "Paul Biya do you know? Out here it hurts, out here things are bad, do you know that Biya Paul?" (Onguene Essono 1996:59). He is not a listening president, he is not informed, and he does not care even for those who have sacrificed so his unproductive New Deal government may keep power in the face of growing opposition, especially from other ethnic groups and regions of the country.

Rightly or wrongly, Paul Biya dismissed the opposition parties of the 1990s as being keener to destroy than to construct the nation, and as irresponsible vandals and illusion peddlers. The *Espoir du Renouveau* appeals to him to demonstrate otherwise: "Vandals cannot build the country, thieves and those who burn down banks are incapable of building the country, those who destroy roads are uninformed of what it takes to build the country, what are you doing, oh Biya, towards building the country? We want a country that is strong, rich and united, unite us for the welfare of our country. Why do you sit by and watch the country destroy itself. Don't you have eyes to see? I am asking this of you, oh Paul Biya" (Onguene Essono 1996:58).

Les Maxtones du Littoral eloquently captures a similar concern with Biya's "callous indifference" to the sufferings, frustrations, expectations and humanity of ordinary people, in a popular tune pregnant with metaphor. Titled "*Doleibe (10f) la suite de l'affaire*," the tune tells the story of a woman who becomes pregnant from a one-night stand with an irresponsible shoemaker she literally has to squeeze to take care of the pregnancy. This is a most unusual pregnancy that lasts 24 months, but what is even more shocking is the attitude of the doctor, who, as an expert, is supposed to reassure the woman with words of encouragement, concern and solutions. But the doctor does none of that. Not only is he delinquent toward his earthly patient, his callous indifference would devastate even the patience of saints. Each time the pregnant woman comes rushing with concern and worry for her life and baby, the doctor says: "*Il faut attendre. Tu es pressé pour aller où?*"(You must be patient. Why are you in such a hurry?). At delivery the child is born already aged, bald headed, bearded, jigger toed, and deformed, with little to warrant a celebration. In sum, he is a freak, not a child. That Cameroonians saw the song as a thinly disguised allusion to their seemingly infinite wait for democracy under an indifferent President Biya was demonstrated not only by its popularity but also by how they drew from it to describe their daily travails. The refrain "*on attend l'enfant, l'enfant ne vient pas*" has been used to describe Cameroon as "*le pays de on attend*" (Cameroon is a country of 'wait and see'). The doctor's admonishment in the form of a question—"*tu es pressé pour aller où?*" (Why are you in such a hurry?)—is a metaphor for the slow pace of political reform. Democracy will come when it will come, not through the agitation of impatient vandals and peddlers in illusion, but through the doctor who is impatient with impatience (cf. Nyamnjoh 1999b).

Elsewhere, "pregnant mothers" were equally impatient with the long wait and labor for democracy. Criticism of the Biya regime did not come from fellow Beti members only (who arguably felt betrayed most by their own *son of the soil*) but soon began to emerge from Douala, the economic capital increasingly without an economy to speak of. The bite of the economic crises since 1987 provided sufficient inspiration to several Makossa players to take their place in the political marketplace of Cameroonian music. Foremost among them was Lapiro de Mbanga, a young and vibrant singer who apparently had lived in Bamenda where he had earned a living as a hawker and taxi assistant. Lapiro epitomizes the strengths and controversies surrounding a protest musician. His music and experiences as a member of civil society inform us of the spirit of the democratic transition in Cameroon between 1990 and 1992, specifically that it was an era plagued by one-dimensionalism both from the emerging opposition and the ruling government. However, his genre of music and his activism as a human rights advocate has inspired several new singers, including Longue Longue, whose *Ayo . . . Africa*, has made waves with its biting criticism of misery, exploitation and dependency in Africa. Lapiro himself has remained steadfast, devoting his career to singing out the daily realities of pain and suffering, rejection and exclusion faced by a multitude of Cameroonians. He deserves to be examined at length.

THE CASE OF LAPIRO DE MBANGA[4]

"I decided to take up music as my weapon for battle. I wanted to show that though there is injustice everywhere, Cameroon's experience is particularly discouraging. For this reason, I took up my guitar to call the authorities to order."[5]

Between 1987 and 1991, Lapiro rose to celebrity and made a name in the Cameroonian musical scene. He was highly appreciated by "common people" for the use of pidgin[6] in his songs but loathed by pro-government politicians for his attack on President Paul Biya. His emergence was timely as this was against a background of a failing economy and growing social disillusionment, which he quickly and tactfully incorporated into his songs. With the worsening of the economic crisis, unemployment rates rose from 30 percent to 35 percent in 1987, and to between 40 percent 45 percent in 1988[7] thereby exacerbating an already desperate situation.

Seen not only as a musician by some, but also as an incarnation of the hawker population,[8] Lapiro released his first of so-called "subversive" albums which was thematic of the burning socio-economic and political issues of the time. Entitled *Kob Nye*[9] Lapiro made use of the popular despair and betrayed hopes of hawkers and many a Cameroonian who suffered the bite of the economic crisis. He eventually became an opposition reference chiefly among the youth and even with opposition leaders such as John Fru Ndi of the Social Democratic Front (the main opposition party in Cameroon). His popularity further increased because of his out-spokenness during the Monga/Njawe trials, which threw Douala into great tension (leading to an anthropology of anger as termed by Monga himself) between sympathizers of the ruling party and civil society. Monga and Njawe were accused and charged with treason for subversion and contempt on the president's person.

The content of Lapiro's songs spoke of the lamentable experience of hunger, the excess of suffering (*souffrance*) and the need for freedom of expression in Cameroon. Most of the lyrics invoked state authorities to remember the *petit peuple*, or rather "the forgotten," each time they dined and wined and smoked cigars.[10] Lapiro accused the authorities (without calling names) of having plundered the state almost beyond recovery, rendering mothers (*reme*) and children (*njaka*) emaciated and starved, like those in Ethiopia. To him, the Cameroonian president was a stooge of France without any genuine concern for his people; his only concern was toward his neo-colonial master whom he regularly visited and consulted on issues of State. Little doubt then, Lapiro contended, that they (*the strugglers*) had been advised by the president to go back to rural areas and till the soil for survival. His songs called for open demonstration and pro-test against an establishment that was careless about the plight of the dis-possessed and disillusioned. He frequently referred to the strugglers[11] as his people, his followers, thus affirming himself as their advocate, for life is a vast arena of struggle—the struggle to make ends meet and keep hope alive even in the most desperate of circumstances. Summed up in his words, no condition is permanent—a modest way of giving reins and spurs the disillusioned not to give up.

Having received much approval from the public, Lapiro came up with more songs such as "Surface de Reparation," "No Make Erreur," and "Mimba We."[12] These songs re-echoed concerns previously raised, but were spiced with newer developments in the political landscape. En-dowed with such popularity, Lapiro quickly became an opinion leader and was bestowed the title *Le President des Sauveteurs*.[13] Later he was in-corporated as one of the six vice-presidents of the Human Rights Organi-zation of Cameroon (HROC),[14] a young NGO consigned with the task of tracking human rights abuses within the country and invoking state au-thorities to respect the rule of law.

Lapiro also became a member of the Coordination, created in October of 1990 to lead the "Biya Must Go" campaign and demand a Sovereign

National Conference (SNC).[15] He stayed at the forefront of civil society politics in Cameroon despite the banning of his music on CRTV—the state's official radio and television channel. He pleaded the case of several university students who had been arrested by the police for participating in strike actions in their solidarity with the demands of the Coordination.[16] Later in the struggle, a rift emerged between Lapiro and his colleagues over the issue of the Ghost Town.[17] While others argued that the Ghost Town Operation was the best and only means to oust President Biya, Lapiro maintained that such an operation would rather worsen the state of an already suffering and devastated people. He argued that if his colleagues insisted on spearheading the cause of the Ghost Town, he would unavoidably isolate himself from such a method of struggle. Eventually, he went to CRTV (Television) and denounced the instigators of the Ghost Town operations. This invited suspicions from his colleagues, as well as prompting unprecedented brutality by "sauveteurs" on his property, who saw his action and opinion as an outright sign of unpardonable treachery. Sauveteurs suddenly became violent against their so-called advocate as they looted and burned Lapiro's house and some vehicles as he escaped to Yaoundé under cover of the police.[18] They argued further that Lapiro had betrayed them by accepting a bribe of 22 million CFA francs to change camp.[19]

Lapiro thus became the center of controversy. On the one hand, he was accused of having betrayed the cause he fought so valiantly for, by accepting a bribe from the government. On the other hand, others defended him as having been a victim of the people's intolerance. In the former camp, the bone of contention was: how come Lapiro could not see in the same light as the other members of the Coordination? It is against this background precisely that we can explore the tensions and cracks in Cameroon's democratic opposition. This can be attained by examining in detail the tensions that characterized Lapiro's fallout with the Coordination and the people he purported to represent.

Firstly, he is accused of having subscribed to the "politics of the belly" or what some have recently referred to as "bellitics."[20] Their "evidence" is that Lapiro met with Jean Forchive (Delegate for National Security) on two occasions during which, it is claimed, he received the sum of 22 million CFA francs. Further, when enraged members of civil society stormed and burned Lapiro's compound and some cars, he escaped to Yaoundé under cover of several policemen sent by Mr. Forchive himself. This protection, his enemies argued, was unusual of the same policemen who had brutalized Lapiro a week before because of their suspicion that he had collaborated with vandals (*casseurs*) in Douala.[21] Others pointed out that Lapiro's colleagues in the opposition overtly dissociated themselves from his actions and saw that as ample proof of his betrayal.[22] Lastly, it was contended that, despite the banning of Lapiro's music on CRTV, which by implication meant that he was not a friend of the government and CRTV most especially, he was seen on the same medium denouncing the Ghost Town Operations as ruinous to the national economy. To crown it, a colleague of Lapiro was said to have revealed that the musician intended to hold a cross-country concert, free of charge, sponsored by some government officials.

Despite the accusations, Lapiro and a collection of supporters argued that he was never bought over to the government's side. Rather, they argued that he had been victimized by a band of intolerant enemies who excelled in undertaking smear campaigns against an innocent musician. In addition, Lapiro denied that he ever received a franc from any one and were he to receive any, he added with bravado, it would not be a meager sum of 22 million CFA francs but at least 50 million to share with his large following. He refuted the accusation of practicing "bellitics" and fired back at the Ghost Town initiators as money-minded extortionists.[23] By selling about 2 million red cards at the price of 100 CFA francs each, they should have reaped about 200 million CFA francs without any effort or exertion. (At the height of the civil disobedience campaign Ghost Town activists took to selling red cards to people they thought unsympathetic to their cause. By buying a red card, one was spared the potential trouble of seeing one's house or property burned down by angry rioters. Yellow cards were also available but sold at a much cheaper price. Apparently, this activity seemed to have yielded a fortune to those who managed the Ghost Town operations.)

Lapiro also contended that were he to be bought over to the government's side, he would have accepted many attempts as far back as 1987 when he started the fight for social justice and political change in Cameroon. He therefore wondered how it was that after persevering for so long, he would all of a sudden betray his "people" who looked up to him as an advocate of social justice in Cameroon.[24] He admitted to have had two meetings with Mr. Forchive as his detractors were fast to point out. However, his mission on the first visit was to plead the cause of some students in detention and on the second to defend hawkers in Douala, who were under constant persecution by the police.[25] It was in this regard that Lapiro defined himself as a "political contestataire" and human rights activist stressing the right to voice his opinion on issues that concerned civil society especially those of the hawkers whom he represented. For him, the Ghost Town operation was a strategy designed by some people to exploit, extort and manipulate innocent Cameroonians.[26]

Lapiro's case demonstrates most vividly the trials and tribulations of *l'artiste engagé* in Cameroon. As previously noted, music and politics have had a love-hate relationship in Cameroon. Lapiro's vociferous criticism of Paul Biya and his government apparently led to the banning of his music on CRTV. Though banning his music made him even more popular with the opposition and his supporters (an indication that his words had struck the right cords), the latter group failed to appreciate the fact that the artist too was entitled to his own opinion. The artist's predicament is thus expressed on two fronts: as spokesperson for civil society and as an enemy of the ruling elite. While the ruling elite seeks to eliminate or co-opt (transform the popular artist) into a praise-singer, his supporters are more than desperate to see him submit to their whims and caprices, even when this is contrary to the very democratic spirit they claim to espouse. What then are the implications of this trend for civil society in Cameroon? Nyamnjoh has discussed these implications in general elsewhere (1999b).

In the particular case of Lapiro, however, we observe that his engagement with civil society—students, hawkers, taxi men, human rights activists and even politicians—is fraught with a huge degree of ambivalence, uncertainties and loopholes. The alleged bribery, as a case in point, was based more on rumor than any trustworthy evidence. But simultaneously, his sudden romance with the government, by going to CRTV for example, or meeting with the director of national security, Mr. Forchive, opened up space for suspicion even to the most astute of skeptics. It is in this light that we need to situate Nyamnjoh's (1997) contention that rumor or *radio trottoir* should be taken into account as a legitimate medium of communication within contexts where access to official information is scarce as was the case in Cameroon between 1990–92.

Moreover, the early 1990s in Cameroon were characterized by recycled one-party fanatics or self-proclaimed democrats, who claimed to be the true champions of democracy (even in an advanced form unbeknownst to the West—*la démocratie avancée*), yet unable to stand or dance to music articulating difference or opinion unpalatable to their frozen positions. It was not unusual for both ruling party elite and opposition stalwarts to invoke democratic precepts only when things pointed to their favor and wonder even aloud "how come the others could not see things their way." This was a vicious reign of intolerance, violence caught up within the liminal field of dictatorship and liberalization. But after several years of artistic/political hibernation while the political elite and Cameroonians hopefully matured, Lapiro has made an influential comeback and this time, he has spared no side. Both the CPDM ruling party (*club de toiteurs*) and the opposition (epitomized by John Fru Ndi of the SDF) have come under fire and, so far, it appears they have accepted his claims to independent observation and expression. With hindsight, it is possible to argue that the *state in waiting* (opposition) could stand Lapiro's criticisms only when he was critical of the *state in action* (the ruling CPDM)—thus failing to recognize that despite all, the artist had rights to independent or alternative expression. This has meant victory not for the CPDM or SDF but for democratic progress, for difference and plurality constitute the stuff of any democratic system (as opposed to monolithic rule).

Lapiro's experience does not only lead to our appreciation of the refractory nature of civil society, but also shows that his music contributed substantially to Cameroon's repertoire of political grammar. In the main, these contributions could be found in the use of certain expressions, words, clichés or phrases that constitute common references to political activities. For example, words like *sauveteur, petit peuple* and even lapiro itself have become common currency. Lapiro, as part of Cameroon's political grammar, was employed to mean treachery, betrayal or being manipulated. To refer to someone as Lapiro was a harsh way of labeling the person traitor. Bole Butake, a famous playwright and university professor, is noted to have published an articled entitled "Refused to be Lapiroed" in which he played with the use of Lapiro as both traitor and a manipulated subject. Hence, the engaged artist does not only interpret the experience of individuals as the shared experience of the community, which he (she) feels a part of, but also he (she) actively contributes to the deconstruction, (re)construction and transformation of political processes, consciousness and political grammar.

CONCLUSION

We have argued in this chapter that the content of political songs in Cameroon has changed with the fortunes or misfortunes of politics and politicians in high office. Under President Ahidjo, protest music was often masked in ways not so obvious to the ruling elite. However, Biya's *rigorous* plunder of the economy since 1982, ironically followed by timid political liberalization, permitted the proliferation of critical voices from several artists such as comedians, cartoonists and musicians. The case of Lapiro became very conspicuous, given his political activism which he carried into his lyrics. Even Bikutsi, which gained notoriety for praise singing during Biya's first years as head of state, began to see dissenting voices, principally among village musicians in rural areas. Biya's determination to hold on to power for over two decades against a backdrop of sharp economic downturn has fueled disillusionment even amongst his most ardent supporters in the music industry. Urban-based Bikutsi singers are increasingly becoming critical, even as they invite Cameroonians to "pedal away" the crisis while hoping and waiting for recovery. This second baby, shall it be real and human? Not if the doctor is the same and has a say. Meanwhile, music, pregnant with political meaning, is there to keep hope alive in the face of current setbacks.

NOTES

1. John Minang's Album—"Issiah," carries ads for "L&B," "Beneficial Life Insurance" and "PMUC." Prince Afo-Akom obtained sponsorship from World Wildlife Fund thanks to his song "Our Environment," in which WWF is mentioned positively.

2. Some Cameroonian musicians, in order to get by, include in their lyrics names of individuals seeking greater social or political visibility, in exchange for monetary payments.

3. Interviewed after one of his concerts in Bamenda in 1980, Prince Nico Mbarga, in a Freudian slip, referred to Ahidjo as "le chef de caisse," instead of "le chef d'état." But the slip reflected the reality of a presidency that had centralized and personalized everything, including the national treasury and economy, to the point that little initiative was possible outside his overwhelming grip.

4. Lapiro is an acronym for La̲mbo Pi̲erre Ro̲ger. He also had several nicknames among them: Ndinga Man, *le president des sauveteurs*, and Tara. *Cameroon Tribune* No. 4912, Vendredi 24 Juin 1991.

5. Original French version: "J'ai decidé de faire de la musique l'arme de mon combat. J'ai voulu montrer que les injustices existent partout. Mais qu'au Cameroun particulièrement, c'était grave. Pour cela, j'ai pris ma guitare pour interpeller les autorités politiques."

6. Pidgin is the lingua franca in Cameroon. It is a mélange of English, French and indigenous slang. It is important to note the medium of conveying one's political ideas such as Lapiro's appropriation of Pidgin. There is a sense of great appeal to speak to common people in the language they best understand as supported by Fela Kuti of Nigeria whose critical, anti-military government songs were all expressed in Pidgin.

7. USAID/CDSS statistics as cited in Times and Life, July-August 1991, pp. 14–15.

8. *Cameroon Tribune*. No. 1206 of June 2 1991, p. 2.

9. This is a Pidgin expression for "Come and See" but *Nyé* also refers to the repressive forces of state violence who regularly unleashed terror in Douala (Cameroon's economic capital) and other opposition strongholds (Bamenda, for example). One could therefore think that there was an interplay of words here, given the fact that the he makes reference to gendarmes in many of his songs.

10. "You wan damé you mimba we, you wan sulé you mimba we yeh, oh mimba weyehe, tara, oh mimba we." Translated into English, it goes thus; "At table remember us, even when having a cigarette remember us, you who are our patron."

11. *Sauveteurs* include taxi men, truck pushers, hawkers and the unemployed, in other words, those on the margin of subsistence who must scrape by to stay alive.

12. Surface de reparation (Penalty Area), No Make Erreur (Don't be Mistaken), and Mimba We (Remember Us.)

13. President of struggling people or the "Strugglers."

14. Op. cit., p. 2.

15. *Le Quotidien*, Vendredi 29, Samedi 30 et Dimanche 31, pp. 3–13.

16. Op. cit., p. 2.

17. The Ghost Town Operations (*Opérations Villes Mortes*) marked a prolonged period during which there was an overt boycott of economic activities except on Saturdays and Sundays. During this period, people organized protests against the state machinery. Some of those who were said to be members of the CPDM ruling party saw their houses or other properties burned. It was a combination of peaceful opposition and overt confrontation. Yaoundé was more peaceful during the Ghost Town period. Most of the violence and protests took place in Douala (where Lapiro resided), Bamenda and Bafoussam.

18. Op. cit. *Times and Life*, p. 15.

19. Ibid., p. 15.

20. As coined by Barrister Alexander Taku in *The Post.* . . . This is a marriage of the two words belly and politics.

21. Op. cit. *Cameroon Tribune*, p. 3.

22. Op. cit p. 2.

23. Ibid., p.5. Lapiro argued that his accusation was a bid by his enemies to cover up their own practices of extortion. In his words, "Ces opérations ne sont rien d'autre qu'une escroquerie du petit peuple. Car si les organisateurs vendent par exemple 2 millions de 'cartons rouges' au prix unique de 100frs, ils recoltent sans effort la somme de 200 millions de FCFA."

24. Op. cit. *Le Quotidien*, p. 12.

25. Op. cit. *Cameroon Tribune*, p. 3.

26. Op. cit. *Cameroun Tribune*. "Les instigateurs des opérations villes mortes ont pour la plupart au moins quatre congélateurs pleins de viande de boeuf, poissons, poulet . . . au point qu'ils peuvent rester quatre mois sans avoir besoin de se ravitailler. Ces hommes, . . . pensent-ils seulement à la pauvre vielle maman qui doit se lever tous les jours à 4h du matin pour faire des beignet, les vendre et aller ensuite acheter la tomate qu'elle revendra avant d'acheter à manger pour les

siens? Pensent-ils aux pousseurs et autres 'sauveteurs' qui doivent travailler tous
les jours pour survivre?"

BIBLIOGRAPHY

Collectif Changer Le Cameroun, (1990), *Changer le Cameroun: Pourquoi Pas?*
  Edition C3: Yaoundé.

Fuller, H. & C. (1997), "A History of Bikutsi Music in Cameroon,"
  http://www.africasounds.com/history.htm.

Mbembe, A. (1997), "The 'Thing' and Its Double in Cameroonian Cartoons" in:
  Karin Barber (ed.), *Readings in African Popular Culture.* James Currey:
  Oxford. (Pp. 151–163).

——. (2000), *De la Postcolonie: Essai sur l'Imagination Politique dans l'Afrique
  Contemporaine.* Karthala: Paris.

——. (2001), *On the Postcolony*, University of California Press: Berkeley.

Mbock, C. G., (ed.), (1996), *Cameroun: Pluralisme Culturel et Convivialite.* Edition Nouvelle du Sud: Paris.

Modo, A. (1995), "La Chanson dans la Communication Politique au Cameroun,"
  Frequence Sud, No. 13, pp. 121–131.

Monga, C. (1992), *La Recomposition du Marche Politique au Cameroun
  (1991–1992): De la nécessité d'un aménagement du monitoring électoral.*
  Forum Démocratique: Fondation Friedrich-Ebert.

——. (1995), "Civil Society and Democratisation in Francophone Africa," *The
  Journal of Modern African Studies*. 33(3):359–379.

——. (1996), *The Anthropology of Anger: Civil Society and Democracy in Africa.*
  Lynne Rienner: London.

——. (1997), "Cartoons in Cameroon: Anger and Political Derision under
  Monocracy" in: Anyidoho, Kofi (ed.) *The Word Behind Bars and the Paradox of Exile.* Northwestern University Press: Evanston, Illinois. (pp.
  146–169).

Mono Ndjana, H. (1997), *Les Proverbes de Paul Biya*, Edition du Carrefour:
  Yaoundé.

Nyamnjoh, F. (1989), *Broadcasting for Nation-Building in Cameroon: Development and Constraints.* PhD Thesis, Center for Mass Communication Research (CMCR), University of Leicester, UK.

——. (1996), *Mass Media and Democratisation in Cameroon*, Friedrich Ebert
  Stiftung: Yaoundé.

——. (1997), "Political Rumour in Cameroon" in: *Cahier de l'UCA,* no.2, pp.
  93–106.

——. (1999a), "Press Cartoons and Politics in Cameroon" in: *International Journal of Comic Art.* Vol. 1(2):171–190.

——. (1999b), "Cameroon: A Country United by Ethnic Ambition and Difference," in *African Affairs*, Vol. 98(390):101–118.

Onguene, Essono (1996), "La Démocratie en Chanson: Les Bikut-si du Cameroun," *Politique Africaine*, 64, pp. 52–61.
Takougang, J., and M. Krieger (1998), *African State and Society in the 1990s: Cameroon's Political Crossroads*. Westview Press: Boulder.

Bibliography

Abbott, G.C. 1994. *African Review of Money, Finance and Banking*, no. 1–2.

Africa. 1975. August–September, no. 51.

——. 1984. August–September, no. 89.

Africa Report. 1983. "Cameroon: The Politics of Presidential Succession," no. 28.

Anderson, B. 1983. *Imagined Communities*, London: Verso Editions/NLB.

Appadurai, A. 1990. "Disjuncture and Difference in the Global Cultural Economy," *Theory, Culture and Society*, vol. 7.

Appiah, A. 1992. *In My Father's House*, Oxford: Oxford University Press.

Arbena, J. 1996. "Nationalism and Sport in Latin America, 1850–1990: The Paradox of Promoting and Performing 'European' Sports," in J. A. Mangan, ed., *Tribal Identities: Nationalism, Europe, Sport*, London: Frank Cass.

Aristotle. 1948. *Politics*, London and Oxford: Oxford University Press.

Baker, W. and J.A. Mangan. 1987. *Sports in Africa, Essays in Social History*, London, New York: Africana Publishing CO.

Bank of Central African States. 1988. *Annual Report*, June 30.

Barber, K. 1987. "Popular Arts in Africa," *African Studies Review*, vol. 30, no. 3.

Bardet, M. and N. Thellier. 1988. *OX Cargo!*, Paris: Grasset.

Bate, B. 1991. *Requiem far the last Kaiser*, Calabar, Nigeria: Centaur Publishers.

Bayart, J-F. 1977. "The Structure of Political Power," in R. Joseph, ed., *Gaullist Africa: Cameroon Under Ahmadou Ahidjo*, Enugu, Nigeria: Fourth Dimension Press.

——. 1979. *L'état au Cameroun*, Paris: Presse de la Fondation Nationale des Sciences Politiques.

——. 1999. "The Social Capital of the Felonious State," in J-F. Bayart, S. Ellis and B. Hibou, eds., *The Criminalization of the African State*, Bloomington, IN: Indiana University Press.

Bekolo, E. B. 1986. "Retrospective d'une decennie de croissance de l'économie camerounaise," *Revue Camerounaise de Management*, no. 3–4.

Benjamin, J. 1972. *Les Camerounais occidentaux: la minorité dans un état bicommunautaire*, Montreal: Presses de l'Université de Montreal.

Beti, M. 1984. *Main basse sur le Cameroun*, Rouen: Editions peuples noirs.

——. 1987. "Le Cameroun de Paul Biya: autopsie d'un chaos annoncé," *Peuples noirs, peuples africains*, 55, 56, 57 and 58, janvier–août.

Bevir, M. 1999. "Foucault and Critique," *Political Theory*, vol. 27, no.1.

Bob, H. and O. Ntemfac. 1991. *Prison Graduate*, Calabar, Nigeria: APCON Ltd.

Bongadzem, V.N. 1996. *State-Owned Media and Partisan Politics: Political Reporting on Cameroon Television 1995*, Yaoundé, Cameroon.

Bonjour l'Amérique. 1994. 27 juin.

——. 1994. 28 juin.

——. 1994. 2 juillet.

Bory, P. 1968. *Ahmadou Ahidjo, pionnier de l'Afrique moderne*, Monte Carlo, Yaoundé: Bureau Politique de L'Union National Camerounais.

——. "Introduction,"*The Political Philosophy of Ahmadou Ahidjo*, Monte Carlo, Yaoundé: Political Bureau of the Cameroon National Union.

Bourdieu, P. 1990. *Outline of Theory and Practice*, Cambridge: Cambridge University Press.

Bourdieu, P. 1986. *Ihzstinction*, Cambridge, MA: Harvard University Press.

Cahiers Upécistes. 1985. January–March, no. 21.

Callum, M. 1998. "Neopopulism and Corruption: Toward a New Critique of the Elite," *Constellations*, vol. 5, no.1.

Cameroon Information. 1997. March. Yaoundé.

Cameroon News Agency. 1972. May 23. Yaoundé.

Cameroon Radio and Television (CRTV). 1989. April 10. Limbe.

Cameroon Post, various issues.

Cameroon Tribune. 1981. May 10. Yaoundé.

——. 1989. June 23. Yaoundé.

Chaffard, G. 1967. *Les carnets secrets de la décolonisation*, vol. 1, Paris: Calmann-Levy.

Challenge Hebdo. 1993. 4 juin, no. 087.

Chazan, N., R. Mortimer, J. Ravenhill and D. Rothchild.1992. *Politics and Society in Contemporary Africa*, Boulder, CO: Lynne Rienner Publishers.

Clignet R. and M. Stark. 1974. "Modernisation and Football in Cameroun," *Journal of Modern African Studies*, vol. 12, no. 3.

Collectif Changer Le Cameroun. 1990. *Changer le Cameroun: Pourquoi Pas?*, Yaoundé: Edition C3.

Cohen, R. 1978. "Ethnicity: Problem and Focus in Anthropology," *Annual Review of Anthropology*, 7.

Conrad, J. 1989. *Heart of Darkness*, New York: Anchor Books.

Dahl, R. 1989. *Democracy and Its Critiques*, New Haven, CT: Yale University Press.

Day Dawn. 1985. June 11. Limbe.

——. 1985. November 6. Limbe.

de Certeau, M. 1988. *The Practice of Everyday Politics*, Berkeley, CA: University of California Press.

Delancey, M. 1989. *Cameroon: Dependence and Independence*, Boulder, CO: Westview Press.

de Mesquita B. and H. Root, eds. 2002. *Governing for Prosperity*, New Haven, CT: Yale University Press.

Doho, G. 1993. "Théâtre et minorités: le cas du Cameroun," in N. Lyonga, E. Breitinger and B. Butake, eds., *Anglophone Cameroon Writing*, Bayreuth African Studies, 30.

Ekeh, P. 1975. "Colonialism and the Two Publics: A Theoretical Statement," *Comparative Studies in History and Society*, vol. 17, no. 1.

Epie-Ngome, V. 1992. *What God Has Put Asunder,* Yaoundé: Pitcher Books Ltd.

Escobar, A. 1984. "Discourse and Power in Development: Michel Foucault and the Relevance of His Work to the Third World," *Alternatives*, 10, Winter.

Eyinga, A. 1978. *Mandat d'arrêt pour cause d'élections,* Paris: l'Harmattan.

——. 1984. *Introduction à la politique camerounaise.* Paris: l'Harmattan.

——. 1987. "Government by State of Emergency," in R. Joseph, ed., *Gaullist Africa: Cameroon under Ahmadou Ahidjo*, Enugu: Fourth Dimension Press.

Eyinga, A. 2001. "Historique de la Françafrique en 5 dates" (suite), *Le Messager,* bftp://wagne.net/messager/0101/10histoire.httn' p. 3, sourced 3/23.

Fair, L. 1997. "Kickin it: Leisure, Politics and Football in Colonial Zanzibar, 1900s–1950s," *Africa*, 67.

Fako Net.1999. "World Bank, IMF, Biya Create Powderkeg," October 16.

Fardon, R. 1996. "Crossed Destinies: The Entangled Histories of West African Ethnic and National Identities," in L. de la Gorgendière, K. King and S. Vaughan, eds., *Ethnicity in Africa: Roots, Meanings and Implications*, Edinburgh: University of Edinburgh.

Fatton, R. 1987. *The Making of a Liberal Democracy: Senegal's Passive Revolution,* Boulder, CO: Lynne Rienner Publishers.

Feder, G. and D. Feeny. 1991. "Land Tenure and Property Rights: Theory and Implications for Development Policy," *The World Bank Economic Review*, vol. 5, no. 1.

Finance Info. 1998. June 30.

Forbes Global Magazine. 2001. October 1.

Foucault, M. 1979. *Discipline and Punish: The Birth of the Prison,* New York: Vintage Books.

Frost and Sullivan/Political Risk Research.1987. *Cameroon*, Syracuse, New York.

Fuller, H. and C. 2001. "A History of Bikut-si Music in Cameroon," http://www.africasounds.com/history.htm.

Gaillard, P. 1989. *Le Cameroun, Tome 2*, Paris: l'Harmattan.

Génération, August 1994—January 1995, Yaoundé.

Geschiere, P. 1996. "Kinship, Witchcraft and the Moral Economy of Ethnicity: Contrast from Southern and Western Cameroon," in L. de la

Gorgendière, K. King and S. Vaughan, eds., *Ethnicity in Africa: Roots, Meanings and Implications*, Edinburgh: University of Edinburgh.

Gordon, C., ed. 1980. *Power/Knowledge: Selected Interviews and Other Writings*, New York: Pantheon Books.

Gorji-Dinka, F. 1985. *The New Social Order*, Bamenda, Cameroon: Unique Printers.

Gramsci, A. 1978. *Selections from Prison Notebooks*, New York: International Publishers.

Gros, J-G. 1994. *The Privatization of Livestock Services in Cameroun*, Anne Harbor, MI: UMI Dissertation Servives.

———. 1994. "Whither Authoritarianism in Cameroon?," in *The Democratic Challenge in Africa*. Working Paper Series, The Carter Center of Emory University, May 13–14.

———. 1995. "The Hard Lessons of Cameroon," *Journal of Democracy*, vol. 6, no. 3.

———. 2003. "Trouble in Paradise: Crime and Collapsed States in the Age of Globalization," *British Journal of Criminology*, vol. 41, no.1.

Hargreaves, J. 1986. *Sport, Power and Culture: A Social and Historical Analysis of Popular Sports in Britain*, New York: St. Martin's Press.

Havel, V. 1985. *Open Letters*, New York: Vintage Books.

Hermet, G., R. Rose and A. Rouquié, eds. 1978. *Elections Without Choice*, London and Basingstoke: The Macmillan Press Ltd.

Hi America. 1994. July 2.

Hobsbawm, E. 1990. *Nations and Nationalism Since 1780*, Cambridge: Cambridge University Press.

Huntington, S. 1968. *Political Order in Changing Societies*, New Haven, CT: Yale University Press.

———. 1991. "Democracy's Third Wave," *Journal of Democracy*, vol. 2, no. 2.

Jackson, R. and C. Rosberg. 1986. "Sovereignty and Underdevelopment: Juridical Statehood in the African Crisis," *Journal of Modern African Studies*, vol. 24, no. 1.

Jeune Afrique. 1989. 11–17 décembre, no. 1410.

———. 1990. 20–26 juin, no. 1538.

———. 1990. 11–17 juillet, no. 1541.

———. 1999. 2–8 mars, no. 1990.

Jeune Afrique Economie. 1995. 20 novembre.

Johnson, D. 1995. "The Case for a United Canada," *Foreign Policy*, no. 99.

Johnson, W. 1970. *The Cameroon Federation: Political Integration in a Fragmentary Society*, Princeton: Princeton University Press.

Joseph, R. 1977. *Radical Nationalism in Cameroon*, Oxford: Oxford University Press.

Jua, N. 1991. "Cameroon: Jump-Starting an Economic Crisis," *Africa Insight*, vol. 21, no. 3.

——. 1997. "Contested Meanings: Rulers, Subjects and National Integration in Post-colonial Cameroon," in P. Nkwi and F. Njamnjoh, eds., *Regional Balance and National Integration in Cameroon*, Yaoundé and Leiden: ICASSART and the African Studies Center.

——. 1997. "Spatial Politics, Political Stability in Cameroon" Keynote Address presented at *Workshop on Cameroon: Biography of a Nation*, Amherst College, Amherst, MA.

——. Forthcoming. "Spatialization and Valorization of Identities in contemporary Cameroon," in J. Takougang, J. Mukum Mbaku and J. Ihonvbere, eds.,*The Leadership Challenge in Africa: Cameroon under Biya*.

——. 1990. "Force of Law: The Mystical Foundation of Authority," *Cardoza Law Review*, vol. 11, no. 56.

Kamga, Z.V. 1985. *Duel camerounais: democratic ou barbaric*, Paris: l'Harmattan.

Kodo-Ela, J-C. and A.M. Masika. No Date. "Il était une fois...les Lions Indomptables du Cameroun," Yaoundé: Collection Hommes et Evenements.

Kofele-Kale, N. 1985. "Ethnicity, Regionalism and Political Power: A Post-mortem of Abidjo's Cameroon," in W.I. Zartman and M. Schatzberg, eds., *The Political Economy of Cameroon*, New York: Praeger Publishers.

Konings, P. and F. Nyamnjoh. 1997. "The Anglophone Problem in Cameroon," *The Journal of Modern African Studies*, vol. 35, no. 2.

——. 2000. "Construction and Deconstruction: Anglophones or Autochtones?," in P. Nkwi, ed., The *Anthropology of Africa: Challenges for the 21st Century*, Yaoundé: ICASSART.

Kuper, S. 1994. *Football Against the Enemy*, London: Orion.

La Nouvelle Expression. 1998. 26 juin, no 381.

Larrue J. and J-M. Payen. 2000. *Jean Ramadier: Gouverneur de la décolonisation*, Paris: Karthala.

L'effort Camerounais. 1991. October.

Le Football. 1969. Yaoundé.

Le Messager. Various issues.

Le Témoin. Various issues.

Lever, J. 1983. *Soccer Madness,* Chicago: University of Chicago Press.

Le Vine, V. 1964. *The Cameroons: From Mandate to Independence,* Berkeley, CA: University of California Press.

———. 1968. "Cameroon (1955–1962)," in D.M. Condit, B.H. Cooper, Jr., et al., eds., *Challenge and Response in Internal Conflict,* vol. III, Washington D.C.: American University, Center for Research in Social Systems.

———. 1971. *Cameroon Federal Republic,* Ithaca, NY: Cornell University Press.

———. 1976. "Political Integration and the United Republic of Cameroon," in D.R. Smock et al., eds., *The Search for National Integration in Africa,* London: Macmillan Publishers.

Lonsdale J. 1986. "Political Accountability in African History," in P. Chabal, ed., *Political Domination in Africa,* Cambridge: Cambridge University Press.

———. 1992. "The Moral Economy of Mau-Mau," in B. Berman and J. Lonsdale, eds., *Unhappy Valley, Conflict in Kenya and Africa,* London: James Currey.

Lyonga, N., E. Breitinger and B. Butake, eds. 1993. *Anglophone Cameroon Writing,* Bayreuth African Studies, 30.

Mangan, J.A., ed. 1996. *Tribal Identities: Nationalism, Europe, Sport,* London: Frank Cass.

Mangan J.A., R. Holt and P. Lanfranchi, eds. 1996. *European Heroes: Myth, Identity, Sport,* London: Frank Cass.

Martin, P. 1991. "Colonialism, Youth and Football in French Equatorial Africa," *International Journal of the History of Sport,* 8.

Marx, K. 1987. *The 18th Brumaire of Louis Bonaparte,* New York: International Publishers.

Mazrui, A. 1986. *The Africans,* Boston, MA: Little, Brown and Company.

Mbembe, A. 1997. "The Thing and Its Double in Cameroonian Cartoons," in K. Barber, ed., *Readings in African Popular Culture,* Oxford: James Currey.

———. 2000. *De la Postcolonie: essai sur l'imagination politique dans l'Afrique contemporaine,* Paris: Karthala.

——. 2001. *On the Postcolony*, Berkeley, CA: University of California Press.

Mbock, C.G., ed. 1996. *Cameroun: pluralisme culturel et convivialité,* Paris: Edition Nouvelle du Sud.

Mchombo, S. 1998. "Democratization in Malawi: Its Roots and Prospects," in J-G. Gros, ed., *Democratization in Late Twentieth-Century Africa*, Wesport, CT: Greenwood Publishing CO.

Mentan, T. 1998. "Cameroon: A Flawed Transition to Democracy" in J-G. Gros, ed., *Democratization in Late Twentieth-Century Africa,* Westport, CT: Greenwood Publishing CO.

Modo, A. 1995. "La chanson dans la communication politique au Cameroun," *Fréquence Sud*, no.13.

Mokeba, H.M. 1989. *The Politics and Diplomacy of Cameroon Sports: A Study in the Quest for Nation-Building and International Prestige,* unpublished Ph.D. thesis, Columbia, SC: University of South Carolina.

Monga, C. 1992. *La recomposition du marché politique au Cameroun (1991–1992): de la nécessité d'un amenagement du monitoring électoral.* Forum Democratique: Fondation Friedrich-Ebert.

——. 1995. "Civil Society and Democratisation in Francophone Africa," *Journal of Modern African Studies*, vol. 33, no. 3.

——. 1996. *The Anthropology of Anger: Civil Society and Democracy in Africa*, Boulder, CO and London: Lynne Rienner Publishers.

Monnington, T. 1986. "The Politics of Black African Sport," in L. Allison, ed., *The Politics of Sport*, Manchester, UK: Manchester University Press.

Mono Ndjana, H. 1997. *Les proverbes de Paul Biya*, Yaoundé: Edition du Carrefour.

Mortimer, R. 1969. *France and the Africans, 1944-1960, a Political History*, London: Faber and Faber.

Moume-Etia, L. 1991. *Cameroun, les années ardentes,* Paris: Jeune Afrique Livres.

Muclimbe, V. 1988. *The Invention of Africa*, London: James Currey.

Mukong, A. 1975. *Prisoner Without a Crime*, Cameroon: Alfresco Books; second edition, 1989. Paris: Nubia Press.

Musa, T. 2000. "Development Bulletin," *InterPress Service*, Yaoundé, September 9.

National Democratic Institute. 1993. *An Assessment of the October 11, 1992 Election in Cameroon*, Washington D.C.: National Democratic Institute.

Ngaya, P. 1983. *Cameroun, Qui Gouverne?* Paris: l'Harmattan.

Ngenge, T.S. 1983. *The Socio-Economic History of the Ndu Tea Estate: 1966–1982* (unpublished masters thesis), Yaoundé: Department of History, University of Yaoundé.

Ngoh, V. 1987. *Cameroon 1884–1985, One Hundred Years of History*, Yaoundé: Navi Group.

Nkwi, P.N. 1989. *The German Presence in the Western Grassfields 1891–1913*, Leiden, Holland: African Studies Center.

Nkwi, P.N. and B. Vidacs. 1997. "Football: Politics and Power in Cameroon," in G. Armstrong and R. Giulianotti, eds., *Entering the Field: New Perspectives in Football*, Oxford: Oxford University Press.

North, D.1981. *Structure and Change in Economic History*, New York, London: W.W. Norton and Company.

Norval, A.J. 1998. "Memory, Identity and the (Im)possibility of Reconciliation: The Work of the Truth and Reconciliation Commission in South Africa" *Constellations*, vol. 5, no. 2.

Nyamnjoh, F. 1989. *Broadcasting for Nation-Building in Cameroon: Development and Constraints*. Ph.D. thesis. Leicester, UK: Center for Mass Communication Research (CMCR), University of Leicester.

——. 1996. *Mass Media and Democratisation in Cameroon*, Yaoundé: Friedrich Ebert Stiftung.

——. 1997. "Cartoons in Cameroon: Anger and Political Derision under Monocracy," in K. Anyidoho, ed., *The Word Behind Bars and the Paradox of Exile*, Evanston, Illinois: Northwestern University Press.

——. 1997. "Political Rumour in Cameroon," *Cahier de l'UCAC*, no. 2.

——. 1999. "Cameroon: A Country United by Ethnic Ambition and Difference," *African Affairs*, vol.98, no. 390.

——. 1999. "Press Cartoons and Politics in Cameroon," *International Journal of Comic Art*, vol. 1, no. 2.

Onguene, E. 1996. "La Démocratie en Chanson: Les Bikut-si du Cameroun," *Politique Africaine*, 64.

Pelczynski, Z.A., ed., 1971. *Hegel's Political Philosophy: Problems and Perspectives*, Cambridge: Cambridge University Press.

Peterson, M.A. 1997. "The limits of Social Learning: Translating Analysis into Action," *Journal of Health Politics, Policy and Law*, vol. 22, no. 4.

Postwatch. 2001. January, no. 006.

Powell, G.B. 2000. *Elections as Instruments of Democracy*, New Haven and London: Yale University Press.

Przeworski, A. 1986. "Some Problems in the Study of the Transition to Democracy," in G. O'Donnell, P. Schmitter and L. Whitehead, eds., *Transitions from Authoritarian Rule: Comparative Perspectives*, Baltimore: Johns Hopkins University Press.

Radhakrishnan, R. 1990. "Ethnic Identity and Post-Structuralist Difference," in A.R. JanMohamed and D. Lloyd, eds., *The Nature and Context of Minority Discourse*, Oxford: Oxford University Press.

Ranger, T. 1983. "The Invention of Tradition: The Case of Colonial Africa," in E. Hobsbawm and T. Ranger, eds., *The Invention of Tradition*, Cambridge: Cambridge University Press.

République du Cameroun.1961. Ministère des Finances et du Plan, *Premier Plan Quinquennal*, Yaoundé.

——. 1961. Article 9 (I) of the Federal Constitution, Yaoundé.

——. 1967. Bill No. 153-PJI-ANF of May 23. Promulgated by Law No. 67/LF/19 of June 6 (relevant sections: 1, 3,5 and 7), Yaoundé.

——. 1972. Articles 1, 2, 3, 4 and 8 of the Unitary Constitution, June 2, Yaoundé.

——. 1975. Law No. 75-1 of May 9, modifying Article 5 of the Unitary Constitution of June 2, 1972, Yaoundé.

——. 1976. *The Fourth Five-Year Development Plan—1976–1981*, Yaoundé.

——. 1981. *Encyclopedie de la République Unie du Cameroun*, Douala: Nouvelles Editions Africaines.

——. 1984. Article 7 of the Unitary Constitution of June 2, 1972, modified on February 2, Yaoundé.

——. 1994. Decree no. 94-125, July 14.

Rodney, W. 1972. *How Europe Underdeveloped Africa*, London: Bogle-L'Ouverture Publication.

Salacuse, J., S. Cohen and A. Blaustein. 1987. "Republic of Cameroon," in A. Blaustein and G. Flanz, eds., *Constitutions of the Countries of the World*, Sidney and London: Oceana Publications Inc.

Schmitter, P. and T.L. Karl. 1991. "What Democracy Is . . . and Is Not?" *Journal of Democracy*, vol. 2, no. 3.

Shapiro, M.J. 1992. *Reading the Postmodern Polity*, Minneapolis: University of Minneapolis Press.

Sidney, T. 1994. *Power in Movement,* Cambridge: Cambridge University Press.

Smith, A. 1983. *State and Nation in the Third World: The Western State and African Nationalism*, Sussex, UK: Wheatsheaf Books Ltd.

Soh, P.B. 1999. *Dr. John Ngu Foncha: The Cameroonian Statesman*, Bamenda: Unique Printers.

SONARA Magazine. 1984. France: Imprimerie SIRA/ASNIERES, October 10.

Spitulnik, D. 1994. *Radio Culture in Zambia: Audiences, Public Words and the Nation State (I and II)*, unpublished doctoral dissertation, Chicago: University of Chicago.

Stevenson, T. 1989. "Sports Clubs and Political Integration in the Yemen Arab Republic," *International Review of the Sociology of Sport*, 24.

Stoddart, B. 1988. "Sport, Cultural Imperialism, and Colonial Response in the British Empire," *Comparative Studies in Society and History*, 30.

Takougang, J. and M. Krieger. 1998. *African State and Society in the 1990s: Cameroon's Political Crossroads*, Boulder, CO: Westview Press.

Tsanga, S. 1969. *Le Football Camerounais des origines à l'indépendence*, Yaoundé.

The Herald. Various issues.

Today. Various issues.

U.S. Department of State.1996. Bureau of African Affairs, *Republic of Cameroon: Economy*, March.

United Nations. 1961. *Resolution 1688 (XV) 994 of the Plenary Session*, New York, New York: United Nations, April 21.

Van der Walle, N. 1990. "The Politics of Non-Reform in Cameroon," in *African Governance in the 1990s: Objectives, Resources and Constraints*. Working papers of the Second Annual Seminar of the African Governance Program. The Carter Center of Emory University, Atlanta, Georgia, March 23–25.

Verschave, F-X. 1998. *La Françafrique: le plus long scandale de la Republique*, Paris: Stock.

——. 2000. *Noire silence,* Paris: Les Arenes.

Vidacs, B. 1997. "Football in Cameroon: A Vehicle for the Expansion and Contraction of Identity," *Culture, Sport, Society*, vol. 2, special issue 2.3, London: Frank Cass.

Vincent, J. 1974. "The Structuring of Ethnicity,"*Human Organization*, 33.

Washington Post. 1967. March 12.

Welch, C.E. 1966. *Dream of Unity: Pan Africanism and Political Integration in West Africa*, Ithaca: Cornell University Press.

West Africa. 1984. July 23.

Williams, B. 1989. "A Class Act: Anthropology and the Race to Nation Across Ethnic Terrain," *Annual Review of Anthropology*, 18.

Williams, M. 1995. "Justice Toward Groups," *Political Theory*, vol. 23, no. 1.

Williams, R. 1990. *Marxism and Literature*, Oxford: Oxford University Press.

World Bank.1986. *World Bank Development Report*, Washington, D.C.

——. 2001. *World Development Report*, Washington, D.C.

——. 2001. *Cameroon: Structural Adjustment Credit*, Washington, D.C.

——. 2002. *World Development Report*, Washington, D.C.

Zartman, W. I. and M. Schatzberg, eds. 1986. *The Political Economy of Cameroon*, New York: Praeger Publishers.

Zizek, S. 1994. *For They Know Not What They Do*, London: Verso.

About the Editor and Contributors

EDITOR

Jean-Germain Gros is associate professor of political science and public policy administration and fellow at the Center for International Studies, University of Missouri–St. Louis. In 1990–91 Professor Gros was visiting researcher at the Ministry of Higher Education and Scientific Research (MINESRES) and Ministry of Livestock, and Animal Industries in Cameroon (MINEPIA). Professor Gros' publications include *Democratization in Late Twentieth-Century Africa*, (edited), Greenwood Press, 1998; "The Hard Lessons of Cameroon," *Journal of Democracy*, 1995; "Trouble in Paradise: Crime and Collapsed States in the Age of Globalization," *British Journal of Criminology*, 2003.

CONTRIBUTORS

Jude Fokwang is a researcher and lecturer at the University of Pretoria, South Africa.

Nantang Jua is *Maître de Recherche* at the Ministry of Scientific Research in Cameroon. Prior to his current appointment, Dr. Jua was associate professor of political science, University of Buea, Cameroon.

Victor T. Le Vine is emeritus professor of political science, Washington University in St. Louis.

Tatah Mentan is associate professor of politics and communication, University of Yaoundé (II). In 2002–03 he was Theodore Lentz Fellow in Peace Studies at the Center for International Studies, University of Missouri–St. Louis.

Minion K.C. Morrison is professor of political science, University of Missouri–Columbia.

Tata Simon Ngenge is associate professor of history, University of Yaoundé (I), Cameroon.

Francis Nyamnjoh is associate professor of sociology, University of Botswana.

Bea Vidacs teaches anthropology at Baruch College, City University of New York (CUNY). Professor Vidacs has written extensively on football in Cameroon.

Index

Southern Cameroons, 100
United Nations, 97
West Cameroons, 8, 18
Football (Cameroon)
    brief history of, 170–171
    domestic dissent, 23
    importance of, 169
Forbin, Boniface, 143
Forces vives, political reform,
    15, 27
Forchive, Jean, and Lapiro [de
    Mbanga], 202, 203, 204
Fossung, Henry, 98
Foumban Constitution, Federal
    government, 64, 65–66
France
    and Ahidjo administration,
        10, 17–18, 47–48
    and Biya administration,
        18–20
    colonial policy, 3–4
    trusteeship, 5–7
Francophones
    on Anglophones, 88–89
    oil industry, 81–82
Fraud
    definition of, 162n.9
    election day, 137–138
    non-classical elections, 132,
        133–140
Freedom Land, 99
French East Cameroun
    colonial policy, 3–4, 5
    trusteeship, 5–7, 168
French Union, African policy, 6

G
Gaillard, Philippe
    on Biya administration, 43

on colonial politics, 35–36,
    37
Galbraith, John Kenneth, 93
Garoua, Astragabdo Ada Kano,
    34
Garoua d'abord (Garoua first),
    Ahidjo administration, 11
"Gaullism," influence of, 21,
    47–48, 54n.34
General Statute for Public Enter-
    prises, privatization strategy,
    116–117
Georgy, Guy, colonial politics,
    39–40
Germany, Cameroon protector-
    ate, 1–3, 89, 168
Gorji-Dinka, Fongum, 66, 97
Gramsci, Antonio, 44, 46
Grand Patron, Ahidjo nick-
    name, 11, 12
Great Britain
    colonial policy, 3, 4–5
    trusteeship, 5, 8
Great Lakes conflict, 20

H
Harare Declaration, 96
Hayatou, Sadou, national politi-
    cal reform conference, 15
Head taxes, German protector-
    ate, 2
Health care, privatization of,
    126, 127
"Hegemonic project," Ahidjo
    administration, 44, 45, 46, 48,
    49
Hermet, Guy, election fraud,
    132, 137
Hirschman, Albert, 102